D1333173

ONE MAN'S ESTATE

One Man's Estate

THE PRESERVATION OF AN ENGLISH INHERITANCE

Dennis Barker

ANDRE DEUTSCH

FIRST PUBLISHED 1983 BY
ANDRÉ DEUTSCH LIMITED
105 GREAT RUSSELL STREET, LONDON WCI

COPYRIGHT © 1983 BY DENNIS BARKER

TYPESET BY GLOUCESTER TYPESETTING SERVICES
PRINTED IN GREAT BRITAIN BY
EBENEZER BAYLIS & SON LIMITED
THE TRINITY PRESS, WORCESTER

ISBN 0-233-97519-5

Contents

List of Illustrations vii
Introduction 1
1 Seeds of Rebirth 13
2 Entertaining at the Hall 33
3 The Keeper of the Gate 42
4 Ragley's Wise Ladies 47
5 You called, Milord? 57
6 Kitchen Talk 71
7 No Ordinary Office 78
8 Battle of the Flowers 89
9 The Heir and His Lambs 101
10 Tenant Farming – a Lasting Tradition? 111
11 Harvest Help 136
12 The Princess at Home 145
13 The Very Idea 152
14 A Fraternity of Horsemen 161
15 The Contemporary Gamekeeper 172
16 Forest Strategy 187
17 The Old Faithfuls 194
18 Parson's Thanksgiving 208
19 Shades of Autumn 216
20 Future Prospects 223

ILLUSTRATIONS

All the photographs apart from those otherwise credited were taken by Duncan Fraser

Between pages 72 and 73
The front terrace of Ragley Hall with its magnificent Palladian portico
The Hall's rear terrace, which overlooks the gardens
Ragley's West Garden, with the avenue of trees in the background reaching to the skyline
The Mauve Drawing Room (English Life Publications Limited)
The Main Dining Room (English Life Publications Limited)
The Great Hall (English Life Publications Limited)
Lord Hertford and Peter Crabtree, the farms manager, outside the farm office
Lord Hertford in his office in the Hall
The sophisticated milking unit at Weethley, Ragley's dairy farm
Jack Smith, Ragley's gatekeeper (the author)
Ragley's lady guides
Mrs Cynthia Bindley in the sweet shop, with the souvenir shop in the background

Between pages 136 and 137
Mrs Maureen Lawrence, Lord Hertford's secretary
Fobbester the butler and 'Mrs Fobb' the cook on the front terrace of the Hall
Mrs Marian Crabtree working with her husband Peter in the farm office
John Lindsey, Ragley's head gardener
The Earl of Yarmouth, heir to the Ragley estate (Lady Hertford)
Harold Heard, one of Ragley's tenant farmers, at work on his farm
The Heards' farmhouse at Alcester Park Farm
The Princess Alphonse de Chimay, Lord Hertford's mother-in-law
Lady Hertford on horseback (the author)
The Ragley stables
Phil Roberts, Ragley's sole groom
Harry Green, the local farrier (the author)
Ken Ward, the gamekeeper
Colin Bindley, Ragley's head forester
The Reverend Arthur Stally handing out harvest thanksgiving parcels (the author)
Miss Marjorie Crick, daughter of a late Ragley butler (the author)

Alf Goddard, a former gardener (the author)
Albert Richards, former head gardener (the author)
Bertie Brass, a retired groom (the author)

Introduction

THE 8TH MARQUESS OF HERTFORD, of Ragley Hall in Warwickshire, can play to perfection the role of the unworldly English Lord, pottering about securely on his country estate as if the twentieth century had passed him by.

'I'm so sorry,' he said in his very first telephone conversation with me, 'but I've completely forgotten your name. As a matter of fact, I often forget in the middle of conversations who I am talking to.'

Such declarations, I was soon to discover, should not be taken entirely at face value. Advising me on which hotel I should patronize at nearby Stratford-upon-Avon for our first face-to-face encounter, he showed another side of his character: 'As it's out of season, you can probably press them for some very attractive reduced terms.'

If at least some of the great estates of England continue to survive, it is unlikely to be by accident. In this portrait of a great hall and its estate I set out to discover why it has survived with such elan, albeit sometimes on a hand-to-mouth basis. The answers will, I hope, throw some light on how the British aristocracy and their country estates can continue to sustain a way of life for themselves, their servants, their tenants and, in turn, their employees. In this sense, the 8th Marquess of Hertford, with his 6,000 acres, his half-a-dozen tenanted farms, his hunting, his cigarette holder, his Berry Brothers Pale Dry Number 3 sherry and his meticulous accountancy and sales graphs, is more than an individual in vacuo. He could be regarded as symbolic of the British aristocracy as a whole, who, widely lampooned in these lean and nominally egalitarian times, have still somehow remained very firmly part of a country landscape that continues to provide comparatively sheltered, if not too grandly-paid, employment. And at a time when British industry – once the backbone of a country that had supposedly consigned mere land-owners to the dustbin of history – is in a deep recession, from which it may or may not fully recover.

It was to see the patterns of survival in action, and to examine their causes and effects, that I visited Ragley. I wanted to discover how an aristocrat like Lord Hertford (pronounced Harford), who can trace his Seymour (pronounced Seemer) family line, however erratically, back to beyond Henry VIII, had apparently managed to make his farming a highly profitable business, to fashion his forestry as a growing concern, and to keep his enormous Hall open as an attraction for the public and a home for himself. A home in the true sense, not one in which he occupies only a flat. I wanted to find out what the people he directly employed, or who were effectively answerable to him, thought about their lives and about their Lord. I wanted to discover whether the traditional functionaries like butlers, footmen, grooms and gamekeepers still existed and what sort of people occupied these positions today if they *did* still exist. I also wanted to know whether the old retainers in their cottages on the estate now felt themselves to be social victims or socially privileged.

The result is a portrait of a country way of life which still exists, though townsmen are only dimly aware of it. It is a way of life with its own customs, rules and social observances which say something about a different sort of English character, a different set of values and beliefs, at a time when the crude materialism of the towns approaches the status of a perversely self-flagellating neurosis with which it is impossible to live comfortably. Those on the upper rungs of the social ladder become neurotic if their cars are one year older than their next-door neighbour's, while muggers in deprived areas earn themselves the scorn of society by trying to rob people who are scarcely better off than they are.

From what I discovered at Ragley, I began to wonder whether there might be an element of truth in the notion that the future of England really lies in our great country estates. Especially as heavy industry and technology come increasingly under siege from the newer world powers: particularly Japan, the USSR and the USA. Is it feasible to think that Britain may go back to the land, the land of Ragley and similar great country estates which are supported by, and support, the Hall? Certainly not as a whole. But there are arguably significant signs of a slight shifting of power in favour of the Marquess and his country estate, and against the barons of big business.

I have not set out to be partisan about the social morality of such estates, though I have allowed all the people I talked to at Ragley their own views on the subject, if they chose to express them. There *are* visitors to Ragley Hall who are heard to mutter such comments as, 'Why should one man have all this when some people are homeless?' To every one of these, I was assured (and my own experience at Ragley tended to bear it out) there are a hundred who say, 'Does Lord Hertford actually live here and am I likely to meet him?' Such paying visitors are often the car workers and foundry-men of the industrial West Midlands – the very sort of workers some revolutionaries expected would put the 8th Marquess of Hertford and his equals on a tumbril long ago.

Lord Hertford's mother actually abandoned the Hall as being too big for modern times, but her son clung tenaciously to his birthright – pro-phecy of 'historical inevitabilities' can be an inexact and perilous science. Ragley is now a business (not quite a sector of show business though approaching it) which survives with comparatively few grumbles from those in its employ or under its influence.

The case for the defence of Lord Hertford and his estate might run something like this: that they are not merely a social eccentricity of the closing years of the twentieth century, but a personification of something deep in the English character; perhaps even an indication of a movement back to the land. The case for the prosecution might be that the 8th Marquess, and men like him, have managed to build a cocoon of unreality around themselves, a false little world in which they can still act out the fantasy of their innate superiority to other men, protected by (as in the case of Ragley Hall) a mile-long drive from the public road.

The case has often been argued out by those totally ignorant of the facts. The English aristocrat (except for the gossip column froth) usually takes some care to make himself discreetly invisible to a possibly unfriendly eye. In these circumstances easy, sometimes ludicrous, stereotypes can grow. Some people assume that the remanants of the British aristocracy are all living in the South of France, the Bahamas, Bermuda, Jersey or Jamaica. There they spend their listless days exchanging banalities with unaristo-cratic and uninteresting fellow tax exiles. Their daughters have taken to interior design, photographic modelling, selling themselves to the more respectable type of crook, and sniffing cocaine. Their sons, driving fast cars and drunk by noon, are pursuing unusual sexual practices while selling unreliable used cars in Tangiers. Both sons and daughters are more than likely to have embraced some unlikely form of lunatic political extremism in the company of people who don't wash or clean their teeth, seeing it as the only way of maintaining their traditional God-given right to order the lives of other people.

Such stereotypes will almost certainly seem fatuous to those who have actually met a present-day aristocrat in his country habitat. But they are perhaps as convenient to the aristocracy itself as to its most vehement social critics: they can easily be laughed aside. A more sober criticism often levelled against today's noblemen is that they still simply have too much luxury in their everyday lives, too much power and influence over those they employ directly, or whose living depends on them indirectly. Can an aristocrat today have a fat life without effort?

Ragley may provide an answer; and a more revealing one than would a statistical survey of the owners of great estates as a whole (even assuming they would co-operate). A survey *might* have been sociology. It would certainly have been tedious. In understanding the way human beings think and act and live, one example may be worth a ton of statistics. Twenty Lords, twenty butlers, twenty sets of tenant farmers and twenty grooms might disappear into statistical abstraction. Lord and Lady Hertford, with their almost fanatical love of horses; Fobbester the butler and his practised deference; tenant farmer Robert Hiller with his own successful business interests and gamekeeper Ken Ward, with his mistrust of shotguns, will, I hope, stay in the memory as living individuals as well as segments of their particular sort of rural society.

Ragley is a picturesque as well as a representative estate, situated almost in the centre of England. It is adjacent to the little village of Arrow with its pub, the Arrow Mill, which looks like a miniature stately home in its own right and has an old water wheel which still turns. The gates of the Hall are only a couple of miles from Alcester, a thoroughly idiosyncratic English town. At the end of its main street (only a few hundred feet long) is the parish church of St Nicholas, with its clock mounted across one corner of the square tower, rather than on a flat wall. Eight miles down the road to the south is Stratford-upon-Avon, with its hordes of American, European and Japanese tourists in pursuit of Shakespearean history. The estate used to stretch right up to Stratford-upon-Avon itself until the Second World War, when death duties forced the sale of many acres. Its 6,000 remaining acres are devoted to a mixture of parkland, tourist attractions, forestry, farming and lambing.

Because the Hall, with its 115 rooms, is a mile from the road, the traffic of the outside world cannot be heard. But harsh economic realities are still experienced by all those who live on or around the estate, whether of high or low degree: Lord and Lady Hertford themselves, their son and heir Harry, the Earl of Yarmouth; their daughters Carolyn, Diana, and Anne Seymour; Princess Alphonse de Chimay, Lady Hertford's mother, who lives in a house in Ragley Park; Fobbester the butler and 'Mrs Fobb' the cook. And, of course, the other functionaries who flit in and out of the great Hall: His Lordship's formidably efficient secretary Mrs Maureen Lawrence (constantly); the farms manager Peter Crabtree (frequently); the head gardener John Lindsey (quite often); the groom Phil Roberts (not infrequently); and the gamekeeper Ken Ward (hardly at all, as he is no longer employed by Lord Hertford himself but by a syndicate consisting of Lord Hertford's tenant farmers and business and professional men).

The decline of Ragley in the middle of this century was on most counts merely typical of what was happening to stately homes all over Britain. The exceptional factor was that Ragley's problems had been exacerbated by events in the Hall's and the family's history. The family line of the Marquesses of Hertford has been chequered. Sometimes it has been distinguished – the 1st Marquess (1719–94) was Lord Lieutenant of Ireland, British Ambassador in Paris and Lord Chamberlain of England. Sometimes it has been raffish – the 2nd Marquess's wife was scandalously friendly with the Prince Regent; the 3rd Marquess lived such a debauched life that he was portrayed both as Lord Monmouth in Disraeli's novel *Coningsby* and Lord Steyne in Thackeray's *Vanity Fair*; and the 4th Marquess lived all his life in Paris, spent virtually nothing on Ragley and left everything *except* Ragley to an illegitimate son. Sometimes it has been precarious – the 7th Marquess was the uncle, not the father, of the present Marquess, but obligingly had no children. The 8th Marquess succeeded him at the precocious age of nine. When the 6th Marquess died in 1912, it was the last time the Hall was actually lived in by the family itself for years. One family of servants lived there in solitary splendour, keeping an eye on it for posterity.

The present Marquess moved back into the Hall, amidst general disbelief, in the 1950s. When he set out to rescue it from what seemed like almost certain destruction, he set himself a huge task. It was undoubtedly more of a challenge than his youthful mind and spirit fully comprehended. If Lord and Lady Hertford are unusual among the aristocracy, it is perhaps only because they had rather *more* to struggle against than most of their class. This challenge only fired their desire to have a lifestyle traditionally associated with their social standing. But in today's economic climate is that lifestyle a personal triumph or a social disgrace? The argument will doubtless continue. Another question has a rather more practical edge. Will this book offer some kind of blueprint for the survival of the British aristocracy as a whole or will it simply be a record, as human and informative as I could make it, of what one aristocratic family, its home and its estate was like in the last years of the twentieth century, as both the British aristocracy, and a previously internationally supreme Britain, were facing an increasing number of formidable challenges from a variety of directions, including the South Atlantic?

After meeting the people of Ragley, readers can be free to make up their own minds. What primarily interested me was the very fact that Ragley's way of life was continuing. Like Mount Everest, it was interesting because it was *there*.

Perhaps the most revealing occasion on which to meet the people of Ragley for the first time is that which is also the most nerve-wracking for them, whatever their rank or degree. This is the run-up to the first open day of the season, with its atmosphere of first-night nerves, as in the theatre. Indeed, Ragley, before and during opening day, is sheer high-tension theatre, with a vigilant eye always being kept on the box office.

It was during the preliminaries to opening day that I first met at least some of the people of Ragley. It was an early April day with uncertain weather and therefore uncertain prospects at the ticket office near the main gates and at the ticket desk inside the main doors of the Hall itself. Lord Hertford, in characteristic blue open-necked shirt, took a sombre look at the admissions graph, always kept up-to-date on the stone wall just outside the door of his office in the south-east corner of the building. It showed that the number of visitors in 1980 was only 104,576, compared with 120,899 the previous year, and that in 1981 the number was down to 88,700. Nonetheless the 8th Marquess of Hertford, for the benefit of his loyal band of helpers, radiated confidence that *this* year more people would be prepared to pay nearly £2 to view the habitat of a family which can trace its ancestors back to Lady Jane Seymour, one of King Henry VIII's queens who did not die at his hands but in childbirth; and perhaps to view the present Marquess himself, who certainly does not shrink away from worshippers of the nobility.

'It was absolutely wet weather in the two bad years,' pointed out Lord Hertford, almost as if the family honour had been impugned. 'There was a general reluctance to spend money on petrol. The weather made as much difference as the money situation, I think.' (In 1982 there were signs of a more prosperous season: the weather was rather better.)

The major innovation of the new season, which was due to open a couple of days after I began my visit, was to be the new restaurant. It used to be the supper room. Now it was having its flagstone floor covered with hardboard and carpet in the interests of hygiene, and a better menu was being offered in the hope of increasing the revenue.

'Once we had sealed the old flagstones they would have been as hygienic a flooring as the one we are laying over it,' insisted Michael Hatcher, the thirty-six year-old self-employed builder who became one of Lord Hertford's maintenance men.

The old Gun Room had been commandeered, under Michael Hatcher's vigilant eye, as the new restaurant's more sophisticated wine cellar. The Earl of Yarmouth had removed his guns and similar impedimenta only a few hours before the public opening. Michael Hatcher regarded some of the cupboards in the room with obvious doubt: 'We're going to be pretty short of room in here, Milord, if we don't strip these cupboards out. There isn't going to be very much room for the staff to sit in here.' Lord Hertford considered this briefly. 'I don't know whether the staff need to sit in the wine cellar anyway,' he commented. Subject closed, as were the cupboard doors on the wine.

Michael Hatcher immediately accepted Lord Hertford's ruling. He turned to tell me something about his job. 'We've never been as rushed as this before. We've had so much work to do in areas other than the house, that's the trouble. We're doing other conversion work on the estate, too. At least I'm never bored! I don't know what I'll be doing from one day to the next. I deal with every aspect of the building trade here, from plumbing to plastering, carpentry to electrical work. I occasionally work on pieces of lovely furniture in the house, which is very interesting for me because I am a carpenter by trade. It's certainly more satisfying for me, after being a self-employed builder, to do building work here at the Hall, rather than be building breeze-block housing somewhere else. The difference is marvellous. I have had years of building breeze-block houses and I didn't enjoy it at all.' This was a theme I was to come across many times in conversation with Ragley workers: the personal satisfaction of working at a job where there was individuality and quality.

The Mauve Drawing Room and its ante-room had to be repainted for the opening of the public season. Fortunately this did not contribute to the last-minute rush. The work was done well before time. It cost the estate £6,000 and these rooms are by no means the largest of the 115, though they are certainly among the most historic. At least the ceiling of the Mauve Drawing Room did not have to be painted: it has remained the same since it was decorated by Wyatt in 1780.

The Italian landscape by Claude Joseph Vernet had to be removed for the redecoration, and so did the Austrian piano with mother-of-pearl and tortoiseshell keys. The card table had to be moved too; but that item is used to the twists and turns of fate. Lord Hertford always describes it, with a not unusual irony about family habits, as 'much-used'. Redecoration of the Mauve Drawing Room can itself be a gamble: its walls were repainted nine years ago, but the modern paint started to flake off, so they had to be redone. Unfortunately, the bill for dredging the lake and creating a new small island – about £5,000 – came at about the same time. Admission had to go up by 20 pence that year, which was barely in keeping with inflation. Unfortunately the price always has to be set the previous September, before the old season has come to an end, and long before the financial results of the season can be reliably ascertained.

It is rarely that the Hall gets one of its public assets for nothing, but John Hayward, a London artist, came as a visitor and afterwards presented one of his paintings. The only other gift Lord Hertford could remember offhand was a grand piano: 'A lady who came here said she admired the way we looked after our possessions and would like to give us her piano. It was an 1860 Bosendorfer which was in store; so she saved her own money by giving it to us. That was twenty years ago. I don't know if it was entirely clear whether it was given to us or on loan. Anyway, we have still got it.'

The calculation of admission charges is partly the province of Mrs Maureen Lawrence, Lord Hertford's secretary and one of the kingpins of his organization. Mrs Lawrence, who has a cosmopolitan background and an experience of commerce, had been working for Lord Hertford for thirteen seasons, and was a trifle too busy getting ready for the fourteenth to talk freely on this occasion, though she was most helpful later. She had had to explain to one of the many telephone callers that he didn't really want Lord Hertford's home but Rag*dale* Hall, the Melton Mowbray health farm. Such matters, with the Ragley opening day approaching, obviously required saintly patience and a brisk manner. Mrs Lawrence, I was to discover, had both.

The fact that the season which was just opening was to be a short one did not really make preparations any easier. The reason why it was to be a short one in *itself* created further work. Lord Hertford's elder daughter, Carolyn, was to be twenty-one later in the year. There was to be a Great Ball at the beginning of October, when the house would normally have been still open to the public.

'It means we shall be closing one week early,' said Lord Hertford. 'That is something you can do if you are a private enterprise, as we are, but not so easily if you are a National Trust property. In fact, two summers ago, we did an extraordinary thing. We shut the house up for ten days for my son's twenty-first birthday. We got so much publicity from it that our numbers for public admissions went up at that time, in spite of losing ten days of the season.' Lord Hertford reconsidered this statement. 'That doesn't really do justice to the significance of the occasion,' he said thoughtfully. 'It was more important than one young man's twenty-first birthday party. It was the twenty-first birthday party I had never had myself. It was the first time that a real party had been given in this house since 1892, which was my uncle's twenty-first birthday party. I made a conscious effort to entertain every single person who could reasonably expect to be entertained. There was virtually no one we know who wasn't invited to Ragley during that week.'

Of his own twenty-first, Lord Hertford will say, in tones that show it still rankles, 'It was a pretty miserable party.' Ragley stood empty, Lord Hertford was in the Army and his mother was living at Kingley, one of the estate's farms. All that happened was that his mother gave a cocktail party for 300 – friends, staff, tenants – in the Great Hall of Ragley, which was undecorated and unheated. Lord Hertford's birthday falls in March, one of the coldest months of the year.

For the 8th Marquess's son and heir, it was totally different. There was a series of parties lasting a full week. On Monday, there was dinner in the Main Dining Room for the farm tenants and their wives; on Tuesday a party for 400 people from the Alcester neighbourhood; on Wednesday a lunch party for 60 old-age pensioner ex-employees; on Thursday a dinner party for the entire staff and their wives or husbands, followed by a disco and, as Lord Yarmouth's birthday chimed in at midnight, the illumination of a 30-foot long banner bearing birthday greetings from the staff. Lord Yarmouth was then tossed twenty-one times into the air by the younger members of the farm staff. On Friday there was a party for family and god-parents and on Saturday night 24 sat down to dinner and 400 attended the ball afterwards, some guests dancing until seven in the morning.

'I remember,' said Lord Hertford, 'that I got out of my white tie and tailcoat, and my wife took off her tiara, at about mid-day and we then entertained 40 people to lunch. They were left-overs from the ball or people from neighbouring houseparties, whose hosts and hostesses found it easier to let them stay here. That afternoon we had tea in the Park, with a birthday cake which was an exact model of the house. This was large enough to give a slice to 2,000 people.'

The 2,000 might have been 'the whole of Birmingham' had the 8th Marquess and the Marchioness not taken precautions. They advertised in the local newspaper saying that the Lord of the Manor of Alcester and the Marchioness invited everyone within the Manor boundaries to tea, and anyone wishing to accept should write in, saying how many tickets they wanted. In this way addresses could be vetted. The weather turned out fine, television was present and when, after allowing a week for recovery, the Hall was once more opened to the public, attendances shot up pleasingly.

Almost, but not quite, everybody who comes to the estate is welcome. Winter vandalism can be a problem at the start of every season. The Adventure Park, one of the most popular amenities for families with young children, is half a mile from the Hall and a favourite target.

'We started putting it right ten days before it was due to open,' said Byrt Edwards, who has run its sweets stall for several years. 'There is no ending to this vandalism. They smash windows in the shop and steal the stock. We had to spend four days just cleaning it ready for the public opening. The coffee and tea machine was damaged, and will cost about

£100 to put right. All the windows were broken and the place was covered in mud. They smashed the lock off the ladies lavatory and there is no point in trying to have it repaired in the winter. I think Lord Hertford has been thinking about having patrols.'

A patrol, I was tempted to think, would need to be a Commando Unit at very least – after all it was just such a unit from the Territorial Army who first inaugurated the Adventure Park. But Lord Hertford himself dismissed the idea of patrols. Too complicated, he ruled. A member of the staff suggested an alarm system for £400. Lord Hertford winced. 'Not worth it. By the time we got there the intruders would be long gone, leaving the smashed windows behind them.'

'Well,' said the staff member shrewdly, 'we could get a simple alarm bell for a fiver.'

'In that case,' said the 8th Marquess, equally shrewdly, 'do it.'

For Lord Hertford, there have been inevitable financial frustrations as each season has opened. Always there is something he would have liked to have had done had the cash been available, which simply hasn't been done. This time it was the painting *Antiochus and Stratonice* in the Red Saloon, which needed cleaning. But it would have cost at least £3,000 to do it and so the job was deferred. Public admissions have brought in about £100,000 a year and the expenses of the house have been roughly the same. Paying for actual improvements has entailed a certain give-and-take between house, farms and forests, and often meant postponement of house improvements. Such postponements are now not uncharacteristic of the British aristocracy.

But, even on the very eve of the public opening, Lord Hertford still maintained his habitual calm – that endowment of the English Lord which today can be one of his most charming and profitable assets. This calm persisted even when, at the very end of a hardworking day, a young salesman, presenting for Lord Hertford's signature documents concerned with the ordering of a new video screen to be used to show films of Ragley Hall, asked the Marquess: 'Who do you work for?' Lord Hertford managed to convince the diligent salesman that he worked for himself.

'Is that *all*?' enquired Lord Hertford hopefully, as the young man left. Were it not for his polo-necked sweater and slacks, he might have been a Marquess of the Regency era, just finishing a game of cards, rather than what he in fact was: a modern impresario stage-managing the opening of a great theatrical revival which could run and run.

Apparently it was all. At six o'clock Lord Hertford bathed, donned a black tie with his green smoking jacket and had his evening sherry. *Always*, of course, Berry Brothers Pale Dry Number 3. The only permitted exception to this rule has been the occasional gin which *must* be Gordons.

'Once I was in a bar in Stratford-upon-Avon and asked for a Gordons gin,' recalled the 8th Marquess. 'The man beside me said, "Can I buy it for you?" I thought I was being picked up, so I declined. Then he said, "I'm a Gordons salesman and you're the first person I've actually heard ask for Gordons by name." '

The ever-realistic and astute Marquess did not hesitate further when confronted with such a blameless opportunity. 'In that case,' he said smartly, 'I accept.'

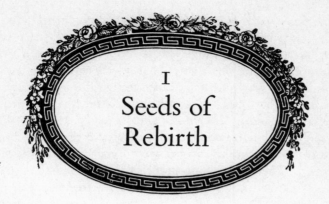

I
Seeds of Rebirth

THE REVIVAL OF Ragley Hall and its estate has to some extent been governed by fate, but it has been made possible by the efforts of many conscientious and loyal workers, who have gained vicarious pleasure from cheerfully identifying themselves with Ragley as few industrial workers are able to identify with their places of employment.

But the rebirth owes itself *primarily* to a few sheets of paper. Though no one except Lord Hertford was really aware of it, the real starting point was a letter his mother wrote to him at Eton when he was just seventeen. It did not seem the beginning of anything good at the time; indeed, its tone was bleakly negative. It contained the traumatic news that he and his mother could no longer afford to live at Ragley and must move to a smaller place.

'I did not believe it, even then,' recalled the 8th Marquess. 'I always meant to live at Ragley. I remember writing back saying, "If we are all that poor, what the hell am I doing at Eton?" I said I had no idea there was a money shortage, but that now I saw no need for any further education at all. It would not have bothered me if I had gone out and got a job there and then.'

The aristocrat whose family line went back for centuries was, in other words, in almost exactly the same psychological position as a poor boy who suddenly realized that money was short, that this situation was something that concerned him, and that therefore he must somehow chip in, even if it meant forsaking the rest of his education. The only difference was that in Lord Hertford's case, the elimination of Eton fees, and the

13

acquisition of any wages he could have independently earned as a seventeen-year-old, would hardly in themselves have produced the necessary financial upturn in the family fortunes.

His response to his mother's letter he now sees as 'a statement of intent' from a youth who was quite determined to live at Ragley, however grim the 'facts' his mother might present to him. 'And I haven't grown up at all,' he asserted blandly. 'I have remained exactly the same. From that moment on, I was intent upon retaining Ragley as the family home.'

Unfortunately, he and his mother were forced to leave the Hall when he was twenty. The conditioning process to which he had been subjected in the meantime had not worked. The estate's trustees, who then controlled it, considered that the house was far too large for the second half of the twentieth century and that the days of great houses were over. 'Their view,' recalled Lord Hertford, 'was that it was well known to be a fact – one or two of us are now proving the contrary – that we could not possibly afford to live at Ragley, whatever I thought and whatever I did.'

That Lord Hertford is a romantic and a showman is clear now that he is an established personality in his fifties. But all the evidence at the time suggested that here was a shy young man who simply did not know much about the cost of living in any house, large or small. Had he known that three decades later it would be costing him £5,000 a year for Ragley's electricity and £10,000 a year for central heating, perhaps he would have given in to 'realistic' thinking. But, on the whole, I think not.

It is easy enough for an accountant to suggest the solution to the 'problem' of huge old houses like Ragley: pull them down and build smaller houses in their place. That was more or less what the trustees' accountants advised. But even the briefest acquaintance with Ragley is enough to make one realize that the reality of the operation would be rather different. The man who removed the first block of stone would be committing an act of gross historic and aesthetic vandalism. This feeling was a thousand times more intense to the young man who had grown up there and saw it, quite simply, as the family home.

'Of course, when talking about the cost of running Ragley in the 1950s, you must divide today's figures by about ten,' pointed out Lord Hertford. 'Unfortunately my income at that time was divided by more than ten. I had virtually no money. But there still seemed some discrepancy between being too poor to live in one's own home and being educated at one of England's most expensive schools. I do now see that the relationship between the two is not very relevant, when one compares the amount we would have saved by my going to a cheaper school for a few years with the costs of living at Ragley.' But the resentment Lord Hertford felt as a youth was very real.

Soon coincidence presented the family with a means of living more cheaply than at Ragley. One of the tenant farmers on the estate moved out of his farm and his house and Lord Hertford's mother went to live at Kingley, a farm with 240 acres. About half was let to a temporary tenant and the rest retained for the dozen Jersey cows which the family had always kept, to provide milk for themselves rather than to sell.

Lord Hertford remembers telling his mother that he had worked out how much their Jersey butter was costing, and that it would be cheaper to eat caviar. 'But darling,' replied his mother, looking at him with her beautiful blue eyes, 'I don't like caviar.'

'I had quite a battle before we actually got rid of the cows,' remembered Lord Hertford. 'I was at Sandhurst, aged twenty, when we moved out of Ragley. I served three years with the Grenadier Guards and left them just before the Coronation of Queen Elizabeth II.'

Then came a significant year, during which the exiled aristocrat acquired the practical skills which would eventually enable him to rescue his home. He carried out the twelve months' farm work that was the necessary preliminary to being accepted at the Royal Agricultural College at Cirencester. This was on the estate of Apley in Shropshire. Lord Hertford lived in the village pub with several other students who also worked on the farms. He himself worked on the main home farm, a friend of his was studying estate management, and two other boys were working on the dairy farms. A student from South Africa left because he couldn't afford to pay the £4 a week it cost to live at the pub.

The young aristocrat *could* afford the cost of the pub out of his wages – just. It was one of the few occasions in his life when he had lived out on his own, away from Ragley, and he was earning £6 a week as a farm worker. This, he remembered with irony, was the same as the income of a Lieutenant in the Grenadier Guards. 'My status altered, but not my income. It would be rather different today. Farm workers are grossly underpaid now compared with Lieutenants in the Grenadier Guards – the former get only £3,000 or £4,000 a year.'

It was in the two years at Cirencester Royal Agricultural College that the young Lord 'began to learn about the cost of things'. But there was an understandably large amount of leeway to be made up and the knowledge was not accrued easily.

But his will was good. In 1956 he married a young lady with an aristocratic background as impeccable as his own. He moved away from Kingley Farm, where his mother remained, into Ragley Hall. At the same time he began to implement his plan to retrieve from his tenants as much of the family land as possible, in order to farm it himself.

He appointed a farm manager whom he remembers as being 'awfully nice, but in a sense as equally reluctant to do office work as I was. We were very active in rushing about the farm, but we didn't do our sums and we didn't make any money to start with.' This manager, a hard-working practical farmer from the north, was only a few years older than his aristocratic employer.

'We spent *too* much,' recalled Lord Hertford. 'When the farm made a loss, we realized it, although it was not a significant loss to start with. When we had been on the farm about a year, a tenant farmer died and we took over his farm as well. Then his neighbour indicated that he would retire if given a little sweetener, so we did that and this added a further 500 acres. That gave us over 700 in all, unfortunately quite widely separated.'

Lord Hertford was beginning to rebuild his jigsaw of land that was ultimately to bring over 2,000 acres of farmland under his direct control, a level which does not really satisfy him nor his son Harry, who casts his eyes towards lands long forsaken in the direction of Stratford-upon-Avon. It was a form of living up to the old military motto: 'When the enemy are punishing you mercilessly, attack.' Though the aristocratic entrepreneur was losing money, he calculated that once they had put together a bigger acreage, they would be able to farm it more efficiently.

'Yes, it did require a steady nerve. But it was perfectly obvious that the only sensible thing for a landowner to do was to farm as much of his own land as he could. Rents of farms at that time were pretty low – about £5 an acre, compared with £40 or so today, which is reasonable in the circumstances. It is true it still presents a low return on the capital value of the land; but on the other hand in today's farming conditions it is not easy for a tenant farmer to pay much more than £40 an acre and still see a profit for himself.'

While the agricultural land was being augmented, plans were also being made for opening Ragley to the public. Workers on the farms recall seeing

Lord and Lady Hertford, newly married, rushing about Ragley with paint brushes in their hands, though Lord Hertford thinks such recollections may be over-dramatic: 'We didn't do much redecoration, except for a little painting, chiefly downstairs, where everything was covered in brown paint. We covered it in pink to cheer it up. It wasn't very nice even then, but still, it was better than it had been.'

The newly-married couple had been there two years when the house was first opened to the public in 1958. The idea then was that the tourist trade would pay the basic running costs of the house and that the farms would produce the spending money.

At this point, Peter Crabtree entered the story. He was two years younger than Lord Hertford and entered his service as 'a sort of foreman'. He appeared to be well above the level of the average tractor driver and eventually, with some hesitation, Lord Hertford made him his farms manager. When I visited Ragley over twenty years later, Peter Crabtree was still farms manager and was helping to introduce Lord Hertford's son Harry to the operation of the farms. With the exception of one farm worker, Frank Gosney, he was the longest-serving farm employee.

Twenty years ago Lord Hertford and Peter Crabtree planned future strategy. 'And it hasn't altered very much,' said Lord Hertford. 'We had a dairy herd of Friesians at Kingley and we moved that up to the new farm at Weethley. Mainly it was because of the drains at Kingley – they went straight into the River Arrow and the River Board wouldn't allow this. To have done anything about it would have been terribly expensive, and in any case, the buildings at Kingley were antiquated and unsuitable.'

At that time, wheat was the most profitable branch of the farm business, and it still is. The advantage of having a dairy herd was nonetheless considerable – and revealing. It showed what a financially thin line the young aristocrat was treading in his attempts to revive what he saw as his birthright. Payments for wheat are traditionally made once a year, whereas payments for milk are made monthly. 'Milk helps the cash flow', is a Ragley maxim.

'We had to start when we were under-capitalized,' remembered Lord Hertford, 'and the dairy was the only way we could meet the necessary expenditure – another tractor or grain dryer, for example. The expense is *always* more than you think it will be.'

Back in the 1960s the estate suffered a setback. The tourist trade diminished, partly because Lord Hertford had gone to London in 1962 to run a public relations business of which he was chairman, living at Ragley only at weekends. He was probably overstretched, trying to run the house as a tourist business as well as working in London. He was at Ragley for long weekends, including Mondays, but it was the Swinging Sixties, when a public relations business with offices in Fleet Street and a flat off the King's Road in Chelsea seemed more fun than it would do today, when Fleet Street has the atmosphere of an elephants' graveyard and the King's Road a Wild West town long after the gold rush has passed it by.

'Opening the house to the public required a lot of publicity, and I appeared to have a flair for publicity,' said Lord Hertford. 'I had made a lot of friends in the Press and television.' He went into the public relations business with one of them, Bryan Thompson, who had come to the conclusion that he would make more profit in an independent partnership. Denis Hamilton (not the man who was to become the head of Times Newspapers) also entered the partnership.

Nepotism undoubtedly helped. Lord Hertford was asked if he would become chairman of an appeals' committee to raise a considerable amount of money in order to keep open the Hertford British Hospital in Paris, which had been founded by Sir Richard Wallace in memory of his father, the 4th Marquess. He wrote back (as befitted an aristocrat in hard straits but fighting form) offering the services of the public relations firm on a professional basis. 'They were disappointed because they hoped they would get me for free, but in fact we did quite a job for them. We raised about £150,000.' There was a party in St James's Palace to appeal for the hospital.

That put the public relations partnership firmly on the map. Fleet Street was impressed that a public relations firm could get inside St James's Palace and other contracts soon came in from British and overseas clients – all of which was good for the partnership but, perhaps, not so good for Ragley. Everyone assumed that Lord Hertford was the social head of the partnership whereas he was, as he puts it, 'just a working partner'. His wife went to London with him on Tuesdays and came back on Thursdays, one day earlier than he did. The Hall was only 'just jogging along'.

The year 1963 brought this pleasant existence to an abrupt conclusion. The architects were asked to prepare an urgent report on the state of

Ragley. More things were going wrong than the newly-married couple had expected, as is apt to be the case with far more modest old houses. The roof was leaking in many places. The front steps were crumbling and there were often blue flashes when the lights were switched on or off. The architects reported that about £150,000 needed to be spent on the place as a matter of urgency.

The days when a nobleman could get such a sum while by-passing the bureaucratic machine were long over. Lord Hertford wrote to the Historic Buildings Council in July of 1963. A year later, he had received an acknowledgement of his letter, but no decision.

Means tests are resented when imposed on the lower orders, but apparently Peers of the Realm are fair game. The council instructed a firm of accountants to draw up a very detailed report on the financial position of Ragley and the 8th Marquess of Hertford.

'I think it was because they took so long that I have never entirely forgiven them,' Lord Hertford will admit today. 'It was a deeply worrying period. I normally weigh about eleven stone. Never before this had my weight fallen below ten stone. I didn't see how we could carry on unless we got a grant.'

The British aristocracy may not be immune to the sort of worries that beset us all, nor to the resulting strain on mind and health, but they are trained by past history and present circumstances to seize every opportunity for putting things right. At this time, Lord Hertford was coincidentally invited to lecture to the Council for the Preservation of Rural England. 'I used my public relations expertise,' Lord Hertford recalled. He saw to it that newspapers, radio and television were all invited to his lecture. Then, in the course of it, he announced that unless he got some sort of Government grant, he would do what the trustees of the estate had advised him to do over ten years previously: demolish the house and build a smaller one on the site.

The resulting shock waves stimulated the Historic Buildings Council into some sort of action. They offered a grant of £30,000. Lord Hertford refused it on the grounds it was not nearly enough. They made another offer, then another, and so on, until there was a grant of £100,000. Some of Lord Hertford's own cash had to be added to this to do all the work immediately necessary. About 1,000 acres of land which had been taken over in 1947, standing on the Worcestershire side of the estate, was sold. That enabled the family to renew part of the roof, rebuild the front steps completely, renew the heating and plumbing systems, and redecorate every room on the main floor.

It was possible to get a grant for those operations because they directly benefited the public who looked over the house. The family's own money went into renovating a lot of the bedroom floors – they were not open to the public and so were not eligible for a grant.

'My weight began to go up again,' reported Lord Hertford. 'But it took a long time.'

For almost a year, Lord and Lady Hertford had to move out of Ragley while the work was carried out. It was not good for morale: 'On the other side of Alcester, I had a farm house converted into flats. I took two of them for ourselves.'

But even two flats used as one seemed like a prison to a couple who had had the run of Ragley, especially when the renovations took rather longer than they had initially expected. 'We were out of the place for ten months,' said Lord Hertford. 'I hated being in a flat. I felt cribbed, cabinned and confined. I didn't worry too much about it in the winter, but come the summer, there was nowhere particularly to take the dogs for a walk, because to get to the west side of the estate meant I had to cross a very busy main road from Alcester to Birmingham. Whereas here at Ragley you are in the middle of the estate and just walk out with the dogs. I missed Ragley very much in the summer. If you have ten minutes to spare before lunch, here you can stroll out into the garden. Oh yes, there was a garden there at the flats. There was a patch about the size of my study here – not somewhere you could *walk* in.'

For the first, and last, time Lord Hertford's life was a commuter journey between two flats – the one in Chelsea and the one near Alcester. He was in Warwickshire for the weekends and in London during the week, and restless without Ragley itself.

There was also the restlessness of the bank manager to deal with.

'Talking the Bank Into a Loan' is a game that almost all successful businessmen have to play with great skill from time to time. The landed gentry with their stately estates have less trouble in winning the game than most. They have an almost invincible trump card.

'I don't think I have ever had to borrow sums of money for the house that weren't quite easily covered by the value of the estate,' said Lord Hertford. 'In other words, they weren't out of proportion.'

I asked him if his bank, the Midland, had ever been difficult. He thought a moment. 'They have never been *impossible*. They have never actually refused my cheque. They have screamed in anguish occasionally: "You can't do this to us!" But they have always done it, mainly because the capital value of the Ragley estate, put on the open market, is very large, though unfortunately it bears very little relation to the income from it.'

His security, said Lord Hertford, was 6,000 acres at up to £2,000 an acre, or roughly £12 million. Of course, part of the land was farmed by a tenant rather than by the owner and would fetch less on the open market: say £1,500 an acre.

'It doesn't really matter *exactly* what it is worth,' pointed out Lord Hertford briskly, 'because I am not about to sell it.'

There has been only one period when the bank got a bit edgy, though no more edgy than Lord Hertford himself. That was in the middle of the 1960s when major work was being done on the Hall. The Government had finally come across with some grants, but were infuriatingly slow in paying out the actual cash.

'I do remember experiencing a great deal of trouble when we first got the Government grants,' Lord Hertford told me. 'The building contractors were beginning to demand weekly chits signed by the architects. What was supposed to happen was that the architects sent me a signed document which said, for instance, "We authorize payment of £2,000." I paid out the £2,000 and then sent the chit to the Department of the Environment – and nothing happened for three months at a time, by which time I had paid out a great deal *more* money.'

At that time, the estate was still run by an agent, who informed Lord Hertford that he couldn't carry on paying out money at this rate. Later he became ill, while Lord Hertford's weight dropped from eleven stone to ten as a result of the strain. There is no record of what happened to the bank manager's health.

An appeal to the Historic Buildings Council followed. They said the procedure could be changed and a new arrangement was made. The architects sent the pestilent but vital chits straight to the Department of the Environment, who then managed to speed up their payments considerably.

'There was a nasty moment,' recalled Lord Hertford, 'when I owed the bank £40,000 and the Government owed me £40,000. But the Government didn't pay me the interest the bank was charging me. That is quite a common problem with grant-aided work. Our particular problem took a lot of working out, but in the end we reached a more or less satisfactory solution.'

The vital factor that decided the issue was the imperishable value of Ragley's land, an advantage not shared by any industrialist trying to persuade the bank to lend against the problematical value of buildings and machinery.

Lord Hertford put it succinctly: 'On the whole, over the past twenty years, land has increased more or less in line with inflation. While it might now be worth up to £2,000 an acre, in 1951 it would have been valued at about £100 an acre.'

Fortunately, while there were frustrations over financing the Hall the farming side was going fairly well. In the late 1960s the estate took over direct control of part of another farm, alongside the one at Weethley, called Park Farm. Gradually more and more acres of the farm were acquired, so that by the beginning of the 1970s the family was farming just over 1,000 acres. The income from this, plus the sale of the land on the Worcestershire side of the estate, helped towards the cost of renovating Ragley Hall (it cost Lord Hertford himself about the same as the £100,000 grant) and keeping it going generally. The estate was, in fact, by this time making a small profit, to which were added rents from the remaining tenants and the profits from public visits to Ragley. The result – which tended to be typical – was a small net loss on the whole undertaking in the course of the financial year, a loss small enough to enable the estate and the family to stay afloat.

A fluke of circumstance then took Lord Hertford himself nearer the centre of the Ragley stage. In 1973 his agent, who was responsible for the overall running of Ragley, became extremely ill and retired. He was an ex-Royal Air Force man who had had some harrowing experiences in the Second World War. He had also been an intense worrier and at Ragley there was always plenty to worry about.

'He worried much more than I did about my finances,' recollected Lord Hertford. 'We were quite a good combination, because he was always a pessimist and I was always an optimist, and the mid-line between our opinions might well be right! But he said he was sorry, he must have an extended period of sick leave. So I took over – someone had to handle the administration. I told my partners in London that I wouldn't be in London more than one or two days a week. Then it became apparent that the agent was not going to come back, and I told my partners I wouldn't be back at all, because running Ragley was obviously a full-time job.'

It was also, probably, the job he had always really wanted.

'I could possibly have obtained another agent,' said Lord Hertford drily. 'But I came to the conclusion that the agent's life was rather better than the life I was living in London.'

He sold his public relations firm, with the full agreement of his partners, to a large company which also ran ferries. Had he ploughed the revenue into Ragley? 'At once!' was his prompt response.

The 8th Marquess of Hertford found that he had at last become what he wanted to be. 'I *enjoy* running the estate. It is the job of a land agent, a manager. I tell the maintenance staff what to do, and the woodmen and the head forester. I deal with the tenanted farms, reviewing the rents every three years. I arrange the allocation of the costs of the drainage system, erect new buildings for them and agree how this is to be paid for.'

Under his direct stewardship, more of the tenanted farms were taken over. One tenant with 1,200 acres who said he would leave if the price was right, was paid a substantial sum of money and went off to develop his other business interests. The following year, another farm was brought back into the control of the family, one of 250 acres. This brought the Hertford farms up to 2,600 acres.

Did that make Lord Hertford content, or did he see the active control of himself and his family as landowners increasing further with the years, thus reversing even more the process of two generations ago, whereby businessmen-farmers took over from the poor old impoverished land-owners? 'Well, I no longer want to *buy* a tenant out, put it that way. But if, for any reason, a farm became vacant I would not relet it. I can make more money out of farming it myself. If the 2,600 acres were bringing in rent, it would be about £40 an acre. We can make an income of, say, £80 an acre by farming it ourselves, and in good years we have done that.'

The relentless determination to stay at Ragley at almost any cost, and the constant search for new ways in which that cost can be realistically met, have undoubtedly been initiated by the 8th Marquess. But every shrewd businessman (and even those who mistrust Lord Hertford's cigarette holder affirm that he is a shrewd businessman) needs a reliable and trusted right-hand man. The estate and the house Lord Hertford has managed himself, but the farms have been managed by the man who, almost from the start of the revival, has been, if the title belongs to anybody, the Marquess's right-hand man. The forestry staff at Ragley will sometimes mutter jealously that the farms are given top priority at the expense of the forests. If true, that may be because of the great influence of Peter Crabtree, who has known His Lordship for many years. When Lord Hertford's son and heir, the Earl of Yarmouth, first took an interest in the farms, concentrating on the sheep, he was given a dog as a present. Peter Crabtree was the man who gave it.

'I have become part of the scenery,' he reflected. 'Lord and Lady Hertford were just married when I first arrived. I have seen the family born, educated and growing up, and the Hall opened to the public. I have seen the farms grow from 300 acres to nearly 3,000. I suppose the difference in working at a place like this compared with anywhere else today, at least as far as I am concerned, is the sense of *intimacy* one gets.'

Peter Crabtree came to Ragley in 1957. Most of his working life – latterly as farms manager – has been spent on the estate, and he has been closely concerned with the growth of the farms. He is a Black Country-man with a realism which sits easily behind his businesslike metal spectacles; but where Ragley and Lord Hertford's family are concerned, he is a sentimentalist. It was plain that he identified strongly not only with the practical details of his complex job, but also with the fates and fortunes of the family at the Hall. They say this is a hard and competitive age and that there is no room for sentiment in successful business. Those who say it are usually townsmen. Even in an era dominated by the idea of passionless professionalism, the great estate seduces its servants high and low into a willing sentimental loyalty, a direct personal identification with the Lord of the estate. The great estate appears to be one of the few remaining features of traditional British life which has within it shades of both nobility *and* survival. That is why people like Ragley's farms manager can successfully reconcile their realism with their sentimental loyalty.

Peter Crabtree did not move from a businessman's farm in Melton Mowbray to Ragley because he was merely in search of bigger pastures. At that time, the Melton Mowbray farm had 300 acres and Ragley had no more. He came, I suspect, because Lord Hertford was then a young man like himself and Peter Crabtree could identify more easily with a man of his own generation than he could with a man whose career was already made: 'At Ragley, there was an agent for the estate, there was a farms manager, there was me and there was 300 acres. At that stage, speaking honestly, I simply wasn't in it – I was simply the farms manager's assistant. But I felt part of the estate.'

After three years, Peter Crabtree took the departing farms manager's place. This was not without some secret soul-searching on Lord Hertford's part because although Crabtree had been a farms manager at Melton Mowbray, he was still comparatively inexperienced. But there was a chance that he would mature alongside Lord Hertford, and that is what actually happened. Lord Hertford tactfully kept his initial reservations to himself and the two of them now, as Peter Crabtree puts it, 'talk about everything – we seem to talk of cabbages and kings'.

'This is probably general with these sort of estates,' said Peter Crabtree when I caught him one day at the headquarters of the Friesian cattle herd – one of his ports of call as he tours around the farms, exhorting a worker here, keeping an eye on a modernization there. 'I mean general where the owner is responsible, as he is here now, and where he is very much in evidence. One becomes very much involved in the family battle, as it were, to retain an inheritance. You become part of them and get taken along with it, if you develop the same attitude as I do. Lord Hertford's enthusiasm is infectious. It is difficult not to be enthusiastic oneself, because of the close involvement with the family.'

This involvement can be almost a round-the-clock business. '*Anyone* who has got this sort of job is responsible twenty-four hours of the day,' admitted Peter Crabtree, 'but that is not to say it is onerous, because it is part of life. It is accepted as such and you really never think anything of it.'

When Peter Crabtree first came to Ragley, the estate and farms were still in the hands of the agent, and Lord Hertford was a 'little bit removed', because he was still with his public relations business in London. But it was obvious, even then, that Lord Hertford's heart was at Ragley, where it had always been: 'Lord Hertford has one reason for living, as far as I know, and that is Ragley. There is no way you can divorce the two at all, and you work to that end.'

When the agent became ill and retired, Peter Crabtree saw this as 'tipping the balance' in his employer's mind in the battle between the possibilities of extending his London business undertakings or taking a more personal grip on Ragley. Perhaps circumstances had forced the issue in the direction that Lord Hertford wanted.

The result had a decisive influence not only on the lives of the family at the Hall, but on the lives of all the families on the estate. Peter Crabtree's wife, who had always worked with him closely on the farms, and kept the farm accounts, began keeping the accounts of the estate as a whole, and Peter Crabtree became involved in the running of the estate as well as farm business. At Ragley, the lion's share of the income comes from arable farming, which means chiefly cereals. Second comes dairying – when I first met Peter Crabtree he was supervising the complete rebuilding of a dairy for over 250 Friesians. Once again he found himself working alongside Lord Hertford on a dairy modernization project, just as he had done twenty years previously when he had helped move the Friesians from Kingley to Weethley. It was perhaps an indication that human beings are still more permanent than machinery and buildings in today's mechanized age. The Weethley buildings were only patched up in the 1960s when the herd was moved in, but by the beginning of the 1980s they had been diverted to secondary uses and a new dairy complex was built to take over 250 cows, compared with the 120 that had been kept there during the past twenty years. But the dairies are still economical in terms of labour, employing only two men and a boy.

Third on the profitability list are the sheep, the branch of the operation chosen as the one which Lord Hertford's heir Harry, the Earl of Yarmouth, would make his own. Forestry comes next – a matter left chiefly to Lord Hertford himself and his forestry experts.

All the buying for the farms and estates – with the exception of the house itself – is the responsibility of Peter Crabtree. He has bought all the raw materials and all the machinery, thus following in his own family tradition as well as that of the family at the Hall; for his father also farmed.

The family tradition of Ragley means – and Peter Crabtree is well aware of it – that eventually the Earl of Yarmouth will take over the running of the estate. At the time I first met them both, the Earl, at twenty-one, seemed little more than a lad who did not bother to shave every day. But one day he would be the master of Ragley, and those around him knew it. Tactfully, he had to be given an opportunity to learn in the present, while he was paid the respect due to his future. The sheep, as will emerge elsewhere in this book, were the hard taskmasters to which the young Earl was introduced after discussion between the Lord and the farms manager.

'Lord Yarmouth has been here six months,' said Peter Crabtree at one point. 'Rather than let him wander about with no specific involvement or responsibility, it was decided, at Lord Hertford's suggestion, that as he was keen on the sheep side, we should put him there. A lad of twenty-one has a great deal to learn, but his responsibility is going to be enormous in due course. We thought it would probably be a good thing to let him – in theory and partly in practice – take responsibility for what is a fairly large enterprise: one, anyway, that has a definite view point, rather than let him wander around willy-nilly. He is involved 100 per cent in the sheep farm. Lord Hertford decided to make him responsible for recording the sheep and handling the marketing side. We want him to organize the operation. But we have tried, in the last twenty years, to make activities compatible. We haven't had watertight compartments. We are trying to encourage him to form his own ideas and standards, to bring in some new thinking. Hopefully, it is going to be beneficial.'

One of the possible sadnesses of working closely with a family not one's own is that the heir will inevitably have his own ideas, which may or may not be good for one's own future. Peter Crabtree said with some reserve that his future prospects had been 'discussed'. Of course, he said, in time, as the Earl of Yarmouth became more and more involved, he would take responsibility which had previously been the farms manager's, especially as he appeared to be more interested in farming than he was in the opening of the Hall to the public.

'You need to be the 8th Marquess of Hertford to do what the 8th Marquess of Hertford is doing,' reflected Peter Crabtree. 'You need to be the public relations showman needed to sell Ragley, if you like. A lot of people would consider it one hell of a bore. Lord Hertford not only enjoys it but is extremely good at it. I believe his son is very conscious of the fact that the tourist trade is very important to the family maintaining residence at Ragley, and that you don't live in a house that size without it. But, who knows? Possibly he won't want to. We all wonder. Who can tell what the future holds? You need to be tremendously enthusiastic and hard working, like Lord Hertford is on the house side of the estate, to maintain the level of income that he does – which is vital.'

In Peter Crabtree's view, Ragley was a successful estate because the place was not 'full of comptrollers' handling the administrative work: Lord Hertford handled it all himself. And the fact that he was there made it more interesting for the staff, as well as for the public. They got swept up in the public interest. 'Everyone around here is fascinated by the estate.

People say to you, "Where does he live?" I say, "In the house," and they say, "But *where* in the house?" I say, "The *whole* of the house." That is why Ragley is different. In some ways the house is just like my house, it is a private house.'

I asked Peter Crabtree whether, in his opinion, Lord Hertford put all his energies into the house and the estate because he liked high living or because he wanted to preserve a tradition. 'You need to know him very well to know the answer. He set out to use Ragley as his ancestors used it, but probably rather better. He has a cook and a butler and a minimum of staff. He strives to maintain not the standard of living his ancestors had, but Ragley as a *home*.'

At Christmas time, he pointed out, the family used all the rooms in the Hall, and you never knew who was going to come out of what door. This made the whole place seem very different from a museum. A week before Christmas there was a staff dinner, now with a disco, for eighty people. Ragley at Christmas time was simply beautiful, he said. 'It takes you back. You can visualize what it was like sixty or seventy years ago, when the number of staff would be fourfold. It seems to mirror the whole thing, somehow, the Christmas dinner. Then I picture it as it was in 1950, when I would have thought it was inevitably going to be something like a town hall; and then Lord Hertford starting to pull the thing back, until the estate was almost what it was at its inception, a private home and a way of life for the family – Lord Hertford's and others.'

Peter Crabtree had little patience with the people who occasionally chanced the comment in his hearing that one man had no 'right' to a place the size of Ragley. In his view, Lord Hertford *did* have the right because he took active pleasure out of providing jobs and homes for the members of his staff. He might or might not be embarrassed at hearing that testimonial (Lord Hertford was a difficult man to embarrass, said Peter Crabtree), but it was true, and it made him the right man for the Hall and the estate.

'How long it can go on for, I don't know. It is like a battle here, a financial battle. To be able to live in a house that size is an enormous achievement, and to maintain the estate as he wants it to be maintained. . . .' Peter Crabtree shook his head thoughtfully, but his reverie did not last long. He had to dash off to another farm on the estate, leaving behind him the impression of a family employee whose life had given him more fun, and more sense of belonging (though perhaps not more freedom) than he would have experienced outside the gates of Ragley – in the industrial West Midlands for example, where he might well have worked had not fate dictated otherwise.

This sense of belonging, quite easily understandable in a man who occupies a senior position at Ragley, is also experienced by those who might be thought, by cynical city dwellers, to have less of a vested interest in the proceedings. It is the good fortune of estates like Ragley that, even in the latter half of the twentieth century, they are able to attract and hold steady workers who are loyal to their crafts without having an especially pressing ambition to 'better' themselves in conventional terms.

When I first met Frank Gosney, at the age of forty-five Ragley's longest-serving farm worker, he was working hard on the harvest, and Lord Hertford himself turned up shortly afterwards to make sure, with great politeness, that I did not excessively delay him in this task by getting his *entire* life story. Frank Gosney, a well-built, greying and balding man who nevertheless looked much younger than he was – helped by his deep tan – was pointed out to me as that unusual creature in modern British society – a man who had been offered promotion repeatedly and always turned it down.

'I am one of those chaps who don't like responsibility,' he confirmed cheerfully when he climbed down from the cab of the combiner he was driving. 'When I finish at five or whenever it is at night, that is it! I can go home and forget about the job. When you're foreman or manager, it doesn't ever stop. It is around you all the time. Someone wants you on the phone at night. As it is, I can forget about it. I am fairly paid. The money is quite good, because I get over the odds. I started this morning at eight o'clock and at haymaking I might not leave off until about eight at night. But after that I don't have to worry.'

Frank Gosney asked me if I had ever seen how worried foremen sometimes looked. That was not for him. 'I think farming is not like it used to be. Everyone is worrying all the time in that sort of position. It is so mechanized, and you have to know so much now.'

When I met him, Frank Gosney had already been at Ragley for twenty-four years. He discovered that the rat-race was not for him even before he got to the estate. He used to work in an engineering works producing back axles and electrical components for lorries. He had previously been employed on a farm since leaving school but, in an uncharacteristic fit of ambition, went into industry 'for the big money'.

'But it didn't suit me,' he said shortly.

His mother, who lived practically next door to the factory, could understand why he disliked the place – particularly the fumes and the feeling of being inside all the time. She noticed an advertisement for a farm worker at Ragley, and pointed it out to her son. When he applied, Lord Hertford asked him where he was then working, and why he wanted to move. He seemed to appreciate Frank Gosney's explanation.

Immediately after Peter Crabtree became farms manager to Lord Hertford, he offered Frank Gosney promotion to foreman and was surprised when the offer was turned down. When further offers met with the same response, Frank Gosney was accepted for what he was: a trusted and reliable worker who simply did not strive to be a Chief rather than an Indian.

'I live,' said Frank Gosney cheerfully, 'in a tied bungalow, a hundred years old – two bedrooms, a sitting room, a living room, a kitchen, and a bathroom built on in recent years. The best of the job is that, at this time of year, you can be outside and not shut in where you can't get the benefit of the good weather. It doesn't irk me to have to work under somebody else. There is not really any aggro, we can all go our merry way. The foreman works it as a team. There is no, "You will do this or that". They just ask you.'

The only disadvantage of the life, he conceded, was that at harvest time help was needed everywhere on the farms, and it was difficult to arrange holidays in this period of good weather. Usually he and his family tried to take a fortnight between Easter and early July, which was not very good holiday weather, unless you were lucky.

'The wife gets a bit down about it sometimes. She works at Dunnington School, in the area of the estate. She has six weeks' holiday when we are smack in the middle of the harvest. Oh well, maybe we might finish early. . . .'

Later I came across Frank Gosney working on harvesting the spring barley at Cold Comfort Farm on the other side of the estate, and it didn't appear that they would finish that year's harvest early. 'It's rather thin this year, mainly due to the weather. It's all right when it's dry, but when it gets a bit damp at night it is a little devil. It was very damp last night. It was about eleven o'clock this morning before we could start cutting it.'

But there were compensations for these working frustrations, as there very often are in a fairly closed, but at least highly personal environment like Ragley's. Working with him was his sixteen-year-old son Philip, employed at Ragley at that time under the youth opportunities programme which aimed to give otherwise unemployed school-leavers a period of work experience, without requiring long-term commitment on the part of the employer. The family spirit had reared its head once again at Ragley, as it seemed to do at all social levels. Family pride, indeed, had been one of the motivating forces behind Ragley's revival and might in future be the means of its actual expansion.

Lord Hertford's son Harry had made it known to me that he would like, when *he* inherited, to regain control of much of the land between Ragley and Stratford-upon-Avon, which had once belonged to the estate, but which had been sold at the time of the Second World War to pay death duties. I asked Lord Hertford if he thought that this was simply a young man's dream, or if it was in any way realistic.

'*I* have never been *realistic* in trying to live here. If I can stay here, why shouldn't he have his ambition? If he wants another 1,000 acres he will have to spend £1,000,000 at least. It is a question of making enough money.'

Indeed it is, and always will be. Financial acumen and managerial skills are vital if the Ragleys of England are to survive. A great estate which can claim to have pioneered new methods in farming has an enormous advantage in attracting forward-looking staff, as well as favourable publicity – its very lifeblood. Here Ragley has recently made at least one major coup. This was installing the first Tribone system of dairy milking in Britain, which drastically cut the amount of time needed to milk the 250 or so Friesian cows. The system, known as Tricon in the USA, uses a triangular milking parlour, in which the cows are put in rows on each side of the triangle in turn, instead of being arranged in the more usual herringbone formation.

With this system, it is possible to milk the herd in about two hours, compared with the five hours it took previously. Milking takes place three times a day – at four-thirty in the morning, twelve-thirty p.m. and seven p.m. One milker comes in at four-thirty in the morning and is off at two-thirty in the afternoon. Another comes in at eight-thirty a.m. and goes on until nine-thirty in the evening, with an hour-and-a-half lunch break and a similar break for supper. The gain in real productivity has been considerable, and the staff have been encouraged to consider themselves professionals in a thoroughly professional environment.

I asked the dairy manager, Barry Percival – a man in his mid-thirties who left South Africa because he didn't like the 'political outlook' – how he liked working on a stately estate with limited staff (two cowmen, one of them, Nick McDonagh, only nineteen) after having numerous black African staff at the two dairies (each with 500 cows) he managed in South Africa.

'South Africa is a very rich country and farmers over there are very up-to-date and modernized,' he replied. 'But I would have thought Ragley compares very favourably now we have the new building. I would have thought this puts us on a par with anything in the world.'

As the 8th Marquess of Hertford stated so bluntly: it is really a question of making enough money. Perhaps that sentence should be incorporated into the family crests of all Britain's surviving aristocrats. As Ragley's regeneration proves, it has been as important to Ragley as the more time-honoured family motto: *Fide et Amore*, or By Faith and By Love.

2
Entertaining at
the Hall

THE PASTA MANUFACTURERS from all over Europe did not, they said, believe in formality. When they went to their dinner at Ragley as members of the Food Manufacturers' Federation Inc, they avoided formal evening dress. But it was very noticeable – somewhat to the amusement of the British paying guests – that they did *not* avoid the 8th Marquess of Hertford.

On the contrary. 'The Europeans were quite overwhelmed by the whole thing, actually,' said one of the British contingent afterwards. 'And they were particularly overwhelmed by His Lordship. They all wanted to rush in to shake his hand at the reception.'

Others noticed this too. 'There were about ninety of us to dinner in the Great Hall,' said a British guest. 'We asked Lord Hertford if he would like to attend the dinner and he said he would. The Europeans don't tend to go in for black tie. It wasn't until we started going in for the meal that we saw the Continentals were hanging back in the hope that they would have the chance to shake His Lordship by the hand. They like an English Lord just as much as the English do.'

Guests at this particular dinner said that the atmosphere of Ragley was 'something special'.

'You can go to many stately homes for a function,' said one guest, 'and you find that the staff care about you, and they are all very super, but you feel you are visiting just another stately home. At Ragley, because Lord Hertford is involved himself, you get the nice feeling that you are being entertained in a home by the owner himself. I didn't realize until well into the dinner that the food was prepared by outside caterers and I was very impressed; obviously it was not as though the kitchen was just off the Great Hall, and the food was excellent.'

'Of course,' said one of the guests, 'it comes down to money. It was £50 a head, inclusive of wines and the champagne reception. One can do it more cheaply, but Lord Hertford didn't charge for his appearance among us. That was another nice thing, because there are plenty of places where you can have dinner with the owner only if you are prepared to pay enormous amounts of money for the privilege.'

The guests at this dinner, in short, did not have it forced on their attention that their presence at the Hall with the 8th Marquess was not purely social. That, after all, is the hallmark of the successful British aristocrat. Even when he is taking people's money in reasonable quantity, he does not leave the customer feeling that he or she is merely part of a commercial relationship.

But commercial it frequently is – it has to be. Entertainment at Ragley Hall is not, therefore, always quite what it seems.

The wealthy American businessmen and the guests of British Leyland who sit down to dinner in the Great Hall are welcome, but they are not always there for reasons of friendship; in fact, it is more than likely that they are there because they are contributing the liquid cash vital to Ragley's survival.

Lord Hertford made no attempt to hide the fact: entertaining on a professional basis was essential if Ragley was to pay its way, and if that meant sitting down to dinner with sixty or so people, so be it. Not the sort of intimate gathering he would be part of for choice, perhaps; but welcome because in that way Ragley could be saved, and because he could indulge in his favourite topic of conversation – the excellence of his beloved estate.

'A dozen, perhaps, for fun. Above this it is for money. I don't think I would ever invite sixty to lunch for pleasure,' he said firmly.

A dozen professional functions a month is by no means unusual. They have ranged from one hundred guests (and possible customers) of British Leyland or Vauxhall Motors in the large dining rooms (or twenty representatives of a trade organization in the small dining room) to two rich Americans from Hawaii. The latter couple so touched Lord Hertford's manorial pride by coming all the way up to Ragley from the Savoy Hotel in London for their visit, that he was glad to have them tête-a-tête in his own private dining room – though he had never met them before and, right up to the time of their arrival, had no real idea who they were.

'We have these three rooms in which to dine. If we have less than twelve guests we tend to dine in our private dining room. All we did for the Hawaiian couple was to give them a much better dinner than the dinner we would have had as a family if they hadn't been here. I don't drink vintage wine every night, but I will do it for paying guests. That is my attitude.' And a very lucrative approach it has proved to be. Representatives of various organizations ring up the Hall asking if they can be professionally entertained, and bookings are also made through travel agencies. The 8th Marquess tends to invite friends and neighbours over to meet paying guests only if he feels that the paying guests will be congenial company. The Hawaiian couple, being an unknown quantity, met only Lord Hertford and his family. 'The children regard it as part of the life,' Lord Hertford assured me.

I asked him to define the sort of people he would invite to meet his friends and neighbours.

'Nice ones.'

'Yes, but how do you judge who is a "nice" person?'

The answer came without hesitation. 'Whether I take a liking to them or not.'

A Lord can *still* afford to be lordly in his own home, however much he may rely on cheques from the outside world to retain his privileged status.

The whole pattern of entertainment, both private and professional, tends to be fairly rigorous. I asked Lord Hertford to let me see his time-table for a fairly average October, with the autumn entertainment season just beginning. There were ten professional receptions or dinners that month, punctuated by a few days in Venice to celebrate his daughter Carolyn's twentieth birthday.

The first weekend that October had been purely social, a fairly typical private weekend enjoyed by the aristocracy of the present day. There were two people to stay: a friend from New York and an attractive young lady from one of the great art salerooms. 'It was an ordinary dinner when they arrived,' remembered Lord Hertford. 'It was not a party. Only the woman was extremely pretty and rather utterly charming, and so dinner with her stopped later the next night, as it were.' What was an ordinary dinner? 'Oh, soup – my favourite is clear consommé. In October, it's a bit early for pheasants, so we would have had partridges, with potatoes and Brussels sprouts. It was one of the few weekends when most of the family were together. One daughter would have been at Cambridge, but let's say there were eight or so of us. I have the most elaborate meals I can when I have the chance, but we don't have them all the time. We tend to have English food, whatever the season. With guests, we probably have pudding; on our own we would have cheese and biscuits or chocolate mousse. I love cheese and have it for every meal.'

Whether the Hertfords are entertaining privately or professionally, stew is unlikely to feature on the menu, especially if it contains pearl barley. The 8th Marquess cannot stand it: 'I don't know why I hate it, I just do. They have it here when I am out. The rest of the family quite like it. We don't buy our meat from the butcher, we get it straight from the farm, and when you do that you realize that an extremely high proportion of the beast is not fillet steak! We have to have things like stews, cottage pie, all those rather dull things. But I try to avoid soup which contains pearl barley and onions, and I can't eat tapioca. Guests would not get soup except with pheasant or game.'

In the past fish was delivered to Ragley once a week direct from the fishing port of Grimsby, but the idea didn't work out. The delivery man stopped first in Alcester High Street, so by the time he reached Ragley all the best fish had gone. It was decided that the cook should go into Alcester and intercept the fish van every Tuesday morning. Vegetables have to be bought locally as Ragley grows only a small selection in its own gardens, but the estate has its own supply of venison as well as beef and lamb.

The motto at Ragley is that the only difference between private and professional entertaining, on any scale, is that more people are brought in to help for professional functions. A footman or waiter to every six guests is the absolute minimum. The ideal is one footman to four people.

'Professional' guests may receive some of His Lordship's fine wines from his cellar of 2,000 or so bottles; purely social visitors are more likely to receive a wine which His Lordship thinks matches their sophistication.

'There are two sorts of people who have the best wine here,' he told me briskly. 'The people I most like and the people I think will most appreciate it. They overlap, but do not necessarily coincide.'

Thus, if there was a party of his daughter's friends who were not really knowledgeable about wine, the best wine would not be produced. It would be rather a waste, and His Lordship was not reluctant to say so.

Funnily enough, his eldest daughter did notice when something rather good was produced and would say, 'Is this a '66?' He himself could not tell what Château a wine came from, though if he were offered a Chablis Latour 1948, he would notice it. A party of twenty teenagers would get Berry Brothers Claret at £2.58 a bottle: 'They put on 15 per cent Value Added Tax and take off 10 per cent discount because I order so much.'

A party of eight adults attending as private or paying guests would be expected to drink about a bottle a head, including the champagne which Ragley always likes to serve before dinner. The eight would probably drink two bottles of champagne before dinner, then have sherry with the soup, then despatch three bottles of claret and a bottle of port afterwards. It usually worked out at a bottle a head, said Lord Hertford, and left enough over for a meal next day when he was by himself.

The aristocracy have a preference for port rather than brandy and few paying guests will refuse port when it is offered.

'Most people prefer port, I think. I have always loved it,' stated Lord Hertford flatly.

When I looked slightly surprised, and said that port played little part in the life of the brandy-drinking middle classes, the 8th Marquess seemed rather taken aback: 'I did not know it was *ever* unfashionable. I assume my guests, who are offered port, will like it.'

In fact, the wily Marquess has tended to stack the deck against any guest who might prefer the obviously lower-class brandy: he plies them with the port first and then asks them if they would like a brandy. At that stage, most guests feel constrained to refuse.

Cigars are likely to be offered to a small party, though Lord Hertford does not smoke them himself. Female guests are usually expected to have their own cigarettes, since Lord Hertford smokes Players, which are not too popular with the ladies. Ladies expect filter tips and often have to accept that Lord Hertford has forgotten to provide any – at least if the party is a private one. Paying guests will most definitely get everything they are prepared to pay for.

That pleasurably punishing schedule of entertainment at the Hall during the month of October meant that there was a fairly generous exodus of bottles from His Lordship's cellar, for both personal and professional reasons.

His diary, and his comments on it, went as follows:

Saturday, October 4. Wedding of member of family of friends in Warwickshire, then dinner with neighbours.

Sunday, October 5. The house was closed to public. Champagne reception for the house staff to celebrate. Small party and presents for the lodge keeper and the tea room manageress, who were leaving after twenty years.

Monday, October 6. Rent audit – a week late. Attend charity event for Save the Children Fund at the Park Lane Hotel, plus the House of Lords.

Tuesday, October 7. Hair cut in London at Carlton Tower Hotel. Train back to Ragley in time for buffet lunch plus tour for a party of twenty. ('This was cancelled. We charge about £15 a head for the whole thing. It frequently happens that they are cancelled.') Four p.m., see man about having model boats in the stable yard. Meeting of Parents Anonymous, a charity. ('I agreed to be their patron.')

Wednesday, October 8. Meeting with Midland Bank farm adviser. ('I find them extremely useful and helpful. They lend me large sums of money.') Lunch in Birmingham for a charity. Four p.m., take tour of house. Seven-thirty p.m., charity meeting near Stratford-upon-Avon – Action Unlimited, affiliated to Action for the Crippled Child.

Thursday, October 9. Pay day. ('I always hand out pay personally. It is one way of keeping contact.') Then to London for House of Lords.

Friday, October 10. Tour for thirty-five at ten-forty-five a.m., plus sherry. Tour for twenty at twelve noon. See new farm man who is due to arrive.

Saturday, October 11. Two Texans for lunch. ('Cancelled. It can't be helped. You forget it.')

Sunday, October 12. At eleven a.m., a number of AC vintage car owners arrive to see whether the drive is suitable for a race meeting. Church.

Monday, October 13. Spend whole day with friend who is forestry expert and gives professional advice about the woodlands. He stays the night.

Tuesday, October 14. Ditto.

Wednesday, October 15. Take restaurateur to lunch to discuss Ragley's restaurant. New Lodge keeper to arrive. Organizer of dog show to pay visit, to see if Ragley is a suitable venue.

Thursday, October 16. Lord and Lady Hertford to London. Lunch at House of Lords, then to wedding of friends of children. ('The wedding invitation was rather sweet. They asked us because they began to get engaged at a ball at Ragley. After the wedding Lord Montagu drove me back here at considerable speed. We left London at four-thirty and he was bathing and changing here in time for dinner in Birmingham.') At Ragley, twenty-four people to dinner from the Vauxhall Motor Company. Three of them stay the night as paying guests – £50 for dinner £50 for bed and breakfast.

Friday, October 17. Morning in office. Meet man suggesting installation of solar heating system in roof. ('This turned out not to be worthwhile. It would have cost too much – like £10,000. And it wouldn't do all the heating, it would only give a boost.')

Saturday, October 18. Hunting.

Sunday, October 19. Court Leet (old Manor Court of Alcester with High Bailiff), marching in procession to Alcester church. ('I am Lord of the Manor. It is the one time of the year when they pray for me, which is rather nice. I also wrote a gardening article for *Homes and Gardens* magazine.')

Monday, October 20. Inspection of cottage roof on estate that needs repair. Meet daughter off two-forty-one train from Evesham. Meet man about holding exhibition of china at Ragley. Twenty-four paying guests from Vauxhall, three of them staying the night at usual rates.

Tuesday, October 21. A party of eighty people connected with the Motor Show to dinner in the Great Hall.

Wednesday, October 22. Discussion group and exhibition of tour operators in Coventry, where Ragley has stand. At one p.m., tour of Ragley and buffet lunch for twenty-five. Evening – dinner with neighbours.

Thursday, October 23. Pay day. Take money round as usual. Meeting with estate agent at eleven-thirty to advise on farm rents and other estate matters. Evening – twenty-four to dinner from Vauxhall, in connection with the Motor Show. ('British Leyland have been here, not connected with the Motor Show, and I hope they come again.')

Friday, October 24. Youngest daughter Anne's half-term. Meeting of Shakespeare Country Association of Tourist Attractions at Ragley – twelve members to stay for lunch.

Saturday, October 25. Hunting.

Sunday, October 26. ('No diary entry. This is rather rare.')

Monday, October 27. Tour for twenty-five people – cancelled. Three Americans to lunch. ('Not cancelled. They had a perfectly ordinary lunch with us. A nice middle-aged couple, rather dull.') 7 p.m. – meeting of Alcester branch of the British Legion.

Tuesday, October 28. Evening – private showing of Roman Polanski's film, *Tess*. ('A friend of ours is the producer. He gave a splendid party in a private cinema, and then twenty of us went to dinner.')

Wednesday, October 29. Return to Ragley for a tour and buffet lunch for eighteen people at noon. Two-fifteen p.m. – Inspection of the farms. ('This was because of a difference of opinion on a management point. Someone else took my daughter to school that day.')

Thursday, October 30. Organizer of survey on Ragley visitors' attitudes comes to Ragley for lunch and examination and discussion of the results.

Friday, October 31. Morning – office work. Afternoon – visit to model circus at Kenilworth, with a view to having it at Ragley. ('I decided not to have it. Not worth it. No public appeal here, in my view. I didn't think it would be a success here, but one has to investigate every possibility.') Evening – attend opening of new interior design showroom, in what was the old Ragley estate office in the village of Arrow.

Such a hectic schedule of professional and personal entertaining puts constant strain on outside caterers, estate staff and the Ragley cellars. An aristocrat who aims to be a success professionally, must have a shrewd eye for business logic and be able to analyse exactly what is happening and why, when people visit Ragley in a private or paying capacity.

'We have got a lot of champagne in the cellar, which will be largely gone by autumn, before we hold the next dance here,' said Lord Hertford.

'When our son was twenty-one we had a series of parties. One was a cocktail party for local people between seven and eleven in the evening, and we had 400 people at that. I put out 200 bottles of champagne and the caterers came up to me after the party had been going on one and a half hours and said, "The champagne has come to an end, have you any more?" I said, "No, I think 200 bottles quite enough." A few days later we had a real ball for 400, and 200 bottles of champagne lasted all night, from ten in the evening to six in the morning.'

I asked Lord Hertford what he deduced from that. Quick as a shot came his answer: 'When people are standing drinking in one room, they drink very much more than they do at a dance.'

It is as a result of such fine calculations that the aristocracy today have managed to preserve some elements of the lifestyle of their ancestors. But the preservation of this way of life is also due, in no small part, to the fidelity and loyalty of their employees.

3
The Keeper of
the Gate

THE PUBLIC are a welcome necessity to great halls like Ragley, but some of its members can be distressingly ignorant of the correct form. For such halls, always delicately poised between privacy and public invasion, a good 'Man at the Gate' is essential.

Ragley's gatekeeper has to be a cross between a good secretary to a busy businessman; a good bodyguard to an actor who is so popular that the public want to tear the clothes off his back; a good sentry at an Army depot; and a good receptionist at a five-star hotel. He should be friendly, but not too friendly. He should always show a welcoming face to those who are going up to the Hall lawfully and a formidable one to those whose business is suspect.

Jack Smith told me that he was in fact a retired engineer, but he had about him something of the old soldier. He had the neatly-trimmed grey moustache of a Sergeant Major and a wary eye for a fishy invader. Twice, before he got used to my face, he overtook my car on the drive and forced me to a halt by pulling in front of it, well before I had a chance to reach the Hall and the high-born within. International terrorists or Jesse James in his prime would have had difficulty in getting past Jack Smith.

Though a comparative newcomer to Ragley, Jack Smith, green fleck suit and all, blended easily with the Hall and its surroundings. He was born in Alcester, but pursued his engineering career in bigger ponds before deciding to get a light job after his retirement at sixty-five. At Ragley, he was offered a rent-free bungalow – the gatehouse – and a wage during the summer. There was also an indication that there might be a light job for him in the winter as well, when the house was closed to the public. He had heard that the previous gatekeeper was leaving, so he applied. All his busy first summer he was also trying to get the garden of his own house into shape, so it was as well he started in one of the recession years, when attendances were slightly down.

When Ragley is closed, the gatekeeper has to be very careful indeed of who comes in through the gold-topped black iron gates. There can be difficulties too when it is open, as he also helps to man the ticket office, which is a small wooden hut a quarter of a mile up the mile-long drive (it used to be at the gates themselves, but there were too many traffic jams).

'The public are generally pretty good,' said Jack Smith one busy open day. 'But you can get one or two who can be a bit clever. They come in and start chatting to you all the time, while you are trying to calculate how much they have to pay. You might have a big car-load of people – children, parents and senior citizens – and you have got to work out all the different prices. This year it would be senior citizens and youngsters £1, ordinary tickets £1.50. You have got to think hard, especially if you get a crowd, one behind the other. It gets a bit hectic sometimes.'

There are usually two or three people on the ticket box at busy times, but there can be up to four lanes of cars coming in. The good gateman, even while flurried, must be wary of the few artful dodgers.

Jack Smith said he worked on the principle that most visitors to the Hall were genuine, but occasionally there would be a person who would attempt to drive past the ticket box without paying, saying he had an appointment with somebody or other, perhaps with Lord Hertford himself.

'It is not our place to argue with him. If he says he has got an appointment, you let him go. Or a fellow will come in a car with his whole family and claim to be working for someone on the estate, although he hasn't got a pass. That has happened on two or three occasions. I asked the person concerned on the estate, and he said he had never heard of the fellow. I have never seen him again; but occasionally you do get this sort of thing.'

There have been minor perversities. Ragley is operated on a one-way system – visitors in cars come in through the main gates, but go out through the gates at the back. Some have persisted, rather to Jack Smith's confusion, in driving back down the main drive to the main gates, despite four lanes of traffic coming the other way. The fact that private visitors to the estate, and Lord Hertford and his family, tend to do this may give a moral licence to others to do it, especially as the family's vehicles are not immediately recognizable as such – Lord Hertford is likely to be in his inconspicuous Japanese estate car and the heir to Ragley is quite likely to be in a rather old pick-up van.

Officious visitors are mercifully few and they generally meet their match in Jack Smith. One, who had a carful of guests with him, hummed and hawed a bit when told the price of admission. Jack Smith told him where he could turn round if he had changed his mind, but the man perhaps regarded getting into the Hall as a sort of initiative test. He went shooting off up the drive, with Jack Smith in hot pursuit, as he had indeed pursued me on two memorable occasions.

'I got him near the house, and I said, "Excuse me, you haven't paid." '

'I wish to see Lord Hertford.'

'I'm afraid you can't – he is too busy.'

'You are being insolent.'

'That is the last thing I would be to a customer, but I am afraid you must pay to go in.'

'Who do you think you are talking too?'

At this point Jack Smith's composure cracked a little, and he gave a pungent answer. The man insisted on storming into Ragley Hall, and Jack Smith insisted on storming in with him. Neither saw Lord Hertford, but they did come across Lady Hertford. 'Mr Smith is doing his job here, which is what he is paid for,' pointed out Lady Hertford, who knows how to make herself very clear if the occasion requires it.

Afterwards Jack Smith reflected that the experience had opened his eyes to the different motives that govern human behaviour – particularly when it comes to contact with the aristocracy. One would-be visitor had a party of guests from overseas with him, and presumably wanted to impress them with the fact that he could get them into Ragley Hall. To pretend to a greater acquaintance with the titled than one actually possesses is no doubt a regrettable vice, but a rather human and widespread one. Lord Hertford appears to have a rule that anyone in his house or wanting to see his house is a sort of guest; and that even interlopers are displaying a form of flattery and should be treated courteously, if firmly. After all, he and the family certainly hope they will return one day and actually pay to get in.

*   *   *

44

Visitors who arrive when Ragley is closed do need to be dealt with tactfully: they may, after all, be Lord This or Sir That, arriving for an event which has in fact been cancelled, or they may be people who have no business there at all, except to get a free look if they can manage it.

Jack Smith well remembered two car loads of overseas visitors who started opening the gates and driving in at eight o'clock one evening, long after closing time. He happened to hear the gates opening, and opened his front door to see what was going on. Seeing the people letting themselves in, he enquired why.

'We want to go to that place over there for a drink of water,' said one of the visitors, pointing to the closed and locked pavilion of the cricket club which is based on Ragley Park.

'I'm sorry, the place is closed.'

'I only wanted a drink of water, I'm thirsty.'

'These are private grounds.'

'But I'm thirsty.'

It took Jack Smith quite some time to convince these out-of-hours explorers that they would have to slake their thirsts elsewhere.

The notices put up by the Automobile Association on approach roads to Ragley, giving directions, can sometimes create difficulties for the loyal gatekeeper. The notices say, in effect, *AA Ragley Hall*. British people tend to get the drift, but people from overseas sometimes trip over the ambiguity, thinking the notice means that the AA is *at* the Hall.

'One visitor said he wanted to join the AA, and swore that Ragley Hall had a sign saying AA,' recalled Jack Smith. 'The little excuses they use to get in free!'

Despite the occasional difficulties, the position of gatekeeper on an estate like Ragley is not without its compensations, especially at a time of high unemployment in Britain, when there is a scarcity of part-time jobs for retired people. 'It's pleasant being in the countryside. The whole atmosphere is very pleasant,' said Jack Smith. 'But, mind you, the work pretty well ties you, which you expect, I suppose. I lock the gates at eleven p.m. unless we have got any functions such as dinners. I put the lights on at night to see the guests out, especially if there are diplomats or people like that coming. I have two days off a week, Mondays and Fridays, when the house is shut and only the park is open. We have a relief standing by on the days off. Having days off in the week is not like having the weekend off, of course – you may not be able to do so much with them.'

However, a conscientious gatekeeper is never *really* off duty. Someone is always apt to press his door bell to enquire, 'Is there fishing today?' or to present some other enquiry or difficulty. The only hope of having time entirely free is to get away from the gatehouse, which is not easy, when one has two separated days off. The gatekeeper's wages are paid only during the summer open months, though the tied house naturally continues throughout the year, and there are always odd jobs connected with Ragley for those in the know during the winter. Jack Smith said he always made a point of keeping well tuned in to the Ragley grapevine, to hear what was happening.

'There's plenty of fresh air, and it's a job when there's so much worklessness about,' his wife, Connie, will say.

'Without a spare-time job when you retire, you go to seed,' asserted the busy man at the gate. 'This at least keeps me fit.' It would certainly need to; but the gatekeeper is, of course, only the first of many estate workers who have to exercise considerable vigilance and diplomacy in dealing with the paying public.

4
Ragley's
Wise Ladies

The two leather-jacketed youths in the Green Drawing Room ignored the Reynolds painting of the 1st Marquess of Hertford, the Chinese Chippendale mirrors and the Gibbs ceiling. They were more interested in giving their own views of the surroundings: 'Why should one man have all this when some people haven't got homes at all?'

Grace Judge suddenly feigned deafness. She turned towards some less contentious Bank Holiday visitors, and started talking to them.

'Rather loutish boys,' she said afterwards. 'I thought it best not to answer them. If they want to get into arguments with people, I don't. Ridiculous! Almost all the comments we get are favourable – people say this is the nicest house they have ever seen and they are *glad* someone is still living in it as a home. I think I've had about two hostile comments, and I suppose I must have had 100,000 people walk past since I've been here.'

Mrs Judge was one of the six lady guides of Ragley Hall. Some stately homes have uniformed flunkeys, somewhat resembling retired Sergeant Majors, who see the premises as a barracks square round which they can march their troops at the double. Ragley will have none of this. The guides are a locally-recruited, part-time cabal of very pleasant, respectable, well-spoken, inconspicuous, twin-set-pearl, and altogether very *English* ladies of sensible years and invariable tact. They might be taken for leaders of the local Womens Institute or (except that one actually admitted to being a Socialist) of the Women's Conservative Association.

These are the ladies who, on open days, simply stand one to a room and sense whether the visitors passing through actually want to know something, or whether they are going to be quite content to glance and pass on.

On Bank Holidays the ladies turn out in force (as do the crowds). Sometimes they have practically nothing to do except keep an eagle eye out for the light-fingered. After an almost unblemished record of communal honesty, someone walked off with an ivory figure recently, and if the genteel ladies can help it, there will *not* be a repetition of this.

Bank Holiday crowds, though gratifying to the coffers of Ragley, are not great askers of questions. Some merely come in to escape the rain. Some cannot relate closely enough to what they see to know what to ask, and others, usually rather nice people, think they would be holding up the traffic on a busy day if they were to start asking whether the damask on the walls of the Red Saloon is the original. (It isn't.) Their reticence is a mistake. The ladies, who have only a little black badge and an air of proprietorial pride to distinguish them from the paying customers, always enjoy questions. 'It gives you a chance to ask a longer-serving guide, or the family, if you don't know the answer yourself,' said one of the Six Wise Ladies. This pleasantly amateur approach is somewhat belied by a typical Bank Holiday at Ragley. At such a time the place is seen at its most public: offering a sophisticated entertainment, with the family of Lord Hertford the star attractions as they go about their ordinary business with well-practised nonchalance.

The nonchalance of the Six Wise Ladies is of almost an equal order. But on the Spring Bank Holiday Monday I saw them in action it was reinforced by sheer hard work.

Well before the front doors were due to be opened by Fobbester, the butler, there were four visiting families waiting in their cars outside the front gates, while Violet Brooks, sitting at a desk in front of the doors to Lord Hertford's study, was ready and waiting to tear the tickets and (she hoped) sell the guide books. Mrs Brooks is the first of the lady guides the visiting public sees. Almost always she is at the reception desk while the other ladies work their way through all the rooms in the house, spending a week in charge of each room. This adds variety to their jobs, for which they receive a modest wage – which, to some of them, is almost incidental to being involved.

Violet Brooks, like the other ladies, came to Ragley on the basis of who-knows-who; a process which makes so public a procedure as advertising largely redundant: 'My husband used to work for Lord Hertford as an accountant on the estate. He was in Birmingham before that, with a firm of accountants. We both wanted to get out of Birmingham. We wanted to better ourselves and to get away from the hustle and bustle of the city. We thought that it would be better, both for us financially and for our children's sakes, when you think of all the upheavals in city life these days.'

When her husband left Ragley Hall to become a company secretary, Mrs Brooks was already acting as a guide at the Hall. She knew Mrs Lawrence, Lord Hertford's efficient and slightly daunting secretary, who, once again, had acted as a recruiting agent among her own social circle, as she had done on countless other occasions. Lord Hertford, with almost feudal courtesy, had asked Mrs Brooks' husband if she would be prepared to continue coming up to the Hall.

'I was quite willing to carry on working here, and I've been here ever since,' said Mrs Brooks as she tore the first tickets of the day. 'I love meeting the public, and they really love seeing Lord Hertford or any of the family if they are here. They like to know it isn't a museum. Most people like to see the family's personal things about the rooms. They look round the rooms and say, "Yes, it is obvious they do live here.' They ask, "Where do they eat?" They don't see their private dining room. They think they eat in the little ante-room off the Blue Room. But they don't, they have their private dining room, and the door is always closed. But the public is always content with the explanation.'

Violet Brooks, having lived with the ups and downs of life in the industrial West Midlands before moving to a village near Ragley, was aware that 'there are a lot of people about who are anti-Royalty and anti things like Ragley.'

'But,' she said, as she carried on her ceaseless but unpressing campaign to sell guide books, 'I rather like working for Lord Hertford. I couldn't work up here if I disliked that sort of thing. I am very much for our Royal Family and I hope they always continue to be with us. You do get visitors going round saying things like, "Why should one man have all this house and property?" I think, myself, that they should not go round it at all if they feel like that about it.'

More discouraging than the very rare visitor who has come to the Hall to grind his own political axe, are the people who shuffle along without appearing to see anything. 'Some people wouldn't be able to tell you at the end of the tour what they had seen,' said Mrs Brooks. 'I am amazed sometimes that they will stand a couple of minutes in a room and walk out without looking up, and so they miss a magnificent ceiling.'

Violet Brooks had been a guide at Ragley for eight years at the time I first met her, and had become skilled at answering even 'daft' questions like, 'Does Lord Hertford wear his crown?' Or 'Are there any ghosts in the house?'

Ann Champion, wife of the Rector of Fladbury, Wyre and Moor (also Rural Dean of Pershore), had developed this Christian art to a nicety. I found her in the Blue Room, a sitting room with delicate blue walls on which there are panels in bas-relief. Here, people who ask why there are so many sitting rooms in the house are told that in the seventeenth century each of the four corners of the house on that floor had bedrooms with private sitting rooms. This left only four main rooms for general use, and explained the apparently excessive number of sitting rooms.

A flip comment by the visitor about what he sees, new to him but not to the Six Wise Ladies, is always greeted with a tolerant smile. Most such jokes come in the Main Dining Room, a yellow-walled room with portraits of Walpole; Queen Victoria; Sir Edward Seymour, Speaker of the Long Parliament; the Prince Regent and King Charles II; and place settings for thirty in Ragley's old solid silver. 'Oh, they were expecting us!' visitors will say. Or, 'What time do we eat, then?' or, 'This is just like home!'

If, as is likely, one of the guides is hearing those jokes for the thousandth time, she will either feign deafness or grit her teeth and smile: 'The customer,' Lord Hertford decrees, 'is always right.' The ladies will be expected to know this, not because they are taught it (they get very little training for their jobs as guides) but because they are ladies.

Which is not to say they are high-born. The one who most looked like a dowager duchess at the time of my Bank Holiday visit, when car workers were pressing on the heels of schoolteachers in the enormous Red Saloon, was the wife of a retired bus driver. Doris Bennett, who had managed an outfitters' shop for thirty-seven years, was the longest serving of the guides. Also she lived locally in the village of Arrow, whereas the others had to drive in, or be collected, from nearby towns and villages.

Mrs Bennett, with her soft Black Country accent, had a way of effortlessly engaging the Bank Holiday trippers in conversation. Her technique was based on apparently artless and simple questions. 'Do you like this colour?' she would ask; and the passing visitors, amazed that this rather regal-looking lady had actually *spoken*, responded to the simple enquiry and were soon in conversation.

'They all say what a lovely room it is,' said Doris Bennett. 'One person may be interested in the porcelain and another in the pictures, but the majority, nine out of ten, want to know about the family, where they are and when they are likely to appear. They say, "How well do you know them?" I say I know them quite well. That makes them happy. Once, on a table in this room, there was a photograph taken at Harry's, the Earl of Yarmouth's, eighteenth birthday party. People used to talk about that a lot. They would say, "Are they *all* Lord Hertford's children?" Lord Hertford will say to me as he passes, "Don't forget to say they aren't all my children." I say to visitors, "No, Lord Hertford has three girls and one boy, that's all." '

Children's eyes are sometimes sharper than those of their adult companions. They usually look upwards in the Red Saloon, and notice the signs of the Zodiac painted in a circle round the fitting in the roof for the crystal chandelier. If they don't see them at first, but look bright, Doris Bennett will say, 'When is your birthday?' And when she gets the answer, she will then add, 'Can you find anything to do with your birthday on the ceiling?' If workers living in a concrete suburb of Birmingham or Coventry are to be encouraged to enjoy and appreciate Ragley, bridge personalities like Doris Bennett must be worth their weight in cash. Small wonder, then, that when one couple pay their yearly visit from North Wales, as they have been doing for the past ten years, they always ask if Mrs Bennett is still there.

When occasionally faced with provocative questions, Doris Bennett told me she did not always turn the other cheek. 'What a lovely ceiling,' said one visitor, 'you couldn't get work like that today.' Another visitor who overheard the remark disagreed. 'Of course you could,' he said dismissively, 'we could still get work done as good as this.'

'But I wonder how long it would be before they went on strike?' murmured Doris Bennett sweetly.

She was obviously very much part of the Ragley inner circle. It started when she was living in one of the estate's cottages and was asked to go and 'help out' when one of the regular guides died suddenly. Once again it was Lord Hertford's secretary who did the asking, so Mrs Bennett went, quickly gaining experience. Only occasionally, she said, did she make what, in Ragley terms, was a mild gaffe. One was characteristic enough: an eighty-year-old woman with the Ladies Circle positioned herself in the Red Saloon and asked, 'Do the family ever come through here? We have come such a long way and would love to see them.' Harry was walking through and Mrs Bennett said, 'Here is Lord Hertford's son, the Earl of Yarmouth.' The old lady asked, 'Would he speak to me?'

'I called him,' remembered Mrs Bennett, 'and he was very young then and blushed and was very shy, but he shook hands with her and she thanked him very much. Afterwards he said, "Phew! Don't you ask me to do that again!" "Right, I won't," I said, "but it made her day." '

One or two guests, even on busy Bank Holidays, have been known to curtsey to the Six Wise Ladies, who did indeed, I thought, have something of a suitably noble air.

Elizabeth Kendrick, wearing a ring of clustered diamonds, was a relief guide on duty in the Library on the Spring Bank Holiday I met her. She had started working at Ragley the previous year when her husband, director of a chain and cable firm in Cradley Heath, in the Black Country, had just died.

'I didn't know what to do with myself. I wrote and asked if they needed any help. A few months later Mrs Lawrence rang me up and said could she come to see me. It was lucky for me, actually. I thought I simply had to do something, I couldn't just sit there and feel sorry for myself. My husband and I had always collected antiques and I like being amongst nice things. I am learning something new every day. Someone asks something that leads to another point, or they tell you something. Once a man told me a lot about the firm of clockmakers who made the clock in the Green Drawing Room. I found it very interesting. If I don't know what a picture is, I go and ask.'

On duty in the Library, Mrs Kendrick encountered comparatively few questions. 'How many books are there here?' was a fairly frequent one. So was, 'Do the family actually *use* this room?' Yes, explained Mrs Kendrick. After the Hall was closed for the night, the family used it as a sitting room. By way of confirmation, she pointed out the less than historic items in the room – the guitar used by one member of the young family, the Sony music centre and stock of records. The Red Saloon, she pointed out, also had its evidence of present-day use: a rack of long-playing records under an ormulu-rimmed French table, for a start.

The guide with socialist beliefs was Miss Peggy Naylor, who wore a rather racy white sweater and slacks, and with sympathy for the Lower Orders may or may not have been invigorated by the fact that she had just been made redundant as a civil servant. She had been, she said, a driver with the Government car service for many years, driving many senior civil servants and Government ministers.

'I needed a little part-time job to make ends meet,' she confessed. It was an incongruous remark in the setting of the Main Dining Room. 'Yes, this room does impress people. One lady yesterday said, "It makes me feel I want to cry, it is so beautiful." '

Peggy Naylor had encountered questions like, 'Who does the washing up?' and ribald suggestions like, 'Oh, do pass the cruet.' But she had personally never come across hostility from visitors and, as a socialist, saw no contradiction between her political beliefs and her job, helping people to enjoy and appreciate Ragley Hall.

'Sometimes you get people saying they wished they could turn the clock back, and that you don't get workmanship like that these days. But you don't get hostility or envy. I tell them, if they ask, that I, personally, am glad those days are over. I think times have improved. Workmen could still make fine things, but there wouldn't be enough money about today to buy them, would there? I am a socialist, but I still admire excellence. I am *glad* the house has been restored. I think the family have done a magnificent job of work. The house is for the public to appreciate. It is part of our national heritage. It is so real – a little image of the past. You will find people of all political convictions who appreciate quality.'

In the next room to the one Peggy Naylor was manning – the Mauve Drawing Room – was her sister, Christine Jackson, widow of an insurance man. 'People are always saying how lovely and clean everything is here,' she said, 'and what a friendly atmosphere there is. Quite a few sit on the window seats – they are allowed to stay in a room as long as they like.'

The guides are not the only Wise Ladies of Ragley. Two other ladies manage the souvenir and sweet shops with great efficiency. Mrs Molly Stephens, a maternal lady in large gold-rimmed spectacles, has sold the souvenirs, which she helps her friend Mrs Lawrence to choose at trade fairs, for many years.

'We start to buy before Christmas,' she told me. 'We go to the National Exhibition Centre at Birmingham in February, various commercial travellers come here, and I go over to the Worcester porcelain works. This year we have two new lines – Glastonbury Galleries handpainted paper weights and pictures. The Beckford silk scarves are the most expensive things we have, at £8.50. We keep a lot of tea towels and book marks, because they are the most popular lines. The personalized stuff goes better, on the whole. People want to remember the Hall and having been here themselves.'

Molly Stephens has habitually driven to the Hall every day of the open season by car, bringing with her two of the guides who live nearby. This co-operative effort has been smiled upon by all, especially by Lord Hertford, who has bought the petrol. Molly Stephens has regarded the job as an enjoyable experience as well as a source of cash: 'I live 11 miles away in a village. It is a different world there. It is a different set of people. I know our village as one little world and this as another little world.'

It has been a little world which takes five hours a day of her time in the run-up to the open season, working alongside the sweet shop and the lady who looks after it, Mrs Cynthia Bindley, wife of the head forester. Cynthia Bindley had, in the past, specialized largely in clotted cream toffees in Ragley Hall personalized packaging, but was now introducing a new sort of Ragley Hall chocolate. She has taken about £250 a week – roughly the same as the souvenir shop – at peak times and schooled herself in patience even when encountering the 'seventeen double-decker loads of children who sometimes seem to arrive all at once'. Thefts, she said, were few: perhaps it was something about the atmosphere of the Hall which deterred it.

On this particular Bank Holiday Monday, rain was coming down so heavily outside that people were staying longer than usual inside the house. This soon led to a long queue of people standing in the pouring rain on the main steps outside the house, waiting to get in. Lord Hertford, who had himself managed to answer dozens of questions and sign innumerable guide books during the afternoon, once actually considered asking visitors to 'kindly move on'. But he finally decided this would be against the Ragley code that visitors, having paid to get in, should *not* be hurried.

The new restaurant, open for the first time that Bank Holiday, was doing good business. The tea room, across the stoneflagged lower level hall, was faring even better. The people of the West Midlands, and some from much further afield, were comparing notes over their plastic trays. Ernest Curnock, a corporation window maker, had brought his wife Valerie and two daughters, Jane, fifteen, and Michelle, fourteen, with him for an indoor 'day out'. The Curnocks, who had been the first to buy tickets at the gate that day, were impressed with the sheer spaciousness of the house, the 'tonnage' of the books in the library and the amount of money that must be necessary for the upkeep of the whole place.

'I don't think it's immoral for the family to live here, not at all,' said Ernest Curnock. 'It has been handed down to them through the years. It could have been any of us, really. It's just the luck of the draw, if you think of it that way.'

This reaction was fairly typical. Could it be that the Bank Holiday crowd felt less threatened by the privileged lifestyle of the aristocracy, who were where they were because they were born to it and history dictated it, than they would have been by the confidence of the new meritocracy, who were often apt to be less tactful and pleasant in their social habits?

Jane, described as the 'knowledge box' of the Curnock family, even ventured a slight criticism of Ragley: she would have liked, she said, to have seen the old kitchens. When I told her that they had all been stripped out years ago, I felt that I was shattering her illusions.

Despite the rain, the day was fairly lucrative. A steady flow of visitors passed by Mrs Brooks' reception desk. 'Most of them were enamoured of Royston, Lady Hertford's beagle dog, which I had in the study with me,' reported Mrs Brooks. 'Well, if people are out for the day and want to look at the dog and not at the house, that is up to them.'

It was left to Doris Bennett, the lady with the very approachable manner, to try to sum up the day, as she has always done on occasions worth commemorating. 'You don't think I'm mad, do you?' she enquired as I encouraged her to comment on this rainy but otherwise typical Bank Holiday in the life of Ragley.

'No more so that the rest of us,' I assured her. So Doris Bennett obliged with:

Another Bank Holiday is here once more,
Alas, not the thousands we had of yore.
What with the weather and pay packets small,
I wonder we get visitors at all.

This verse proved to be over-pessimistic. Even on a rainy day, with the national economic depression even deeper than the meteorological one, some 1,570 people proved that Ragley's Six Wise Ladies were unlikely ever to join the unemployment queue.

5
You called, Milord?

Fobbester was summoned, as Fobbester often is. William, the golden spaniel, had been sick behind a screen in the study, where Lord Hertford was about to receive a guest. Hence the call for Fobbester the butler, who shortly appeared in black jacket, striped trousers, black tie, immaculately-ironed plain white shirt and kindly spectacles.

'There isn't much of it, Fobbester,' said Lord Hertford, pointing behind the screen.

'Quite so, Milord.'

Having taken exact stock of the situation, which included the fact that the footman was unavailable, Fobbester retired and reappeared almost immediately with a roll of kitchen tissue to remove the evidence of the dog's indisposition. Such was my first sight of Fobbester, a fine example of one of the rare treasures still available to the noble classes – who, I suspect, now outnumber the willing butlering classes. Is it better to sit behind an office desk and say, 'Yes sir, no sir' than to dispose of a dog's vomit, however well-connected the dog? Many would say yes. Fobbester did not agree.

Shortly afterwards Fobbester, his mane of white hair as unruffled as ever above his round and tactfully expressionless face, appeared once more in the study. No beating about the bush, no humming and hawing. 'Are we open early today, Milord?'

'No, why?'

'Two cars have just drawn up on the terrace, Milord.'

'Well, we should have a chain up already so they stay down on the car park, shouldn't we?'

'Quite so, Milord.'

'Will you fix that?'

'I will, Milord.'

It is often assumed that butlers are a thing of the past in Britain, except perhaps at the homes of rich Arabs and Americans. Ragley Hall is blessed not only with Fobbester as butler but also with his wife Iris as cook, which must be a double bonus.

Fobbester, six feet tall in his plain grey socks, is a social phenomenon of interest to all those who feel that any self-respecting worker should consider personal service demeaning. He plainly doesn't. Born not far from the greyhound stadium at Harringay, London, in 1920, he was the son of an electrician, and after being educated in various schools in London, he became an electrician himself. During the war, he went into the newly-formed Royal Electrical and Mechanical Engineers achieving the rank of Corporal. 'Lovely rank!' Fobbester will confide. Under a Sergeant Major in a unit of only fifteen men, he went from one regiment to another, enjoying a fair degree of independence as a technician. He met his future wife when stationed in Aberdeen, and after the war he stayed on there and ran both his father-in-law's country hotel and a bar.

Entertaining me on a corner of Lord Hertford's dining table, well before the lunch party was due to appear, Fobbester confessed to me why he had become a butler in an age when many men would regard serving a master as against the spirit of the times.

'Having done weddings and other big functions at the hotel,' said Fobbester with the merest flicker of a feline smile, 'my wife and I decided that one boss would be better than every customer being a potential boss, if you know what I mean! So we went into private service.'

Such a move was rather like going to work in the rush hour when everyone else was going home. At the time people were drifting away from private service towards jobs in industry, commerce or the public service. Fobbester did not question his own direction at the time, and still didn't at the time we met.

'We were well versed in personal service by that time. We moved down to England and worked in Yorkshire, for a Lord. We went to that job because it was available and suited our needs. There was a nice house with the job and our children were still at school,' he recalled. 'I went as pantryman, working under the butler. I cleaned shoes, pressed suits, washed dishes and cleaned silver – to learn about it more than anything else.'

Did he feel that this had been a come-down? Fobbester said he would think better if he could smoke; he went away, returned with a packet of cigarettes and his own ashtray, and carefully lit up, keeping the ashtray in his hands so that it did not sully the dining table, which had to be polished by him or his solitary footman before every meal. 'No, it wasn't a come-down at all. We were very happy. It was a totally different life, you see; we were responsible only to the *one* master and not every customer. You call every customer Sir, so it was not a come-down to call one master Milord. As far as I was concerned, we had stepped into an entirely different life and it was very good training, because the atmosphere was strictly to protocol – much more than it is at Ragley.'

For instance, remembered Fobbester (dropping his cigarette ash neatly into the very centre of the ashtray so that none of it floated down on to his knife-creased, striped trousers), when a pair of shoes were cleaned there were strict rules about it. 'The laces were taken out and ironed before being put back in again. The morning papers were ironed before being put on the breakfast table. If His Lordship was walking down the corridor, the staff disappeared into any convenient corner so they would not be seen – even to the extent of walking into a cupboard. It's true. I've seen it.'

Staff would not speak unless they were spoken to by the aristocratic family. What was the name of these high-born employers? The lips of the Fobbesters of this world are sealed on such matters; wild horses would not have prised the name from his lips, and when I assumed that ironing shoe-laces and newspapers was not on his agenda at Ragley, he agreed, but added immediately, 'mainly because we haven't got the staff. It just shows you the difference between even the 1950s and now, when you think of the number of staff available. My wife had a kitchen maid and a kitchen porter. There was also the butler, myself as pantryman, a parlourmaid and four housemaids. Now they themselves, I gather, have got only a butler and a cook.'

During Fobbester's time at this particular country estate, the butler retired. Fobbester stepped into his shoes at the age of forty – a thing he would not have expected to do for many more years had staff not begun to thin out because of the drift out of personal service. As butler he thus sat at one end of the table in the staff room, while his wife sat at the other, other members of the staff being positioned in strict order of seniority.

Such were the rules, and they moulded Fobbester during four martinet years.

He then went as butler to a businessman in the North of England. Here the etiquette changed in a way that caused him mixed feelings. 'It was quite a good atmosphere, but not the same. He didn't treat you in quite the same way. There was no protocol, the relationship was just one of master and servant. The Lord had been used to having staff; the business-man was a self-made businessman and hadn't been used to having his own domestic staff. That was the difference.'

Plainly what had preoccupied Fobbester was his own title, or rather, the lack of it. Just as a consultant surgeon will go a little stiff if addressed as Doctor instead of Mister, an English butler will go a little stiff if he is called Mister So-and-So, or anything else but plain unadorned So-and-So, by anyone other than junior staff or persons who are dealing with him *ex-cathedra* – such as, for example, bank managers, lawyers or insurance men. It appeared that *I* had set the right tone by calling him *Mr* Fobbester; but had I been his employer, or a purely social guest of his employer, I would have committed not exactly an impropriety but certainly a slight affront to his professional pride.

'When I went to the businessman, he called me Joseph,' said Fobbester in carefully non-committal tones. 'I got quite used to being called Joseph, but it was just a difference I noticed. I would prefer to be called Fobbester, because that is my title.'

At Ragley, he was pleased to say, the children of the family had devised a 'nice way' of addressing him which did not *per se* imply that they were either his employer, or an equal, as his bank manager would be. 'They call us Mr Fobb and Mrs Fobb in a friendly way.'

Just as he had joined the businessman to better himself (that gentleman, though undesirably progressive in matters of protocol, had paid the couple £18 a week all found compared with the previous Lord's £10), Fobbester left him for the same reason. He went to another businessman in the South of England – and experienced another of those subtle changes in atmosphere to which the English butler must be eternally sensitive.

This master had been knighted for his charitable work. 'The atmosphere was very Victorian,' said Fobbester. 'I don't think I had better say too much, really, but I practically lived at the end of the bell. They were for-ever ringing the bell. They were nice enough people but every weekend there was a party.' Plainly it was less than a butler's heaven.

*   *   *

The Fobbesters moved to Ragley in 1971, when it became clear that they 'couldn't see much future' where they were. Their employers were well into their eighties and it was obvious that their children would not take over the large house.

Fobbester answered Lord Hertford's advertisement in the *Daily Telegraph*, went to Ragley for an interview, liked what he saw, and received a telephone call the next day from Lord Hertford telling the Fobbesters that the job was theirs. 'For the first time in my life, I got three weeks' holiday at the start,' said Fobbester. 'His Lordship had employed a temporary couple for a month, so we started work after a three-week holiday.'

It was not only the material comforts of Ragley that appealed to Fobbester, though a self-contained, rent-free flat on the ground floor with its own front door, rent-free telephone, free heating and lighting, was not a negligible icing on a £120-a-week salary cake. What he had really liked was the 'friendliness' of Lord and Lady Hertford and (one suspects) the fact they did not presume to call him anything other than Fobbester.

All this reinforced his instinctive view that being a butler was a highly desirable occupation, especially in a house like Ragley. 'I think we are well paid. There are plenty of these jobs available, and we never have any strikes or that sort of thing – you know what I mean. Certainly I would advise young chaps to go into this business, if they have got the right manner, because there is work available, even these days.'

What, I enquired delicately, *was* the right manner? 'To know your place,' said Fobbester instantly, and then added hastily, 'No, that doesn't sound right, it makes it sound subservient. I can't quite explain. But some people don't like calling people Sir or Milord. They wouldn't have the right manner. They also dislike the anti-social hours of work. Yes, it is weekend and evening work, but we like it. Having Tuesday and Wednesday off, we find we can go out on those days and park the car easily, and the shops aren't so crowded. When we have our break my wife leaves prepared meals, which have only to be heated in most cases, and the family look after themselves.'

No, insisted Fobbester, flicking his wrist to check the time without disturbing the ash on his cigarette (it was getting very near lunchtime), a butler did not have to be subservient, but he had to have the ability to be one step ahead of his employer's wishes.

'Doing something before you are told to do it gives you quite a lot of satisfaction,' said Fobbester. 'You have got to be able to see that a job needs to be done and do it without being told.'

Hence the intervention when the motorists were driving up on to His Lordship's terrace because the chains weren't in place. Hence, too, his intervention when one of his previous employers came down into the dining room for dinner with his immaculately-clad guests in a dinner jacket from which the braces were dangling at the back. The employer was oblivious of this and so, it appeared, was the lady on his arm as they made their stately way into the dining room. But Fobbester, awaiting the company and ready to bring on the first course when all were seated, spotted this unusual sartorial situation.

'Falling into step beside him,' recalled Fobbester, 'I tucked his braces back into his trousers as we walked along. This was a big social occasion, you realize; but I think it happened without anyone having noticed it at all. He didn't take any notice whatever of what I was doing. He took it in good form and, having his lady on his arm, he didn't want to make any comment. It passed by naturally, and no one was any the wiser.'

A butler's expertise can also be sorely tested by gastronomic difficulties. On one occasion, also with a previous employer, Fobbester inadvertently left the gravy boat on the table with its silver salver at the end of the first course. When the lemon souffle arrived, one lady guest picked up the gravy and poured it over the souffle, under the impression it was chocolate sauce. The impression did not long survive the first taste.

'She gave a cry of horror,' sighed Fobbester. 'Everyone joined in the laughter. They took it in good part. So did she. But I was never allowed to forget it. It is the one thing you aren't supposed to do, leave things on the table after courses.'

I found it difficult to resist the conclusion that Fobbester's ex-employers had rather rejoiced in having found *something* wrong in their paragon. But when I asked Fobbester if he hadn't felt like retaliating by suggesting a rather closer inspection of the liquids one was ladling on to one's plate, he replied, as shocked as if I had suggested converting a cathedral into a bowling alley: 'One might feel like it, but one would not dare say a thing like that. Oh no!'

What a butler actually *does* is something that remains a mystery to many people who would probably regard a cleaning lady one afternoon a week as a luxury. Certainly one of the first things he must be able to do is to attend a society function in his private capacity, while at the same time giving no suggestion that he is about to clap his employer on the shoulder and tell him a *risqué* joke. This would not be 'friendly' (which is good) but 'familiar' (which is bad). This ability almost automatically means that he can hold his own in aristocratic company without either rivalling it in conversational sparkle or presuming to argue with it. The Fobbesters of the small world of the remaining British country estates possess such ability in abundance.

Fobbester's technique was well able to handle, for instance, the Earl of Yarmouth's twenty-first birthday party. There was a dinner for close relations in the Main Dining Room, followed by a ball.

'Lord Hertford said, "When you have finished after dinner I want you to come to the ball not as staff but as guests." I was already dressed, but my wife went down and got out her evening dress and we went to the ball as guests mingling with the aristocracy, all in their marvellous tiaras and jewels. We appreciated that very much. The ball went right through the night and we had a marvellous breakfast cooked by somebody else for a change – the caterers.'

But, said Fobbester firmly, no one had called him Mr Fobbester even in those comparatively informal conditions. 'The occasion', he said austerely, 'did not arise.'

Any notion that the butler in a country house which is opened successfully to the public, and also used copiously in private, can be a sort of figure-head would be woefully mistaken. The Fobbesters' day begins at seven in the morning. That is when they get up. Mrs Fobbester starts to prepare the breakfast. At eight Fobbester, who is responsible for security, goes round the house unlocking and undoing the shutters.

Further facts about the working life of this rare and rather exotic species emerged in other talks I had with Fobbester, the first one having fallen victim to His Lordship's lunch, which naturally took priority. When afterwards I asked Fobbester who had been entertained to lunch, I was given only a reproving look. Poor form, it plainly said. The Fobbesters of this world do *not* reveal the identity of their employers' guests.

They will, however, reveal in more general terms the content of their working day. At Ragley, the unlocking of the shutters takes twenty minutes. It is followed by the setting of the breakfast table upstairs for Lord and Lady Hertford. The table is in the nursery, because the family like to get up when they want to and have breakfast in their dressing gowns. The meal is left on hot plates from eight-thirty till ten. At eight-thirty Fobbester walks into Lord and Lady Hertford's room with orange juice for His Lordship, opens the curtains and says either, 'Nice day today, Milord,' or 'Pouring with rain today, Milord.' Or sometimes he says nothing at all, depending on his interpretation of his employer's mood and receptivity.

The next job of the butler's day is to see that the fires are lit if the day is chilly. Fobbester may do this himself or ask the footman, a twenty-one year-old, to do it. There are two enormous fireplaces which nevertheless look small, in the Great Hall, another one in the library and one in the study. Each will have a fire in cold weather. Other rooms will have fires only when they are specifically needed. The cost of keeping the whole place warmed by coal fires as well as the central heating would be enormous: the volume of the Great Hall itself is probably that of twenty private houses put together.

'This is not a cold house,' said Fobbester with the same pride as a man would exhibit when discussing his own home. 'The sun is on the west side of the house and keeps the private dining room warm until the evening. Sometimes, when His Lordship sits in the Green Drawing Room on the west side of the house, we just put a match to the fire there later in the evening.'

All the fires in the house are made with logs from trees grown on the estate, and pieces of coal are occasionally put on the Green Drawing Room fire because it has a raised grate. 'I get my footman to fill up the log boxes every day,' said Fobbester. 'That might take him until ten in the morning.'

By ten, Fobbester himself will have brought down Lord Hertford's suits and shoes for pressing and cleaning. These are the ones the Marquess has been wearing the day before. Fobbester will sponge the suit, jacket and trousers, take any marks out, and press the clothes with a damp cloth and an electric iron. He will do this in the ironing room and the bootroom, which are both on the ground floor.

If Lady Hertford has any shoes that need cleaning, Fobbester will clean them as well – at least, in theory. In practice, Her Ladyship is quite prepared to clean her own shoes, and does so quite often.

'That is not absolutely normal!' insisted Fobbester, almost as if I had accused him of dereliction of duty. 'I do her riding boots and things like that, because they get pretty muddy. But she does a lot of chores of that sort herself. Not Lord Hertford. He is quite a busy man and hurries to get down to his office as soon as he can, to deal with estate work.'

I asked Fobbester if he actually felt insulted when Lady Hertford chose to do her own chores. 'No,' replied the ever-diplomatic Fobbester, 'Her Ladyship knows I have a great deal to do. Normally I would clean her shoes; but this morning, for instance, I did not. She does her own pressing herself or sends the clothes out to the cleaners. In the olden days they would have had a lady's maid especially to do that for her.'

By ten-thirty, a start is made in the private dining room, although it is at least two hours before it will be used. Cleaners do come in daily to vacuum clean and dust, but Fobbester prefers to attend to the condition of the table himself. He polishes both the table and the table mats, consults Mrs Fobbester about the menu, and sets the table accordingly. The best silver will always be used for lunch and dinner. It will be polished about once a week when Fobbester and his footman can best fit the job in, probably on Thursday mornings. There is a slight difference in the menu depending on whether the family are dining alone or with guests.

I eventually managed to establish that there had been only eight to lunch that day – Lord and Lady Hertford, the four children, Lady Hertford's mother, and a friend of the eldest daughter who was staying at Ragley. For such a family meal, there would be no starting course. For first course, roast lamb, creamed potatoes, courgettes and spinach. For second course, strawberries and cream, then cheese and coffee.

The aristocracy still favour linen table napkins, at a time when the middle classes tend to regard them as being as 'common' as table cloths or garden gnomes. Fobbester leapt up from the chair from which he was conducting our resumed dining room conversation, and opened the drawer of a sideboard, from which he extracted a number of immaculately laundered white linen napkins.

'I see to these myself,' said Fobbester intensely. 'You see the phoenix rising from the ashes which is part of the crest, the coronet and then the number? Each napkin is numbered. They must be well over a hundred years old. I think I make a better job of them than the laundry. Laundries sometimes spoil things.'

At eleven-thirty, it has been Fobbester's habit to take a coffee break with his wife in the kitchen, which is also the butler's pantry; the two being combined in what, in middle-class circles, would be called a dining-kitchen. Here the butler and cook prepare meals, keep the plates hot in a dish-warmer directly under a serving hatch, serve Lord and Lady Hertford through the door or the hatch, and receive their own friends or relatives for coffee and a chat.

The napkins are usually ironed around noon, although on one day of the week at this time (usually Thursdays) the clocks will all be wound. The napkins can take up a formidable amount of time. 'I might spend an hour ironing them,' said Fobbester. 'Take a typical weekend like this. We had a dinner party last night for ten, seven for lunch yesterday, eight for lunch today. There are quite a lot of napkins, because you can't always put the same one out for two nights. Twenty napkins take about an hour to wash and iron. I usually do the napkins in any spare time before lunch.'

At one o'clock lunch will be announced. Fobbester will go to the particular room where Lord Hertford and his group are, and say simply, 'Lunch is served.' This is usually said, in a clear but unassertive voice, in the library or study, where the pre-lunch drinks are normally taken. '*Just* those words,' insisted Fobbester, 'no more and no less.' He then makes sure he is in the dining room before the lunch party, so that he can put the guests where the hosts have instructed him to place them. At larger and more complicated meals, especially in the Main Dining Room, there may be a placement (list of the seating order). But in most cases it is left to Fobbester's memory.

The butler then starts to serve lunch. Through the hatch between kitchen and dining room, well-heated plates are handed to Fobbester one at a time. He takes them, also one at a time, to each guest, starting with the main guest, who is seated on Lord Hertford's right. Individually-served plates are a way of reducing the clattering sounds which would be inevitable if a pile of plates were to be brought in at once and distributed.

A guest in a refined middle-class boarding house in Bournemouth might consider himself insulted if the waiter did not help him to the main course and the vegetables; but in aristocratic circles this is not *de rigeur*. The butler presents the first course on a serving salver with a fork and spoon and the guest helps himself to what he wants. Very occasionally a guest not used to mixing in such circles will simply stare at the proferred dish and wait for Fobbester to serve him. 'Would you care to help yourself to what you require, sir?' is always the deferential but firm reaction to this.

Ensuring that the wine is poured into the guests' glasses before the first course has disappeared is a technique of some sophistication. Fobbester himself will fill the glasses – two-thirds is the correct amount – at a small lunch or dinner group. For anything over six people, he will call in the footman to assist. There can, of course, be exceptions. The day I was having this particular conversation with Fobbester, the footman had had to take a car to collect the guides and the staff of the tea room; this ferrying process took precedence over the finer points of serving the wine – in itself a significant indication of present priorities at the Hall.

The footman has all but disappeared as an institution in many stately homes. These days his role is often that of a sort of combined general handyman, driver and emergency waiter. This has certainly happened at Ragley. Lord Hertford has lately been adopting the practice of not even mentioning the word 'footman' when advertising such a post, but asking simply for a driver-handyman. Realism has thus won over pride – on both sides. 'Driver-handyman is a more accurate description,' Lord Hertford will now say. 'He collects the staff from their homes and takes things like ice cream and Coca Cola down to the Adventure Park. Or he picks up litter and brings in firewood and keeps the fire going. A hundred years ago, the footman would still have made the fires and helped serve the meals, but he would also have cleaned the hunting boots and invariably polished the silver. I want someone with good references if he is going to handle the silver; apart from that I just want a pleasant personality. He has got to be someone who will not scream with horror when he is told to pick up a whole lot of litter. One can't afford to employ nowadays the sort of person who says, "That isn't my job." At Ragley it helps if he also has a good head for heights, because one of his jobs is to put up the flag. He has to climb up onto the roof up a fairly steep ladder and he has to do that in the summer every day, unless there is a very strong wind.'

As for Fobbester, one of his favourite sayings is that the difference between now and a hundred years ago is that the same work is still done, but that there are far fewer people to do it. City dwellers used to working trade-union hours and protected by trade-union demarcations, may not be surprised that there are fewer people to do it.

The loyal professional butler at a hall like Ragley is likely to be too absorbed in the techniques of his vocation to indulge in regrets: not even at the occasional absence of a footman, whether he is called a footman or something else. In our conversations, Fobbester was always more interested in the finer points of the profession than in his own deprivations.

Indeed, it was he who firmly brought me back to the subject of his lunch routine: having served the wine, he said, he would always withdraw, leaving a little silver bell near Lord Hertford's hand. The skill of the butler's art at this point is to be *ahead* of that bell. Ideally he should have returned to the room to replenish the wine glasses just before His Lordship's hand starts to move towards the silver implement. Fobbester must weigh up each lunch party and make a mental assessment of the correct period to wait before reappearing to recharge glasses: 'If, for instance, there are a lot of men dining, I would go in to top up their glasses more quickly than I would for mixed company.'

At the end of the first course (if Fobbester has not already reappeared as if by magic) the bell will ring. The plates are removed by Fobbester, one at a time, and handed individually through the serving hatch. In come the plates for the next course, also one by one. Then in comes the sweet, perhaps a dish of strawberries, proferred to guests so that they may take as many as they require, followed by the cream, almost certainly from the estate's dairy farms. The plates are removed the moment they are empty or when the bell rings, to be replaced by the cheese plates and the cheese board.

This method, favoured at Ragley and at most aristocratic establishments, whereby everyone helps themselves to whatever is going, is called Russian Service. The alternative, where guests actually have the food deposited on their plates by the waiter or the butler himself, is called Silver Service.

There is no Silver Service at Ragley, not even for coffee. The bell is rung again in the dining room and the host will tell Fobbester, 'We will have coffee in the library/study/other room.' Fobbester takes a tray with a jug of coffee to that room, and leaves it there.

The energetic butler then comes back to the dining room, clears the table, and washes up with Mrs Fobbester. Here the mechanized age has made welcome inroads. There are two dishwashing machines at Ragley. 'In the old days it would have been done by the pantryman and underfootman,' said Fobbester.

It is usually around two-fifteen that the dishes go into the dishwashers, and a quarter of an hour later before Fobbester and his wife arrive at that part of the day which is, roughly speaking, their own. Fobbester is off duty until five. Often he will twiddle the buttons of his television set to see if there is any golf on. Or the couple will go out shopping, or just for a drive. Or, if it is Tuesday and the couple are looking forward to their usual Tuesday afternoon and all day Wednesday off, they may get into the car and drive down to Dorset, to see their daughter, or to Somerset, to see their son. Another son lives in Harrogate and is not quite so accessible.

If it is not a Tuesday or a Wednesday and it is five in the afternoon, Fobbester returns to duty and one of his first evening tasks on open days. This is locking up the house and securing all shutters, except those in the rooms the family are to use for the evening – probably the study, the private dining room and the library, though perhaps also the Green Drawing Room (Lord Hertford's own personal favourite) and sometimes even the Red Saloon, where gramophone records can be played in a setting almost as vast as a concert hall and twice as grand.

By six, Fobbester is polishing the table yet again, asking the cook about the menu and setting the dinner places accordingly. By seven, he is in the sitting room emptying ashtrays, making up fires and plumping up the cushions, having probably already restocked the drinks cupboards from the cellars. At eight, the same routine will be followed for dinner as for lunch, Fobbester having changed from his black jacket and striped trousers to his dinner jacket.

By nine-fifteen, if the dinner party is a family one, the Fobbesters will be putting the dishes into the dishwashers. The time is more likely to be ten or ten-thirty if the party includes guests. It may well be midnight if it is a big party in the Great Hall for over a hundred guests – not the usual form at Ragley, but far from unknown. After this, the rest of the shutters will be secured by the butler's own hand.

'Then,' said Fobbester, with the faintest flicker of a dry smile, 'I am finished for the day. I believe there is a famous saying, "The rest of the day is my own". When I say this, it amuses a lot of people.'

Even the names of the dishes served in a noble establishment like Ragley may differ from the terms used by the rest of us. I well remember last having *Boeuf Wellington* at a smart restaurant; had I had the same thing at Ragley, it would have been *Boeuf en Croute*. 'That is a thing about private service,' remarked Fobbester. 'You always call it *Boeuf en Croute* whereas in a hotel you would call it *Boeuf Wellington*. It is just one of those strange things.'

Those who imagine that life 'below stairs' on a great estate is now confined to television screen fiction would be disabused of the notion at

Ragley. One day I walked into the kitchen-cum-butler's-pantry to discover Fobbester's son John there with his wife, having coffee. John Fobbester is now a builder, but he first helped his father wait at table when he was fourteen, and doesn't mind lending a hand behind the scenes at Ragley. There is something of an inclusive atmosphere about the place that makes this quite understandable. 'Much more of a family atmosphere here,' said John Fobbester. 'You don't mind helping.'

'We have attended the Christmas parties and there is always a present for us,' said his wife. 'We get involved in giving a bit of help. Father was doing the boots today and so we did other things for him.'

It is still one of the aristocracy's great talents that they can make people feel flattered at being needed. It used to be a peripheral skill. It is now a vital part of their survival kit as staffs become smaller and money tighter. 'We socialize with them more than anyone else, after all,' said Mrs Fobbester senior. 'We are more involved with them than with anyone else.' They are indeed. It is a unity that will strike many outsiders as strange but to the participants on both sides it appears still real enough to be effective.

6
Kitchen
Talk

Mʀs Iʀɪs Fᴏʙʙᴇsᴛᴇʀ, Ragley's cook, and wife of its butler, told me she had kept for many years one of the little notes she had received from Anne, the youngest of Lord Hertford's children.

'Mr and Mrs Fobb,' she wrote after incurring her parents' wrath, 'thanks very much for the "exile" lunch. Here is the plate and spoon. I am going to be at Alcester all afternoon, if Mummy wonders! So I'll be safe until dinner! Well, thanks so much again for helping me out. Love Anne x x x.'

One of the advantages of living in a stately home, when it comes to dealing with youthful high spirits, is that there is so much more space in which they can be absorbed. Another advantage, no less crucial, is that there tends to be an alternative social centre for the young, which is usually the kitchen or the butler's pantry. As both rooms are one and the same at Ragley, and as this single room is immediately adjacent to the family's dining room, the cook also tends to be the provider of out-of-hours cake, the shoulder to lean on in time of trouble, and the ear always ready to listen and understand. This tends to be so with all stately homes, even if the nobility do not deliberately keep such a cool distance from their off-spring as they once did. Because of Ragley's geography, and because staff are now so scarce, the lives of the family and the Fobbesters have tended to inter-twine more than they did in the stately homes in which the Fobbesters previously served.

Mrs Fobbester, born in Aberdeen, met her husband forty years ago and her own family was grown up by the time the couple moved to Ragley. She soon became fond of the young members of Lord Hertford's family, and they, in turn, tended to gravitate to the kitchen for everything from biscuits to surgical plasters.

'In the other houses we have served in,' said Mrs Fobbester, making me a cup of coffee and facing me from another kitchen stool, 'the butler's pantry and the kitchen were well away from the main rooms. I may not have liked the interaction with the family here at first, but I have got used to it; it was just that we had been so used to working on our own. In one house we never used to see the children, because they were in the nursery with their nanny. The same down in Dorset. It was a separate nursery in the grounds. Nanny used to tell me what she wanted. As staff get scarcer, you get closer to the family. It is a good thing, really. It is a very happy atmosphere here.'

The servant who becomes a sort of honorary aunt is evidently *not* a thing of the past, even though many people believe that the breed disappeared with the British Empire. Mrs Fobb has many anecdotes about all the younger generation, but especially about Anne, who was not at school when the Fobbesters first came to Ragley Hall.

'If I have had to tell the children off, then I have done. When Anne was very small, she comes down to breakfast one day in a mood. I had to get her up at seven, and the bus took her at eight o'clock. She sat down there at the end of the kitchen, and would not have her breakfast. I said, "I will give you five seconds to have that." She didn't. She gave me an answer. I was down off the stool and smacked her bottom. I thought afterwards, what had I done? What is Her Ladyship going to say? But she gave me permission to chastise her if need be, if she got out of hand. I never had to do it again. Once was enough. No, Anne didn't hold it against me. She is a nice girl.'

Once, after a clash of wills, Anne was told in the kitchen: 'You will not come here again.' She was about seven at the time, and had been particularly naughty. 'Probably raiding the kitchen for something I needed for dinner,' remembered Mrs Fobbester. 'She would be forbidden to come into the kitchen for a fortnight or so. She would send a little note down in the lift saying, "Sorry, I do love you." I would then let her back into the kitchen.'

Mrs Fobb supposed the kitchen was one of the human focal points of Ragley. The children were in and out all the time. Harry came in for his tea every night at five. He usually had home-made scones, which he loved, even if his mother and father were sitting in the Green Drawing Room

The front terrace of Ragley Hall and the magnificent Palladian portico (*top*) are now an attraction, though when Lord and Lady Hertford moved into the Hall as newly-weds the front steps were crumbling. The rear terrace (*centre*) overlooks the gardens and an avenue to the skyline (*below*), which Lord and Lady Hertford themselves began to cut through the forest.

The Mauve Drawing Room (*top left*), one of the favourites of visitors, is regularly used by the family, whose personal photographs are an added attraction for tourists. The Main Dining Room (*top right*) is now used frequently by industrialists for professional entertainment, but during the two world wars, when Ragley Hall was a hospital, it served a rather different purpose. There are numerous professional receptions and private dances in the Great Hall (*above*), where Roland the huge mountain dog loves to hear his own reverberant barking.

Lord Hertford (with cigarette-holder, *top left*) and the farms manager, Peter Crabtree, who joined Ragley as a young man, confer regularly at the farm office at Weethley about work, but also find themselves chatting about 'cabbages and kings'. Lord Hertford usually works in his own office (*top right*) with William, his golden spaniel, under or near his desk. The informality is now backed by modern technology, including (*below*) one of the most sophisticated milking units in Europe.

The gatekeeper of any great estate, like Ragley's Jack Smith (*top left*), must show a welcoming face to the public while being on constant guard against the ingenious efforts of those who try to enter without paying. The guides (*centre*) are local ladies who take vicarious delight in explaining Ragley's history to American tourists or workers from the nearby industrial towns. The sweet shop kept by Mrs Cynthia Bindley (*below*) is backed by the equally profitable souvenir shop run by Mrs Molly Stephens.

with their afternoon tea and biscuits. Harry would tend to gravitate to the kitchen after he had been working, feeling it to be more informal – and a more likely venue for scones. He would help himself to bread and butter and jam, or make toast, which might be more to his taste than the chocolate biscuits on offer in the Green Drawing Room.

'They come to raid the cupboards, mostly,' said Mrs Fobb cheerfully. 'Or they come in for coffee in the mornings. They come in for anything, really. When they were younger, they came in for help with their homework. I used to help Carolyn with French lessons, because my French was much better than hers, and I used to help her with her maths. Before I had decided to become a cook, I had passed the entrance exam to university, but I didn't want to go – I couldn't stick another five years of study. I preferred cooking, anyway.'

Diana would come in for coffee or biscuits at tea-time, or she might come in for apples for the horses. And Anne might want a quick repair job done: 'She went to a Pony Club camp a week ago, and an hour before she went, she said, "Dear kind Mrs Fobb, will you sew this on my hat?" It was the elastic. Things like that.'

Both the Fobbesters maintained stoutly that they would be bored stiff if they retired at the normal retirement age. There is certainly plenty going on in the butler's pantry to prevent them getting bored; even if much of it comes under the heading of 'unofficial', rather than 'official' duties.

It may be helping Anne to collect peacocks' feathers. The fine birds of Ragley – over twenty of them – drop their tail feathers in the month of July. Anne and Mrs Fobb have been in the habit of collecting as many as they can, for sale in the Ragley shop at about 25p each. In a good July, there will be 300 or more feathers for sale in this way, and Anne has been allowed to keep some of the proceeds as pocket money. Or the butler's pantry concentrates on picking mushrooms, which are used for breakfasts or other meals. There is no nonsense about Continental breakfasts at Ragley. The full English breakfast is the rule. Bacon, sausage, tomatoes, mushrooms and perhaps kidneys.

Sometimes that habit leads to trouble for the cook. Once an American couple who were staying overnight said, 'Don't bother about breakfast. We only have a piece of toast.' The Fobbesters took them at their word, but sent up the usual full breakfast setting for Lord and Lady Hertford themselves. 'But the American couple were there first for breakfast,' recalled Mrs Fobb, wincing. 'When His Lordship came down for breakfast, they had sat in his place, and had eaten Lord Hertford's and Her Ladyship's breakfasts.'

'I said to Lord Hertford,' chipped in Fobbester, 'that he should have sent down for more breakfast. His Lordship said, "It would have looked too obvious." He put politeness above his breakfast. When Her Ladyship came down, she just said diplomatically, "I think I will just have toast this morning." There was no chance of her having anything else.'

Such difficulties are almost expected by the Fobbesters of this world, who must learn to keep a straight face when their best efforts go awry. Mrs Fobb said she was still not sure, to this day, whether the Americans who spread marmalade on her carefully cooked scrambled eggs did so because they thought it was chutney. Guests who come to be professionally entertained have been known to be made so comfortable that they have been busy chatting with Lord Hertford in the library over a scotch when they should have been in their coach for the return trip. In such cases, one of the guest bedrooms has to be made instantly ready. Sometimes guests turn up for events which have been postponed, and have to be humoured, and perhaps even entertained on an *ad-hoc* basis.

Mrs Fobb recalled one such occasion. 'We had a dinner booked for eighty surgeons in the Great Hall, and it was cancelled on the night of the do. Lord and Lady Hertford and one of the girls were here for dinner. At seven-forty-five a Rolls Royce drives up, and out steps a lady and a man dressed in evening dress. My husband went to the door and they said, "We have come for the surgeons' dinner." He said, "It's been cancelled." Lord Hertford went to see what was wrong. These people were from Australia. He offered them a drink and was waving them goodbye when he said to my husband, "Do you think that duck will stretch?" The Australians brought out champagne for dinner and they enjoyed themselves and went back to tell their friends they had had dinner with Lord and Lady Hertford.' Plainly there is business acumen as well as good manners behind such spontaneity.

Even with the unexpected comings and goings of a young family and their friends, life at Ragley is comparatively orderly, according to the Fobbesters. They certainly have had experiences elsewhere which have conditioned them to cool action under pressure.

One such anecdote has become a family favourite. They had previously been employed by an elderly couple in their eighties and one day they asked the Fobbesters for lunch in their separate bedrooms, as they did not wish to get up until later. They asked for lunch to be served at one p.m. and their lunch trays were all ready when there was a ring at the front door. Two ladies were standing there. 'Good afternoon. We are relations, and we are expected to lunch.' Thinking quickly, Fobbester said without hesitation, 'Certainly. Would you care for a sherry?'

'Then,' remembered Fobbester, 'I hot-footed it to the kitchen and said to the wife, "Lunch for four!" Up the stairs to the lady of the house, and told her, "There are two relations of yours who've come to lunch!" She promptly fell out of bed on to the floor. I went and got her husband out of bed, ran down to the cellar, got a bottle of wine, set the table for four, lit the fire and, by one-fifteen, I announced lunch. No one knew the difference. It was only twenty-five minutes previously that they had arrived.'

At Ragley, the human beings are usually more organized, but the dogs also tend to regard Mrs Fobb's domain as a social centre. If Lord Hertford goes away for the day, he will usually leave his spaniel William in the butler's pantry-cum-kitchen, with the Fobbesters. On their days off, Lord Hertford is diffident about bringing in William, but William is not diffident about coming in by himself. If Lord Hertford is away, William will start hammering on the door of the only other person he fully trusts: Mrs Fobb. This will start at ten in the morning, and go on until William is admitted. He either stays in the Fobbesters' flat or goes out with them on car rides, keeping company with their own spaniel, Mr Pickwick.

The two dogs have occasional growling contests over food, but otherwise get on well. They remain in the car during shopping trips to Alcester, and have proved to be a marvellous deterrent to car thieves. While Lord and Lady Hertford and their family were at the Turf Club's enclosure overlooking The Mall to see the Royal Wedding procession on its way to St Paul's Cathedral on 29 July 1981, William was with the Fobbesters. So was Roland, the enormous shaggy Pyrenean mountain dog who, Fobbester swears, only barks so loudly in the Great Hall because he loves to hear his menacing voice magnified.

'Roland is very good,' Mrs Fobb told me. 'But he is too fond of cake and biscuits. Her Ladyship would not believe it. He had a dinner, but he was barking in the dining room and Her Ladyship said, "He's hungry." I said, "He's cake-hungry." I offered him the rest of his dinner and he took no notice. Then I offered him cake. He lapped it up. Now Her Ladyship doesn't pay any attention when he barks after dinner.'

Coping with the aristocratic tastes of Roland may have its difficulties, but Lord Hertford's family do make return gestures. Anne, at fifteen, was fond in dull moments of trying to train the Fobbesters' Mr Pickwick to do tricks.

'Much to his disgust!' reported Mrs Fobbester. 'He loves Anne, but he is not too keen on the training. He does it for her.'

Sometimes the butler's pantry is an intelligence centre as well as a place of social gathering. One evening, just before dinner, Lord Hertford asked, 'Where's Carolyn?'

'Out to dinner, Milord.'

'Where's Anne?'

'Out at the Pony Club.'

'And Harry?'

'Out to dinner, Milord.'

'Where's Her Ladyship?'

'Out to dinner, Milord.'

'Tomorrow, at this rate, all I shall need is a picnic,' said Lord Hertford drily. He always likes having his family around him and admits to a sense of depletion when they are not.

The Princess Alphonse de Chimay, Lord Hertford's elegant mother-in-law, who lives in the Kitchen Garden House on the estate, is one of the rare members of the family not prone to pop in on the Fobbesters. If the grandchildren meet her, it is usually at her home. The Fobbesters know her likes and dislikes without the need of frequent discussion: all joints of beef are *not* turned in the oven, so that one side is rare (as Lord Hertford likes it) while the other side is well-done (as the Princess likes it). If she sees Mr and Mrs Fobb at a staff party, and says, 'In the Autumn you must come down and pick apples,' that is more of a Royal Command than a casual remark. A plea of 'pressure of other business' may not be accepted in mitigation of failure to turn up in the Autumn.

'But she is a charmer,' said Mrs Fobb with enthusiasm. 'She was absolutely marvellous about six years ago, when she was crippled with arthritis. She used to drive herself to London to a bone manipulator, against everyone's advice. She did it weekly. She comes for meals at the Hall, but the only time we chat to her is at staff parties, when she tells us to come down for apples. She has a lovely house, a beautiful garden and a very good dress sense. She is a very elegant lady.'

The butler's pantry-cum-kitchen may be more of a social centre for employers as well as servants than it would have been in the past, but the Mr and Mrs Fobbs of this world know that correct form must be preserved.

'One old gardener,' remembered Mrs Fobb, 'called Lord Hertford "Lordie", which is always the done thing behind the scenes, but never to his face. We would never have a joke about the family, though we sometimes have a joke with them.'

'Like His Lordship a few years ago,' put in Fobbester. 'He did some modelling for suits. One day he came through looking very formal and I said, "Oh, Milord, have you been modelling for Moss Bros?" He took it in good part.'

Mrs Fobb made it quite clear that, as far as she was concerned, no criticism of His Lordship's family from outsiders was allowed. 'I would be most annoyed,' she summed up, 'if anyone joked about the family. If anyone says anything against them, I really go to bat for them. *I* can say it, but I wouldn't let anyone else say it.'

Such devoted service has helped the aristocracy to cope with the demands of a changing world, as they now must if they are to stay solvent.

7
No Ordinary Office

THE LOCAL NEWSPAPER REPORTER who rang the Ragley estate office with a query about some changes on the estate, asked to speak to the estate manager.

'Speaking,' said a man's voice, which then proceeded to answer the young lady's enquiries in detail.

At the end of the conversation, the grateful reporter put in her final two questions: 'Do you mind telling me your name, and can I quote you?'

'My name is the Marquess of Hertford, and you can.'

Recalling the incident with a laugh, Lord Hertford commented, 'I said I was the estate manager with perfect truth, because I *do* manage the estate. But she sounded shattered. People expect to reach me only through an intermediary.'

On another occasion, a man rang the estate office with a query at eleven o'clock at night, and found he was speaking direct to Lord Hertford.

'He told me,' Lord Hertford recalled, 'how impressed he was to find me still at the office at that hour of night. But the estate office number can ring in the library, where we spend our winter evenings. I didn't let on that the phone was ringing in the comfortable library.'

It is Lord Hertford's proud declaration that if he is at home, he is available to any phone caller: 'It is pure luck. It depends which room we are sitting in; we do move about a certain amount. The private number usually rings in the Green Drawing Room, where we spend our summer evenings. I always tell my friends, "If you don't get an answer to one number, try another." I don't find this arrangement amusing, not really. I get people ringing up and saying, "Can we order a load of firewood?" And I say, "May I have your name and address and I will tell them about it in the office tomorrow morning." I don't call that amusing – I call that sensible.'

To a certain extent, Lord Hertford is like the tortoise who carries its 'office' around with it wherever it goes. Of course he does have an office as such, the smallish room on the ground floor, at the north-east corner of Ragley Hall. He shares it with his son and heir, two desks, one smallish conference table and, more often than not, his golden spaniel William, who is fond of lying under his master's desk, noisily licking himself.

Those who have office talks with the average tycoon rarely have to compete with the enthusiastic slurp-slurp of endearing spaniels. But there are superficial resemblances to big business. On the 8th Marquess's desk, as on many a tycoon's, there are *three* telephones. Grey for the estate office, white for the tourist trade, and green for (theoretically) private calls. All with different numbers.

They are all routed, by a process obscure to me at the outset and just as obscure today, so that they ring either on Lord Hertford's desk; or where he happens to be at Ragley at any given time; or in the combined estate and tourist trade office, accessible from Lord Hertford's office via a worn stone staircase and a narrow passageway, and staffed by three willing ladies who constitute (with a fourth in the farm office outside Ragley Park itself) the entire office staff of the whole enterprise.

It is a slender staff, fully in tune with hard times. But at least the staff have no reason to complain, hard-worked as they may be, that the office is just a run-of-the-mill affair you could find in any Black Country foundry or Birmingham nuts and bolts' factory.

'Office life here,' remarked Lord Hertford, 'is complicated only in the sense that it handles the tourist trade as well as the estate. Some establishments probably have separate offices for the two branches of the operation. We do the whole thing from here. A lot of stately homes have a house manager, who runs the place. I have never really wanted such a man here. I have rather enjoyed doing it myself.'

I said that I got the impression that he regarded Ragley Hall as very much his own home and that he would not really want someone else there, running it. 'Yes! That's it exactly! Also I can't quite think what a house manager would do all day. I suppose all those house managers do keep themselves busy. I seem to run the estate *and* the house. Perhaps I don't do it very well, but I do it. It never seemed to me to be quite a full-time job – not the house by itself. Possibly the present office set-up is not ideal: I think there are times when the three women don't like working together all in the one room, with those three different telephones all busy.'

The regulars in the office for many years have been Marian Crabtree, wife of Peter Crabtree the farms manager, and Maureen Lawrence, Lord Hertford's secretary. Marian Crabtree does the accounts for all three sides of the enterprise – estate, Hall, and farms. Maureen Lawrence, effectively the administrator of the office, handles most enquiries that require complex decisions – for instance, requests for bookings of special events, of which Ragley receives a very large number. All of them have to be sifted. In this she is helped by a third lady, who was away ill during the time I was at Ragley. Jane Whitmarsh, the only unmarried lady in Ragley's offices, was secretary at the farm office at Weethley Farm, working with Peter Crabtree and with Marian Crabtree when she is busy on the farm accounts.

I found it difficult to think of these human beings as women: *ladies* is the inescapable term.

'Lord Hertford,' said Maureen Lawrence, explaining how the telephone system had great flexibility, 'sometimes says, "It's a call for you, Maureen," and sometimes I say, "It's a call for you, Hugh." '

Hugh? She called the 8th Marquess of Hertford Hugh to his face? 'Yes. It is only the Crabtrees and myself who do that. Other people would not use Christian names. Lord Hertford looks upon us as senior management, I suppose. Actually, I am one of those people who prefer, really, to call him Lord Hertford in front of people unless we are among friends. It is more polite and courteous. On the other hand, he calls me Maureen and it should work both ways in my opinion. I think there are some people to whom I should be "Mrs Lawrence" in public. That is the way I feel – that in front of strangers we should be more like an office. But Lord Hertford asked me to call him Hugh some years ago. I have been here thirteen years, and that was possibly ten years ago. If we get a new lady she will never call him anything else but Lord Hertford.'

Such are the fine social distinctions involved in working in the office of a Marquess – not all of them imposed by the Marquess himself.

The licence to call a Marquess by his Christian name is certainly earned by the ladies in the Ragley office. Their work has become even more concentrated in the past few years. In the days when Ragley was managed by an agent and the 8th Marquess was newly married, Marian Crabtree used to work in the farm office all the time, and there was a separate estate office out in the village of Arrow, in what had been the old village school. This was closed a few years ago in the course of rationalization. The estate office then had a staff of five and Lord Hertford thought the estate could be managed on a smaller salaries bill. So he opened a new office in the Hall, and closed the old office in Arrow, making one or two workers redundant. The farms office is fairly safe from a similar pruning, as it holds only Peter Crabtree himself, his secretary, and Marian Crabtree on a part-time basis, when she is dealing with the farm accounts sector of her duties.

I arranged a lunch appointment with Maureen Lawrence in the Arrow Mill, the local pub, so she could tell me how the lean operation worked. Her apology for being rather late immediately gave me some idea of her own well-stretched office life. 'Sorry. A chap on the gate came up to the office. It was someone trying to get in, saying they were the parents of a person working in the restaurant. The man at the gate came straight to me, and he was quite right to do so. There should have been a pass signed by someone like Lord Hertford.'

Office life at Ragley, said Mrs Lawrence (even to write 'Maureen' feels wrong) was certainly no less hectic than it would be in ordinary industry or commerce. She was in the position to make comparisons, having worked once for a general sales manager in commerce. 'This is as busy as any office I have been in,' she maintained. 'In the past I have always had more staff than I do here at Ragley. In any industry you don't have three phones to look after all day. You usually have someone on the switchboard. The workload here is quite heavy because we have to do everything between us. There are two telephones actually on my desk – one number and the extension of another number. Whichever one rings, we usually pick it up in the office.'

Every Monday morning, Mrs Lawrence is in the office before nine o'clock, ready for the first of the morning telephone calls. Completing the cash records for the weekend, when the house is open to the public, is usually a two-hour job on Sunday evenings. It sometimes spreads over into Monday morning if other matters have been pressing on Sunday night. Mrs Lawrence's own correspondence might be two hours' work, especially in the summer time, when ideas for the *next* open season are being considered. Lord Hertford will usually be in his own office by ten o'clock, having read his letters over breakfast, and, shortly after this, will go through his mail with Mrs Lawrence. This can take an hour, an hour and a half or sometimes longer, depending on the Marquess's other appointments.

The morning mail, more often than not, contains an enquiry, perhaps several, about the possibility of hiring part of Ragley for a special function. All such enquiries are discussed in principle at this point. Then, if the Marquess thinks the suggested event would not damage Ragley morally, socially or physically, an appointment is made for the organizers to look over the Hall, view the facilities, and specify their exact requirements – then they are told what the cost will be.

Mrs Lawrence will give a price for these special functions after either she or Lord Hertford has shown the organizers over the Hall. The Marquess is fond of doing this himself if he is there – he is always in his element when showing off Ragley and what it has to offer.

'The pricing takes quite a bit of time,' said Mrs Lawrence. 'If someone wants a dinner-dance, I have to find out how much it will cost to hire the band and a portable dance floor, and to get a suitable menu at prices they are prepared to pay. We must establish what sort of drink they want – wine and fruit juice or a full bar? Each function is costed individually.'

Fortunately, said Mrs Lawrence, when people came to look over the Hall before an event, they usually didn't ask silly questions. On the whole people were very sensible: 'Most people realize it is a very beautiful private home, containing things of intrinsic beauty and value, and that it must be treated with great respect. We lay it on the line with people who want dances that we have a drugget (linen cover) for the carpet in the Great Hall, to protect it against food stains; and that we have a bar in the North Staircase Hall and the floor must be covered with plastic, or else we find that drink stains ruin the polish. All this has to be explained at the time they view the premises. We have learned by experience that if you leave any point unmentioned then you can get caught. They might *not* put a cover down. You can't always expect everyone to look after the place as if it were their own home. Sometimes both Lord Hertford and I go round with the organizers. We want to have functions here, we want people to come to Ragley, but we want things to be done properly.'

Lord Hertford is rather fonder of hiring out parts of Ragley to organizers of events than he is of staging events with his own cash. This has proved to be a shrewd attitude.

'Lord Hertford,' explained Mrs Lawrence, 'doesn't like staging big events himself because (a) we are short-staffed and (b) in his early days he arranged outdoor events and it poured with rain and he lost money. He finds it better, for instance, to allow things to be staged in the Park which are organized by the people who want to hold them – like a village event, or a horse show, or a car owners' club, or a kite festival. We let them come into the Park, for which we charge a rent. They then bring more people into the Park and the individual customers have to pay an entrance fee. For us there is a certain amount of planning involved with each outdoor event – for instance, I have to get extra staff to cope with the gate.'

While Mrs Lawrence is showing would-be function organizers around the Hall – she is the only office employee to do so – someone else is answering the telephones and there is usually a pile of memos on her corner desk awaiting her return.

Often there will have been telephone enquiries from organizations who wish to bring over a party of people to view Ragley in the open season or even, by very special arrangement, in the officially 'closed' season. Women's Institutes and old age pensioners' groups all ask specialized questions. So do disabled groups. Not many enquiries about group visits to Ragley can be answered simply by sending out a leaflet, though Ragley periodically orders 50,000 copies of its leaflet at £1,000 a batch and 5,000 copies of its guidebook at about £2,000. Often organizers ask if wheelchairs can be taken upstairs, and Mrs Lawrence has to explain that Ragley has no lift but that it does have one or two strong men who would be prepared to lift the disabled person up the stairs if he or she can be taken from the wheelchair. (There are now ramps up the front steps for wheelchairs.)

Mrs Lawrence usually goes for lunch at about twelve-thirty and she makes a point of leaving Ragley to do so, so that she can come back to the task fresh. Her departure is far from being a complete break from duty. She will usually fit in odd errands – going to the bank, the post office or to the shoemakers to pick up Lady Hertford's shoes, or fetch matches or ballpoint pen refills. The estate has four houses available for holiday lettings and though they are managed by an agent in the village of Broadway, they are run on a day-to-day basis from the Ragley office, and Mrs Lawrence often finds herself buying necessities for the holiday houses too.

Apart from always being on duty on Bank Holidays, arranging the holiday and duty-day rotas ('it is like being a secretary and personnel manager rolled into one'), and doing the buying for the Hall during its open season, Mrs Lawrence is involved – as, very much, is Lord Hertford – with trade politics.

She is secretary of the Shakespeare Country Association of Tourist Attractions (SCATA) of which Ragley is a member together with Blenheim Palace, known as the gateway to Shakespeare Country, and other stately homes in the area. The organization was started by Roger Thompson, who runs a travel association called Guide Friday in Stratford-upon-Avon and modelled SCATA on the lines of the Cornish Association of Tourist Attractions, the first in the field. Members include the Royal Shakespeare Theatre at Stratford-upon-Avon, heavily visited by American, Japanese, German, Dutch and other tourists. Having visited the theatre, the tourists can pick up a SCATA leaflet in the foyer, telling them what other attractions are available to them in the area, including Ragley. If they come first to Ragley, they will take away the same leaflet, pointing out the charms of the Royal Shakespeare Theatre, Blenheim Palace and the other country houses. Lord Hertford stoutly maintains that all twelve members are in competition, but only friendly competition, and that none of them have anything to gain by double-crossing each other: 'When people come here, I warmly recommend Blenheim or some of the other places, hoping they will do the same for me. After all, once they have come to me, I already have their custom, and the same applies to the other members.'

The Shakespeare Country Association of Tourist Attractions meets to exchange ideas once every couple of months. But there are running secretarial duties which fall upon Mrs Lawrence, not the least of which concerns the most ticklish subject within the association: how much money each of the members should pay towards the cost of their communal self-promotion. It cost £2,000 in the first year of its operation to print half a million copies of the leaflet, but the cost fell in subsequent years to only a fraction of that sum as the stock of previously paid-for leaflets was gradually used up.

Apart from trade politics, Mrs Lawrence tends to get involved in the personal and domestic concerns of Lord Hertford and his family, in a way a secretary in conventional commerce or industry might not. 'That applies to the other ladies as well. They all get involved with the family if things need to be done. But you wouldn't be here in the first place if you didn't expect it. It has never been an issue as far as the staff are concerned, as far as I know. It is, after all, part of the charm of the place. Lord Hertford has a lot of interests and activities, but it's not like big business, not really. It has got something of a personal touch to it – the whole office. The mere fact that Lord Hertford does his work, and then goes out riding to see what is going on, tells you it is very different. It is a very basic office, and we probably have to work harder than we would do in industry. But it is a *pleasant* place to work and the ladies obviously like it.'

Undoubtedly the most mobile office lady is Marian Crabtree, wife of the farms manager, because she is responsible for handling both the farm accounts and those of the estate.

'It does mean that I am the one on wheels, as it were,' said Marian Crabtree. 'I am the one who is fetching and carrying things from the farm to Lord Hertford. I like to spend at least an hour in the farm office at Weethley every morning, and usually two hours once I am there. I try to be there to open the post, and to deal with the profit and loss account, VAT and personal letters. But I often have to leave at ten, to do other jobs, before the post arrives.'

Not for the office ladies of Ragley the luxury of their city sisters: a more or less punctual arrival of early morning mail. Sometimes the post comes at eight-thirty in the morning and sometimes not until twelve-thirty or later in the afternoon.

'You can't predict within four hours when it will arrive,' said Marian Crabtree. 'It happened last week. We got it at twelve noon on Friday. But I see the morning doesn't go to waste, because I don't wait for the post before getting on with other things. You have to use every hour effectively.'

The decision to close the original estate office in the village of Arrow, which seemed prudent on grounds of cost-cutting at the time, has led to complications: 'We moved from the village up here to the Hall to save costs. But when the farms doubled in size, it doubled the work. Had we had the foresight to see that would happen, we could have all moved into the estate office in the village, where my husband could have worked in liaison with everyone and I would have been able to liaise without carrying paper backwards and forwards from the farm office to the Hall. But the advantage, to Lord Hertford, of having staff here at the Hall is great, particularly in terms of savings in heating and lighting, and for the sake of general convenience.'

Marian Crabtree, like her husband, is very sensitive to Lord and Lady Hertford's best interests. There seem to be threads of real friendship between the two families despite the fact that, as Marian Crabtree put it, she never forgot they were of a different class. The Crabtrees came to the service of the newly-married Lord and Lady Hertford when they were a young married couple themselves, and later on their children were invited to each other's birthday parties. The Crabtrees can remember what Lord Hertford was doing when they first arrived – writing his first guide book for the opening of the Hall. Marian Crabtree had her young family, then got drawn into doing the farm accounts.

Was there, I asked her, ever a tug of war between the demands of her children and the demands of her aristocratic employers?

'Strangely enough,' she said, 'it has been a unique thing. Even with my last child, who was born twelve years ago when we had a part-time farm office staff, I used to pick the phone up and the child would sit quietly – perhaps he knew that was a priority over him. Perhaps I gave more to the job than I should have done, but I don't think so. The older boys worked for a year on the farm at Ragley. They both loved shooting and took part in anything they could. They were brought up to be competely proud of the estate and Lord Hertford's interests. We have liked the fact that our families have grown up together, and we have wanted to do the job. I never feel the slightest irritation when Lord Hertford rings me at eleven-forty on a Sunday morning when I am doing my lunch. Lord Hertford has this very friendly way of treating us as a part of the family, and I think we have a quite unique relationship as employer and employee. It's a strange thing, isn't it? I don't think other people would understand it at all, but my own family, my sisters, have accepted that this is the way Marian and Peter carry on.'

Did her relatives think of her as being what, in kind terms, could be described as socially aspiring? 'I don't think so for a minute. Lord and Lady Hertford came to our son Andrew's wedding. They sat right at the back of the church, because on that occasion it was *our* family and they were the guests. At the same time, one doesn't think of oneself as being in the same class. This relationship is something quite unique and I am proud that it can work.'

Marian Crabtree said she never thought about what would happen when she and her husband retired. They might buy a house of their own somewhere in the Cotswolds, but they had only discussed it vaguely. She didn't think, one way or another, that she and her husband would ever lose the connection with the family of Lord and Lady Hertford.

Like all the rest of the staff, Marian Crabtree obviously worked hard within the pattern of this friendship. She is off Tuesday and Thursday afternoons and on Sundays, though she is on call Saturday mornings. But there is one great advantage for Marian Crabtree in the singular office life of Ragley. She needs to leave at four every afternoon so she can meet her youngest son Matthew from school; so it is arranged that she *will* leave at four.

To some extent, the routine of Ragley can be modified to suit the staff in a way that would not be possible in an ordinary office – unless, perhaps, there was a *very* hard-nosed shop steward.

'For years,' Lord Hertford will explain, 'we opened Ragley Hall from two o'clock to six o'clock, and then we altered it to one-thirty to five-thirty, because there was always a queue at two o'clock. The main reason we don't open till one-thirty – though the restaurant opens at twelve-thirty – is that we and our staff like to have lunch. Some stately homes are open from ten in the morning, but that requires a bigger staff, because you have got to have relief staff when others are having lunch. We have got the system quite well organized here. The cleaners, for instance, are cleaning the house at nine a.m. They work over until one o'clock on Sundays or eleven-thirty other days. To do it all by eleven, for us to open earlier, would be a bit of a push unless they started at seven, and I don't think they would want that.'

The office and the cleaning staff tend to respond to such obliging compromises by providing willing successors when they leave. As I left the offices one morning and walked out into the stone-floored passageway, I met an example of this.

Phyllis Clarke had been cleaning at Ragley for four years, she told me. Her mother, Mrs Keyte, had the job before her for seventeen years and carried on till she was eighty-six, at which point she recommended her daughter. Her mother had first heard about the job from someone at Ragley, said Phyllis Clarke, and now *her* own daughter, Barbara Taylor, worked at Ragley as well.

Call it tradition, call it nepotism or call it a very hard slog, but Phyllis Clarke was obviously very content with her lot, as, apparently, were all the ladies who service Ragley's offices.

'I have done other sorts of premises,' said Phyllis Clarke, 'and this is dirtier work, because of all the people who come to Ragley. But I like being here, I *enjoy* it. This is partly because of the other ladies. We are all one happy family.'

The 8th Marquess of Hertford, with his sense of family solidarity and financial wisdom, would have liked to hear her say that.

8
Battle of the Flowers

THE GARDENS of Ragley were left untended for decades before they were taken in hand by Lady Hertford. Soon they sprouted a rich crop of colour, and captured public interest. What the public did not know was that they sometimes caused – and still cause – disagreements between the pioneering Lady Hertford and her more cautious husband.

'My role as gardener, up to now, has been mainly one of a destroyer,' explained Lady Hertford. 'The gardens were covered by yew trees, so no one could see anything. I wanted them down, and I wanted blocks of colour. And men do hate change, don't they? They are terrified of change.'

But more than mere resistance to change was involved. Ragley's gardens run all round the house and, via a newly-cut avenue, stretch up to the western skyline. They were created by Lord Hertford's great-grandparents, and to him they symbolize the continuing traditions of Ragley and its family. His bride was Louise de Caraman Chimay. The only daughter of Lieutenant-Colonel Prince and Princess Alphonse de Chimay, she is a vivid and forthright lady with little liking for either gloom or half-measures. To her the gardens were merely a mass of dull green yew and vine, often so thick that her husband could not find a path through them on the horse he loves to ride around the estate.

Standing on the grassed west terrace of Ragley, and looking out not merely on its ancient stone wall but also on the remains of the yews, one can sympathize with both points of view. Lady Hertford's claustrophobia and Lord Hertford's conservatism can easily be understood.

'I don't think, really, that gardening is a thing you can hurry,' admitted Lady Hertford as she enjoyed the new vistas her benevolent destruction had opened up. 'But I *am* in a hurry because really I am twenty years too late. I feel I must make up for lost time. I always swore that by the time of our son's twenty-first birthday I would have renovated and improved every room in the house. So the house had to have priority.' According to Lord Hertford the restoration of Ragley could not have been achieved without Lady Hertford's twenty years of hard work.

Only after that was a diversion of attention to the gardens possible, after years of 'fiddling around spasmodically', as Lady Hertford put it. 'I really got going with a vengeance a couple of winters ago,' she said. 'It took me twenty-three years, but I reckon, actually, that in the last two years we have done ten years' work, because I have very good support from the two men who work in the garden. I think they were rather relieved when I arrived. I said, "You are doing marvellously, thank you," but it was slightly difficult, because any daughter-in-law is treading on eggs in trying to make changes.'

Members of the lower classes may be secretly relieved to realize that such domestic tensions also exist among the aristocracy. Perhaps more so: the Wimbledon housewife who wants to prune the roses is merely tampering with her husband's handiwork, whereas the new bride at the Hall is battling with both filial loyalty and history itself. Lord Hertford admired his mother, a lady of some magnificence and charm, and her garden at Ragley was the only one he had known.

Lady Hertford kept her peace for a long time, her energies being fully absorbed by the restoration of the house itself. 'But what I found I detested here was the saturation of the garden in yew trees and laurels. And I found my husband was not frightfully happy about my removing them. If I had my way, I think I would remove practically every single yew tree in the garden, starting right outside the office window, because the ones in front of that are mostly self-seeded, they are not *meant* to be there. But my husband's mother never objected to them and therefore, to him, the yews and the laurels are part of his home. So I have to be very careful when I come in with fresh ideas.'

Lady Hertford's idea was to remove as many as possible of the ivy-covered yews which surrounded the house, often totally obscuring fine copper beeches. At the same time she wanted to plant flowers and bushes in the gaps to produce positive blocks of colour. As an ambition, it was a clear dramatization of her character. She set about realizing it surreptitiously at first, which was totally out of character; she is very obviously offended by anything underhand and hole-in-corner. Some yews came down without Lord Hertford noticing. (Or perhaps, diplomatically, he simply failed to admit noticing.)

One copper beech which had been planted by Lord Hertford's mother, so as to be visible from the urn in the centre of the gardens, had been almost completely swallowed up by the surrounding brambles and laurels. The tree was between 30 and 40 feet tall and the laurels were over 20 feet tall. Lady Hertford, borrowing her husband's talent for diplomacy, pointed out that the historic wishes of the family had been thwarted because a tree planted to be seen from the urn could hardly be seen from anywhere.

'You have a point,' said Lord Hertford and so down came the brambles and laurels.

Lady Hertford cheerfully admitted that her attitude to gardens was like the Philistine's attitude to pictures – she was no expert, but she knew what she liked. 'My base as a child was London. I was brought up as a reluctant London sparrow, and I was always in other people's houses when outside London. I was never brought up to understand anything about a garden. But I know what I like.' Such certainty of aim was necessary in a situation where a professional gardener, looking over Ragley's gardens decades ago, could say to Lady Hertford: 'Somewhere here is a marvellous garden, but no traces of it seem visible.' Apart from restoring the visibility, Lady Hertford set out to provide colour and smell, introducing roses, honeysuckle and philadelphus where both the family and the public could appreciate them.

The roses are a recent innovation, diplomatically not replacing but augmenting the ancestral herbaceous borders at the foot of the rear terrace wall. The borders have been retained, but they are now used for roses which have been trained to climb up the wall and over the top of it, falling on the side of the wall facing the terrace itself, and breaking up its stark stone. One June day when the roses were still being trained, a party of disabled people on the terrace were enjoying the view over the top of the roses – a view that took the eye straight through the avenue cut westwards to the trees on the skyline.

'Twenty-four years ago,' remembered Lady Hertford, 'we had this idea of making an avenue through the woods. My husband started with a machette. You would have thought we were in Borneo. When we emerged, we found we had cut a path very much off to the left. We couldn't see what we were doing.' But the avenue, now straight, commands the attention of most visitors. They sit out on the terrace on warm days and, for an hour or so, know what it was like to be an aristocrat when the view was indeed commanded from the terrace in every sense.

Eighteen months before the roses were put in place, a pair of wisterias were planted at the back of the house, in the ground immediately below the ends of the stone balcony, and trained up the wall and across the balustrade, ultimately to meet in the middle of the balcony. 'When they do meet,' said Lady Hertford, 'I will try to get this central creeping ivy thing down. I am egg-treading, I know, but I hope to! I hope to put in an Ena Harkness rose, so that it runs right up the central column to the balcony. I said to Lord Hertford, "Can I get rid of the yew trees at the end." He said, "No, I couldn't bear to have them removed." It's so boring, there is nothing there at the end to excite your attention. In a garden you want moments when you stop and say, "How marvellous, just look at that." '

The lavender bushes in pots at the corners of the terrace have green plastic grilles around them, which Lady Hertford admits is *not* a wonderful sight. The grilles are utilitarian, and have at last enabled the family to grow lavender there. Bushes perished in fair numbers when they were 'naked', as Lady Hertford put it. 'It took us a long time to realize that the dogs were lifting their legs against them and killing them off.'

At the time Lady Hertford and I talked, a young balsam poplar at the side of the terrace was about to be freed of its imprisonment of laurels and yews. They were to be replaced by honeysuckle. 'Anything I put down has to have either colour or smell or preferably both.' *Elaeagnus* – a present from Northern Ireland with green and yellow leaves – has also been tried. But further down the side of the lawns, there was still 'an awful great mess' of various plants. 'We must have solid blocks, instead of little bits,' insisted Lady Hertford. 'Pinks and mauves will be allowed to sit together, but we will take out all the other colours and put them somewhere else. I am also trying to establish a peony bed. I put them in a few years ago and they have done terribly well. We are now trying to make a solid bed of peonies instead of fiddling around with a little bit here and there.'

A device of steel arches, probably at least a hundred years old, has been revealed at the side of the lawns as the result of Lady Hertford's passion for cutting away dense undergrowth. It is rather like a gazebo, but with traceried supports and no roof. It has been termed the Mousetrap – whether because it is like a trap or because it is reminiscent of an Agatha Christie mystery is not quite clear. Yew trees had once covered it, but they had now been hacked away.

'I want to cut down that yew tree behind it, too,' declared Lady Hertford forcibly. 'Behind the yew is a lovely chestnut tree, which you could see if I could remove these beastly things, but still Lord Hertford says "No," so there you are! I don't mind a yew tree when it is well shaped, but all this striggle-straggle. . . . If I could be a bit more ruthless, I would wait until he is in London and get a mechanical saw to it! But I don't like doing underhand things like that – you've then got to live with yourself. I suppose it is more his place than mine, but it is *frustrating*. Really!'

One success which has thrilled Lady Hertford as well as the paying public is the fact that virtually every tree has been stripped of the ivy which made it impossible for it to be seen. Since she began to work seriously on the garden in the late 1970s, virtually all the ivy has gone. 'But,' said Lady Hertford, scowling at the yew behind the Mousetrap, 'I wouldn't dream of taking the ivy off that yew. With any luck, it will kill it! And all this tiggle-taggle stuff between it and the lawn! Revolting! I would do away with the lot!'

Some problems faced by the gardening aristocracy are distinctly similar to those faced by the rest of us. Some are rather different. The moles who make mounds on the lawn could bother anybody. The peacocks who roam so freely around Ragley Hall are hardly likely to be a problem to honest gardeners of Darlington or Devizes, but the gorgeously-plumed creatures have been known to eat the buds off the Ragley roses, a sight which severely displeases its owners. Visiting children in humbler homes are also hardly likely to start pulling the plants up, as a minority of them are prone to do at Ragley. Lady Hertford usually writes such depravities off as a debit item on the balance sheet, inseparable from having one's home open to the public. But occasionally some really horrific incident causes her to roar out of the nearest window something like: 'You horrible child! Stop doing that immediately!' Rows of faces tend to look up at her, possibly chastened and possibly thoroughly enjoying the sight and sound of an offended aristocrat repulsing an attack on the ancestral amenities.

There is little really serious vandalism to the gardens of Ragley. But there has been some fairly professional, thoughtful thieving. One of the holes left by Lady Hertford's gardening was filled by Polar Bear, a white rhododendron. Lady Hertford took some trouble to locate a suitable plant, had it brought back to Ragley, and then put a barbed wire and green plastic fence round it. But even so, one evening the plant disappeared. 'So we started all over again, which at £12 a time . . . ! We are changing the system. We are going to have barbed wire on a triangular frame which will be difficult to climb or reach over.' Thus the more vulnerable plants of Ragley will be protected by fencing similar to that used on some football pitches.

'Anyone in the family who was a *proper* gardener would make all this into something really lovely,' said Lady Hertford fairly cheerfully. 'I hope *my* daughter-in-law will be a better gardener than me. But I will have prepared the patch for her, if you see what I mean.'

Ragley's patch has had the benefit not only of Lady Hertford's fresh eye but of a luxury now beyond the reach of most British home-owners: a full-time gardener. In fact, two.

It is true that even the head gardener today is a figure far removed from the traditional image: that of a man wearing baggy corduroys tied up with string below the knee, a floppy hat and smoking a smelly pipe upsidedown. John Lindsey, I found, was a man in his thirties who looked more like a factory technician than a loyal yokel, and who was in fact a refugee from industry.

It is likely that the gardens of great halls like Ragley would be in a sad state of repair were it not for people like John Lindsey, so very different in stamp from the men they replaced. 'I have a staff of one,' said John Lindsey philosophically as he sat in his spacious but chilly flat at one corner of the stables block. There is a sitting room, kitchen, three far-flung bedrooms along a dead straight passageway on the first floor; all rent-free. 'My assistant,' added John Lindsey, his metal spectacles giving him something of the look of a keen computer operator, 'is named Philip Gooding, and he is twenty-five. When I arrived Ragley had an old gardener who had retired and was working part-time, Albert Richards, and there were two students who helped with the grass cutting. Then Albert went into full retirement and for a while I was in the place on my own. Two and a half years ago, we advertised for a gardener and we didn't get too many good ones for interview. You will not easily get, nowadays, the old sort of experienced gardeners. There are very few who want to go into private service.'

In this situation, which has hardly been affected by higher unemployment in Britain, voluntary refugees from industry, men who on the whole prefer a tree to a pylon, are a godsend to the great estates. John Lindsey, who had been head gardener at Ragley for five years when I spoke to him, was born in Yorkshire, into a family which knew more about power stations than the land. One of them worked as an engineer in the nuclear power station at Bradwell in East Anglia. John Lindsey himself was drawn into working at power stations through the family connection. 'I was working at Keadby power station. But it wasn't really me. I had been in the power station ten or eleven years when I met Mary, my wife. We bought a house with a large garden – quite enormous – and that is how my interest in gardening started. I started gardening steadily and soon Mary and I talked about going into business on our own.'

But he was offered a job in South Wales as under-gardener on an estate, and the family decided to move to quieter pastures. Six weeks later the head gardener left the estate and Lindsey applied for his job and got it – the competition was not fierce even then. The estate was a private one in the charge of a retired Army Major who lived in the farmhouse and rented off the land. Later John Lindsey moved back to Lincolnshire, this time acting as gardener, groom, gamekeeper and general man-about-the-estate; and then, after that, a shepherd on the estate farms. This line of employment, like industry, turned out to have its strains and shocks. One night the farmer, who was scarcely older than John Lindsey, had a heart attack and died. His brother had no interest in keeping the farm going, and John Lindsey found himself without a job. He advertised for one, praying for a position offering some stability as well as fresh air. He did not need to analyse the replies, because in the Situations Vacant advertisements of the same issue of the farming magazine, Lord Hertford was advertising for a head gardener. John Lindsey applied for the job and got it. At the age of thirty he was almost a veteran in a declining trade.

John Lindsey had been initiated into the rights and wrongs of private service by a cook of the old school on one of the previous estates on which he worked. So he was, to some extent, prepared for the rites and social observances of Ragley, the largest and grandest estate he had worked on.

'It is hard to describe the employer-employee relationship,' said John

Lindsey. 'We have a reasonably good relationship with the boss, but not the same as in industry. I have seen industry and I have seen private service and it is definitely not the same relationship at all. There is a clear line drawn here. We are friendly, we talk to one another about the job and there is no barrier in that respect, but there is definitely a sort of social barrier. This is still so – though perhaps not on their side, but more on our side. We know how far to go. It would be inconceivable, if I can give you an example, for me to say to Lord Hertford, "Should we go down the town for a drink?" In industry would I say that? Yes. Certainly in power stations I would.'

For the head gardener of modern-day Ragley, the problems are indeed social in more senses than one. The niceties of class are only one aspect, though they are such that sometimes constraints are introduced into what might otherwise be an open relationship.

'In power stations, you get a lot of socializing at all levels right away,' said John Lindsey. 'The station superintendent, who is effectively in charge of the power station, will socialize with the electrician. It comes about because, in most power stations, there is a big social club. You meet while doing the job, *and* on a social level. There are bars, and so you mix in that way. On an estate like Ragley, I always find – and it is probably me, because I am not a very good socializer anyway – that at the social level I cannot get over that barrier of the boss-worker thing. So that you might go to a party at the Hall and have a bit of conversation with Lord Hertford or Lady Hertford and yet be conscious – or I am conscious, anyway – of the fact that you have got to go to work tomorrow when the party is over. So be careful of what you say, don't swear and don't go telling rude jokes just because this is a party. This is not so in industry. The following day the boss is back in his office and things are normal again. And then probably the following night you might be playing in the power station cricket team together, and it is Jack and Ron again.'

Perhaps this degree of familiarity would be risky in the closed atmosphere of a country estate, but the distance deemed necessary between one Lord and his employees does inflame the other main social difficulty of the head gardener: the sheer lack of social contact of almost *any* type. At one time Ragley used to have sixteen gardeners, compared with the two at present. Thus there was more social life for the hard-working breed in those days.

'Mary and I get out of the place very, very rarely,' reported John

Lindsey. 'We go shopping at Evesham once a fortnight and that is about all. Neither of us drink, and we are both lovers of the countryside, so we can find all the pleasure we want on the estate. This probably makes us rather worse off, from the point of view of seeing what is happening outside, than other people. We don't often buy a newspaper. We watch television, yes, as it is our only contact with the outside world. The friends we have got all work on the estate. It is really a very tight-knit community. We do get a limited amount of contact with visitors in summer time, but we have literally gone for over a month without seeing anybody, other than at work. We went a month without moving off the estate at all one winter.'

John Lindsey, the refugee from industry, plainly valued the spaciousness and rural peace of Ragley. But men like him may well wonder on occasion whether they are, mentally, almost dangerously cut off from the world outside. John Lindsey admitted that he sometimes thought this was so. One of his hobbies was rural social history. He had observed that when economies went into recession, first there was a slump in agriculture, then in industry and finally in the service sector. 'We have nearly always had a war after that, and that has resolved the industrial thing, anyway. When there hasn't been a war, there has been a run-down in agriculture for five years, then in industry for five years, then in the services sector for fifteen years. We hit the agricultural depression in 1974, so it will probably be 1989 before things start picking up again. The thing that worries me a lot now is that it leaves the way open for the extremists to move in. It is rife for the extreme Right or the extreme Left to start stirring things up.'

In the days of good old Albert Richards, head gardeners were rarely heard analysing social trends in such detail. It is the modern gardener, possibly with town experience, who is apt to wonder sometimes if life at Ragley, among its 25 acres of unforced but increasingly colourful gardens, is too good to be true, or at least too good to last.

'The first thing we would know if there was civil war,' brooded John Lindsey, 'would be the Luddite thing – the crowd outside the gates with their pickaxes and scythes. We wouldn't feel anything before that.'

John Lindsey's more immediate concern when I met him was the muted civil war between Lord and Lady Hertford about whether more yews should come down or whether an ancient laurel should stay or go. While respecting Lord Hertford's liking for conserving old trees and bushes, he shared Lady Hertford's view that expanses of solid green were not likely to make the public stand and stare. He also tended to agree with her that a few daisies on the lawn were not a mortal sin but a sign of spontaneity: 'It is a peculiar charm of the English that they cut their lawns too short. If they see a daisy, they are out with the weed killer. It costs a fortune.' Conceivably the head gardener may have been helped towards this view by the practical fact that, though the gardening labour forces of National Trust stately homes have tended to stay roughly the same size as they were twenty years ago, those on private estates like Ragley have shrunk drastically. Thus gardeners are always reminded of the harsh financial demands on the great private estates.

But John Lindsey was adamant that, though the work might be harder on a great private estate than on a National Trust property or a public park, the private estate was where the gardener could really learn his trade: 'If you go to work on a nursery or a commercial enterprise, too, you get stuck more or less with one sort of work. You grow tomatoes and you do nothing else all the year round. Or you grow geraniums or whatever. The thing most professional gardeners lack these days is this – they have a very specialized knowledge of only one type of enterprise. They may be brilliant on tomatoes, but they have a very poor all-round knowledge. Private service is the only type of job in horticulture nowadays where you can get a really good all-round experience.'

So why the lack of genuinely keen young men eager to get gardening jobs on great estates like Ragley? For dearth there is, though in days of economic slump and high unemployment advertisements for gardeners at Ragley do get results of a sort. John Lindsey said with regret that, yes, there were a lot of replies, but a good proportion of the job applicants weren't really interested in the job itself. They came chiefly for the house they thought might go with it. 'In fact what you're doing, if you are not careful, is attracting the wrong man for the wrong reason. He has come for the cottage. And once he is in the cottage, especially nowadays, it is fairly hard to get shot of him. If you are unfortunate enough to take the wrong man you can be stuck with him.'

John Lindsey said he was especially on his guard against young men with a belligerent or 'bolshie' attitude to Lord or Lady Hertford. He is usually cautious about employing students direct from agricultural college, who, in his experience, tend to be highly qualified but unprepared to work under anyone else. They had taken farm management at college and when they left they wanted to be managers, not what they saw as *servants* – irrespective of the fact that anyone who is expected to do a job is, in a sense, a servant of someone else.

Thus the gardens of Ragley, as with those of many stately homes, are torn between two cultures – that of the dying, cap-touching, faithful old retainer and the modern, nose-thumbing big-head or 'bolshie'.

'I stand between the two,' said John Lindsey, the modern gardener who had found diplomacy to be very important when dealing with Lord and Lady Hertford's differences of opinion. 'I have never been one to be subservient. I am not prepared to pay someone respect just because they happen to be Sir Somebody. There has got to be some justification for respect. But I try, I hope, never to be rude, though I don't always succeed. I had a strict upbringing as regards being polite.'

The pruning of laurel and yew has certainly been done only with considerable tact and dedication, both on the part of Lady Hertford and a head gardener who is not a traditional countryman steeped in the countryside's ways. If there has been an objection to cutting down a yew, John Lindsey has pointed out that the operation would better reveal an oak or beech. If there have been objections to cutting a way through dense bush and bracken, then John Lindsey has pointed out that it would be one more route that Lord Hertford could take when he took his regular morning ride on his horse. If there has been an occasional daisy or pat of moss on the lawns, then it has been pointed out not merely that they both look nice but that – an argument likely to appeal to any beleaguered aristocrat – the weed killer necessary to assure their departure would cost a fortune.

Economy as much as taste shapes the modern nobleman's lawns, rose beds and woodland walks. The staffing is cut to the bare minimum. 'National Trust gardens have worked on a ratio of one gardener to 3 acres,' John Lindsey will point out with some pride. 'Hidcote in Oxfordshire is 11½ acres and it has thirteen gardeners. With two gardeners to 25 acres here, there is no way you can be told you aren't working hard enough.'

The gardens of Ragley may well be a necessary compromise between the amount of labour and love that should be poured into the gardens of a great Hall and the amount of labour and love that are available; between the money that should be spent and the money actually available to be spent; between the semi-feudal working day that created such gardens and the modern working codes through which they are maintained. A compromise, in short, between the ideal and the possible. But the increasing patches of colour amid those controversial yews, and the increasing comments from visitors who suddenly realize that just sitting in such gardens can make one feel regal, indicate that even the apparently least 'commercial' aspect of Ragley life has had a survival plan which has paid dividends.

9
The Heir and
His Lambs

IT WAS HARDLY a self-indulgent setting in which I found the heir to Ragley at two in the morning. It would have been a spartan one for an average farm worker, let alone a young aristocrat. Wearing his father's old gumboots as some defence against the rain and the mud at the height of the lambing season, the Earl of Yarmouth was settling his differences with 'a bitch of a ewe' whose own lack of interest in hereditary factors was such that she refused to pay the slightest attention to her newly-born lamb.

The twenty-two-year-old Earl, at a time of day when many of his contemporaries and peers might be spending a lot of money in Tramp or some other fashionable London night club, was trying to tempt the stubborn mother sheep to leave the big barn where she had just given birth to her offspring, and to follow him to one of the ninety pens outside.

This he did by picking up the lamb bodily and walking out into the rain. Usually a dutiful mother follows, but on this occasion the mother refused to help Lord Yarmouth in his lonely nocturnal task. Unlike a previous mother, who moved so fast that she crushed the Earl's hand between her head and an iron girder in the big barn, this one wouldn't budge.

'This is what takes up the time,' said the Earl, his old trousers, gumboots and worn leather jacket covered in mud. 'Normally I can get a ewe into the pen in two minutes. But if she's frightened and confused or tries to run away, you have got to catch her and drag her to the pen. Then you have to stand and watch for a quarter of an hour, to see the mother doesn't start butting the lamb with her forehead because she thinks it isn't really hers.'

Lord Yarmouth had started his night turn of duty in charge of Ragley's 1,400 sheep at nine o'clock. There was an almost immediate problem – because although the sheep make a vital contribution to a great estate like Ragley, acting as 'mobile mower' of the grasslands and earning perhaps £50,000 a year in lamb sales, they tend to be stubborn and are not at all quick-witted. A newly-born lamb had been separated from her mother and Lord Yarmouth had to try to find the mother and reunite them. This he did by walking round all the seventy pens set aside for the recently-delivered sheep, presenting to each ewe the dangling umbilical cord of the lost lamb. 'The theory,' said the Earl with commendable patience, 'is that the real mother will take an interest in her own lamb when it is presented to her like this. So much for theory!'

In fact, none of the seventy sheep took the slightest interest as they lounged around in their straw pens. So, rain or no rain, the Earl had to make his tour of the animals again. It was not until halfway through the second tour that one of the sheep took a revealing interest, enabling Lord Yarmouth at last to get out of the rain.

'I am totally on my own on this night duty,' said Lord Yarmouth. 'Lovely! Very peaceful. There is not a lot you can think about, apart from the job, because there is usually something happening. One sign of impending birth is that the sheep arch their necks and make a bed with their feet. Sometimes the process takes two or three hours, other times it's about ten minutes.'

Watching a mother sheep walking around trailing bits of after-birth might seem less desirable to many twenty-two-year-olds than a hectic social life. The Earl of Yarmouth, who gets a salary of £200 a month as a partner in the estate that will one day be his, did not agree.

'If I was that way inclined,' he said, never taking his eyes off the 600 sheep in the barn, in case one of them gave birth, 'I would naturally join that set. I would be living in London, going to clubs every night and writing to my father every day for more money. I have never been very enamoured of that sort of life. So many things put me off it – I can't put it into words. The whole idea of it – I find it hollow, though I hate putting a tag on anything to do with people. People are the most difficult animals in the world. That is why I like sheep – they are quite easy. If I was not who I am and where I am, I would still have the same character, and I would quite happily find my niche in the world as a shepherd somewhere. If I had a major row with my father and I had to push off, I would not have to think twice about it. I would look in *The Farmer's Weekly* – there is almost always a job going.'

Fortunately no major row has erupted. Lord Yarmouth followed his father as a student at the Royal Agricultural College at Cirencester. He talks with touching surprise about his life there: it was the only time of his life when he did the sort of things young men with no assured future are permitted to do and enjoy doing. He shared a small cottage with another student and two cats that belonged to the cottage's owner.

His friend, the orphaned son of a professional soldier with 'no land and not much money' was, he said, the sort of man who very definitely knew what he was doing and where he was going. He would probably finish up as a farm manager somewhere on the strength of his merits alone. It was a friendship that might not have come about had it not been for Cirencester, and is unlikely to be repeated if the future 9th Marquess of Hertford spends all his time on the estate, where he has a special identity, whether he likes it or not.

At Ragley he can never hope to enjoy the companionable limitations of a four-roomed cottage, where one of the occupants had to invent an excuse and leave if the other happened to be entertaining a young lady. At Ragley, though he may prefer to be called merely 'Harry' – and is so called on the farms – he cannot escape the fact that he is known to be the future owner.

'I suppose one does have to play a part sometimes,' he said a trifle sadly, 'But it is a part I don't mind playing, because I do it so seldom.'

When we talked, lambs popping out all round us, it was April and his sister Carolyn's twenty-first birthday ball was due in October. 'I tend to let things like that roll,' he admitted. 'They happen of their own accord, as it were. I had the same attitude with my own twenty-first. My father organized it, as he loves organizing these kind of things; and Carolyn is a very social person, too. I will go along with it and sort of be the big brother and not much more. That's it.'

The heir to Ragley looked quite comfortable in his old clothes, his curly fair moustache untrimmed and his chin unshaven. His appearance did not seem part of a trendy game of social rebellion, but simply suggested that he had a genuine disregard for convention. The big barn, with its 600 ewes divided among three paddocks and giving erratic birth at an accelerated rate with the coming of day, seemed very much his domain: 'They have been in here since the first week of February. We generally aim for April 1, but we were a few days earlier this year. Lateness solves quite a few problems. It is not until a little later in the year that the grass starts to grow. It is always nicer to turn them out to grass which has grown, and to warmer weather. We bring them in when there is nowhere left for them to go outside.'

As a mobile mowing machine, said Lord Yarmouth, the sheep went round the cow pastures of the entire estate. That usually kept them going until the middle of February. Then they stayed in the barn until they lambed. 'The bad thing about lambing inside a building is that everyone is in such close quarters that unless you keep a sharp eye out, you can mis-match a mother and lamb.'

Though it was his first lambing season, the Earl behaved as if he were very much at home – participating, at last, in an activity in which he could become thoroughly involved.

'I left Harrow at sixteen,' he volunteered. 'Academically I am a total failure. I am quite happy to be a failure. I like farming – and sheep. I did no good at Harrow, whatever that means. Winston Churchill may not have done, either, but he went on to better things than I will ever achieve. Anyway, I left Harrow at sixteen – I left, I wasn't sacked. It was a close thing. I reckon if I had stayed on for much longer they would have asked me to go. I was having problems with school life. I had never liked it. I don't really know why. Not being a psycho-analyst I have never been able to understand myself. It was one of those things I could not really cope with. I left and got a job as a farm labourer in Buckinghamshire with Timmy Whiteley. He has got about 1,000 acres. I think the main reason I got the job was that he was an ex-boyfriend of my mother's.'

Attitudes in public schools, according to the ex-Harrow pupil, were basically the same as they always had been, except that the standard of academic teaching was higher. 'If you are academically minded, you will do well there; and you can still do well there if you can play rugger. But I have never been good at sports. I have always preferred the solitary type of sports. I used to go for runs because I had to do *something* – play football or rugger or go for a run.'

Lord Yarmouth moved out of the way as the shepherd, Ivan Davies, walked out of the barn enclosure carrying two lambs. He was followed by the mother ewe and a student called Sarah, who was helping with the lambing.

'Sarah is very good, much better than she was at the start,' said the Earl judicially. 'We usually take students. Last year we had a couple of veterinary students and from what I've heard, one was quite good and the other was pretty well hopeless. I think our foreman put his finger on it when he said they were more interested in watching than actually *doing* anything. You learn much more by actually doing something than by just watching somebody else do it.'

He spent nine months working in Buckinghamshire, and went to a crammer outside Worcester for a year, having failed all his 'O' levels except English language. 'That did me no good at all. I think I got another "O" level there – English Literature. I took it at "A" level and failed it by one mark. My father was pretty . . . *aghast* is too strong, but he was upset and disconcerted at my leaving school. But at the moment I think he is very happy. We are all working together, which is all he wanted. I don't think he wants me to go off and do marvellous things. My father doesn't tell me what to do. He would rather have me here than making a fortune being a banker, which I am not at all cut out to do. My office is over there.'

He pointed to a bale of straw, on which rested one folder, one writing pad and one pen.

While we had been talking, Ragley's heir was breaking off periodically to attend to lambs which were popping out so frequently that even I, a squeamish townsman, became acclimatized to it. Lord Yarmouth was not in the least perturbed from the word go – even when a lamb failed to come out feet first, as it should have done, and the Earl had to insert one finger into the mother to free the baby's tiny legs, which were jammed under its chin. The older mothers had seen it all before, he pointed out, and were apt to behave. It was the younger ones you had to watch. 'The older ones will sometimes walk in front of you as you take the lamb to its individual pen outside: they are so familiar with what is happening. But the others . . . quite often you have to introduce the lamb to the ewe. You persuade the ewe to turn round after the birth. Some of them just feel enormous relief and don't bother to turn round. You have to say, "Oy! There's a little baby behind you!" Generally the younger ewes are totally unaware. There is no sex education among sheep. They have no idea of what is happening. Ewes turn around and are really frightened and may run straight into a brick wall or something. So you have to keep an eye on them. If you do the initial introduction, they tend to settle down quite well . . . There is one over there by the water trough, just look at her – she is about to have twins, I should think.'

Lord Yarmouth was proved 50 per cent right in two minutes, and 100 per cent right in another two minutes. This sheep was lucky: another had had to be sewn up after a nasty birth a few days previously, and was still lying at the entrance to the barn. Some lambs die because they are trampled on before they are spotted.

Five hundred of the estate's sheep had been left outside the main barn. They were mostly young ones, whose birth problems were easier to cope with in the open. Here, what was happening could be more clearly seen and there would be less chance of a mismatch between lamb and ewe.

Lambing at Ragley is carried out on intensive farming principles, which might not delight sentimental townsmen who want, so to speak, to have their lamb and eat it. Lord Hertford, arriving on Peter, his son's horse (his own had gone lame) to oversee his son's progress, put his own ever-realistic point of view. 'It gets the ground cut and manured, but we don't keep sheep entirely for that. It is *profit*. We have grassland because of the rotation of crops: that hasn't changed in a thousand years and the sheep eat the grass. It is a profitable process.'

His son took me off to what he called the Slammer, or adoption unit. This was a sort of corral in which four ewes are tethered head first to a feeding trough and collared so that they cannot push away lambs not their own. Mothers who have given birth to only one lamb can, in this way, give milk to a lamb who happens to be the third of a family and would not be able to drink from its own mother's two teats.

'They stay there three days,' said the young Earl. 'The only way the sheep can stop the lamb feeding is by sitting down, in which case we lift her up with a bit of string. She will take to the lamb after her milk has gone through the lamb once. Why intensive farming of sheep? Most farmers today are financially minded – they are in it for business and not for pleasure, and *have* to farm intensively. Really you are a damn fool not to farm intensively – you are just asking to go broke.'

Neither the present Marquess nor the future 9th, it was reasonably clear, would ever deliberately commit such a folly. Not for nothing has the 8th Marquess kept his children on a realistically tight financial rein. When

Lord Yarmouth went for a six-month visit to the United States in 1980, he took £900 with him. He managed to earn enough from casual jobs while he was over there to put £300 back into the bank when he returned. A Texas cowboy hat, which he bought when he was doing that job for a month, is now used as a paper weight on the wire basket of his office desk, next to his father's at Ragley Hall. At the time of his first lambing season, he had been to Russia, too, and was planning a return visit. He was also planning to cross from Russia into China, though the Russians had warned him that the Chinese 'imperialist aggressors' were quite likely to shoot him if he tried. These visits were expected to involve him in greater expense than the £25 a week he allowed himself to live on in the USA ('a very cheap place'), but his taste for 'paying for travel with work' was undiminished.

'When I worked in the USA, I worked very hard for short periods. I tried to turn over the hours in quantity, so I could earn quite a bit of money. I worked in Canada for a month, and I didn't spend anything. I was on a dairy farm on Vancouver Island. A lovely place. I just settled down to two hard weeks. They were working an average of fifty hours and I turned over a hundred hours. I asked for $3.50 an hour, the barest minimum. The farm manager thought about it for a while and then said, "You have worked very hard, I'd like to keep you on. I will pay you $4.50 an hour." That nearly paid for my travel expenses between Vancouver and Montreal. I gave quite a lot of money away. I am not very good with cash. If I have money I like it to be in the bank. I don't like carrying the stuff. I don't even know how much is in my wallet now.'

To oblige me, the Earl looked. 'Nothing,' he reported.

His earnings were paid into the bank and he had a cheque book but, like his father, no credit card. 'I am not in favour of plastic money. A cheque book is quite different. I keep a close watch on what I do spend. I open my cheque book and say, "How much have I got?" It varies. I hardly spend anything at all at present. I live at home and I have no expenses. I don't pay for water or electricity or food, unless I want to eat out somewhere, which I don't do often. I don't have a social life outside the estate. I suppose I ought to, but I am not that kind of person.'

A young man who has just achieved his majority is justified in wanting to prove he can achieve something worthwhile, even if he is an Earl. Hence the sheep. As even more lambs were brought out of the barn and into the individual pens, Lord Yarmouth pointed out that his father had proved himself to be a very astute businessman. And now, said the Earl of Yarmouth, *he* had to prove himself too.

'I think I will take over here soon,' he said. 'I think my father is going to retire, I don't think he will carry on until he drops. In the old days he would have gone on until he died. Nowadays this is a business, and you have to do things in a fairly businesslike way. I will probably take over when I am thirty or when I get married. I don't have a girl friend at the moment. I have really not bothered. Again, you have to be on the social scene for that.'

At that precise moment, Lord Yarmouth was more concerned about getting a mother to lick her newly-born lamb: 'It encourages the lamb to produce body heat it would otherwise not do.' He showed signs of having acquired quite a lot of knowledge quickly, and of being prepared to put his own ideas into practice one day. He also showed that he had a strong sense of dynasty.

'It would be lovely,' he said, treading nonchalantly in the latest after-birth, 'to turn this place into a farming empire. That is my aim at the moment. This estate used to be huge. We used to own ground from here to Stratford-upon-Avon, but most of it was sold to pay death duties. It was sold for 1s 6d* per acre, which was the lowest price that land has fetched this century. I must say I am pretty sick about it . . . I would like to see Ragley Estates get pretty big. That is what I really want.'

One of the reasons for this, said the Earl, was that he thought that no single individual should personally farm more than 2,000 acres. So a huge estate would create employment for the sort of people who had studied alongside him at the Royal Agricultural College. 'It would present oppor-tunities for employment in what is otherwise a pretty hopeless situation for them. If I was able to get the land, I would be a full-time professional landlord. People seem to have only bad things to say about landlords, but if you are a landlord, you can do an awful lot of good for people. I would put up my rents about as high as I could get them – not to get money, but if a tenant went under, I am afraid that is business life. A more efficient one could take over. If you can't pay your bills, you are not good enough, so get out and let someone else have a go.'

To this extent, said Lord Yarmouth, he would reverse the policy of his father, which had been to reclaim as much farming land from tenants as

---

* about 7½p or 18 cents US today.

possible and to restore it once more to family control. His father's policy was sensible *at present*. 'But I have, perhaps, more social sense in that I would like to see more people get jobs. It is quite a shock to go to a dole queue and find out how many people are there: people with qualifications.'

At the moment, visions of ultimate control must remain visions. An Earl in his early twenties has to be more conscious of the harsh realities of the present. At the time of his first lambing these included, amongst other things, the depressed prices for young lambs at Stratford-upon-Avon market. Lambs produced by other farms at Christmas time had a 'certain excitement' as the first lambs of the year, and fetched something like £46–£47 a head at 18 to 21 kilograms. But Ragley didn't try to compete in that market. 'Because we are late ... well, last year's lambs we sold for about £35 a head, at normally between 20 and 24 kilograms.'

This ability to deal confidently with the business side of sheep farming is an essential talent for a landowning aristocrat who wishes to make his estate pay. In taking his first season's 2,000 lambs to market, and in his cheerful acceptance of being called 'Harry', the future 9th Marquess of Hertford showed himself to be far removed from the chinless idiot of caricature.

Even lack of interest – or apparent lack of interest – in his title may all be part of the survival plan. The Earl of Yarmouth is well aware of the antecedents of his title, but does not regard them with hushed awe. 'I try not to use my title. We have already got one Lord, my father. He is called Milord. I just don't feel comfortable if people use words like Sir and Lord and all that to me. I am not in any way *ashamed*; I don't *hide* the fact. But if I go into a shop and they say "Mr", I don't correct it, I go as "Mr Yarmouth". I am really The Earl of Yarmouth. My father is Marquess of Hertford, The Earl of Yarmouth, Viscount Beauchamp and Baron Conway (I think *twice*). As long as my father is alive, I am known by his second senior title, Earl of Yarmouth. But I am not very good, frankly, at all our titles.'

My final impression of the Earl of the lambs? That perhaps this contemporary and functional Earl was underplaying his part in the proceedings for practical reasons, while being quite conscious of the family's place in history. His own son, he said, should be called Viscount Beauchamp while he himself was alive, but instead would be called Baron Conway – 'because we used to own Conway Castle and there is a whole history behind that name, the castle and the town.'

It will be interesting to see whether, as British industry contracts in search of a new and shrunken reality, aristocratic landowners and farmers of the Earl of Yarmouth's breed slip back into their former role as men of real power and influence. In the meantime, the Earl will presumably continue to lend a hand stitching up a miscarried ewe, to calculate in cash per kilogram and to live on an income that a middle- or working-class young man of his age would regard as an incitement to riot and revolution.

10
Tenant Farming
– a Lasting
Tradition?

IN FORMER DAYS, the tenant farmer was the man the presiding aristocrat at the Hall perhaps invited to lunch but never to dinner. He could do what he liked with his farm, provided it was what the aristocrat at the Hall wanted. He could do what he wanted to on a Sunday, if what he liked was going to church. He could pay his rent as he liked, provided it was in sovereigns and proferred, in person, on Lady Day and Michaelmas; and he could respond to the invitation to the tenants' lunch on that occasion as he wished, provided he wished dutifully to attend it.

It was indeed at one time rather like that with the tenant farmers of Ragley. 'Now all that is changed,' one of them told me. 'Lord Hertford is still very much the landlord, but he is very much the businessman too.'

Yet even a social revolution which has made tenant farmers' true wishes more visible, and forced many aristocrats into the defensive posture of good businessmen, has not entirely eradicated the tenant farmer as a distinctive breed. He is still deeply attached to his rented plot of land, and is, perhaps, able to trace it back through several generations of his own family; he is certainly as jealous of its integrity and peace as any old-time nobleman or squire. It would have amazed the tenant farmers of Ragley a century ago to see some of their descendants emerge as independent-minded and efficient businessmen of the land. But it might equally surprise many townsmen today to discover how, at Ragley, an almost mystical affinity with one's rented plot still persists, and how men whose fathers and grandfathers farmed at Ragley before them can now still expect their sons to take over where they leave off.

It surprised me a little when I met Harold Heard, one of Ragley's tenant farmers. He was a tall, stocky man in his forties whose dungaree suit gave him, superficially, the appearance of a modern motor mechanic rather than the deeply-entrenched tenant farmer he is at Alcester Park Farm, one of the six at Ragley which are still tenanted. Ah, he said, he loved tinkering with farm machinery, and only wished his nineteen-year-old son Adrian was fonder of it than he seemed to be at the moment.

Alcester Park Farm, on the north side of the lozenge-shaped Ragley estate, is three hundred years old and has 320 acres, given over to a hundred cattle, 160 ewes with their lambs, and to cereals. The farmhouse itself is L-shaped and venerable, with an uneven courtyard set in the middle of buildings which sag in a picturesque way that is perhaps more appealing to sentimental townsmen enjoying a visit than to the hard-working farmers who have to use them. There is an arched-roofed cellar, probably used to house cider barrels. It also contains the original butter churn used in Harold Heard's grandfather's day, and the old wires of the pull-bells' system employed to summon the servants in the days when tenant farmers had their own maids. The old lavatory, filled with ash and emptied by pulling a lever at the side of the pedestal, was taken out thirty years ago and replaced with a modern flush toilet, but bats still fly in the upper floors. It is a vast place.

The Heard family have been the tenants of Alcester Park Farm since 1908. Harold Heard's grandfather – a picture of the short, heavily-bearded man is still in the house – came from a farm in Devon in September of that year. He farmed until 1932, when his son took over; and he in turn farmed it until 1963, when Harold took it over with his brother, and they have farmed it ever since. Harold Heard has spent just four years of his life away from the farmhouse. This was when he was newly married and lived in a smaller house just down the road; he did so until his father retired and then father and son exchanged homes.

'Three generations of tenants, *and* I have a son,' said Harold Heard with the sort of ancestral pride that could hardly be beaten at the Hall itself.

There were about 80 acres less land in his grandfather's day, but the place had to be virtually self-sufficient. The postman used to walk from farm to farm, and delivery took most of the day. It was some years before signs of progress were visible. The telephone was put in shortly after Harold Heard was born (at his birth, someone had to troop across ploughed fields for many miles to get the doctor). It was not until the late 1970s that the dustmen started to call for the refuse.

'We used to have to dig holes and bury it,' recalled Harold Heard. 'We also had some dry ponds. We would empty the dustbin into one every couple of weeks, and then tip soil over it. We filled some ponds in, in this way, and used the land afterwards.'

Electricity did not arrive until 1958, and it was four years later when mains water was installed. There is still no mains sewerage. Nor is there central heating – the cost would be prohibitive. There are electric fires and portable gas heaters. Harold Heard can remember, as a child, waking up in the morning and finding ice on the glass of water by his bed.

The six tenant farmers of Ragley – only half the number that were there before Lord Hertford started to take an interest in farming the land himself – were not in the past wedded to the life because they expected luxury. Nor are they today. The seductiveness of the life of the tenant farmer (the man who rents his farm from the estate and pays the landlord a rent proportional to his profits) is something quite different. It has certainly been felt by tenants like Harold Heard who, unlike some of his colleagues on the Ragley estate, has no great amount of land of his own (only an interest in 35 acres with his brother to supplement the acres he rents from Lord Hertford).

The fact of being only a marginal land *owner* could, in at least one way, prove to be an advantage to his family line in the future. The legal position of tenant farmers is complex, but under the 1976 Agricultural Tenancy Act the lease of a tenant farmer is virtually secure for three generations. It is usually held that once the tenant farmer has accepted the first of the three-year rent review findings, this security comes into force: he himself is secure, and may pass the tenancy to his son, who may then pass it to *his* son. But in practice – a fact not unknown to the shrewd tenant farmer – this security can be tested in law for a number of reasons. A tenant's security may be lessened if he is proved to be a bad farmer, or if he has another farm of his own from which to earn his livelihood.

Though Harold Heard may lose a little in prestige through being almost entirely a tenant farmer, he and his kind may well find it easier than other tenant farmers with land of their own to pass on the Ragley tradition to their descendants. It was obvious he had watched carefully the way the tradition was being perpetuated at Ragley.

'I could put a name to quite a lot of sons who have followed fathers on farms within 10 miles of here,' insisted Harold Heard. 'It is still a way of life. You are brought up to it. Unless you have a thorough dislike of farming, you come into it if the chance arises. It is not like a city job where the father goes away to his business and the son has no real idea of what he is doing. In the case of a farm, you are nearly always living at your place of work. That enables sons to be brought up in the farming tradition. I have definitely never thought of a life in a town. I am a country person, and I like the country things around me, without having to get into a car to see them. If I go into the town, I want to get back here as soon as possible. Even when we take our holidays, we usually go to a quiet village in Wales.'

Not that holidays and days off come high on the list of priorities of a tenant-farming family. Harold Heard told me that he was constantly being surprised, on a given day, at how few people seemed to be answering the telephone; then he would realize that it was a Bank Holiday. To any farmer, Bank Holidays mean little. To the tenant farmer, working on shoestring resources of labour, they mean practically nothing.

There is a sort of programme of family and friends self-help available at the crucial times of the year, and when workers are on holiday. Everyone is expected to weigh in.

'There is myself and my brother, plus my son Adrian since April of this year,' said Harold Heard, sitting in his kitchen (old hob still in place) and counting off the available volunteers on his fingers. 'Then there is casual help, mostly from within the family, and mainly during the haymaking. That is when we start at seven in the morning and go on sometimes until eleven at night. Then my brother has two sons, one of whom has left school. Clive is twelve, and helps where he can. I also have a brother-in-law who comes in to help. We have a man in a cottage who gives us a certain amount of help, plus his son. My wife's brother's son helps with the hay in June or July.' And so on.

Some of this help is paid for, but much is given as a friendly gesture. Harold Heard has got a workshop as well as cattle and sheep sheds, and can mend things as well as oblige with a load of muck for the garden. He insisted, and I believed him, that he would just as soon be in his workshop after a full day's work than watching television. The tenant farmer of the more traditional sort – and Harold Heard must fall into this category – tends to prefer feeling useful to feeling inert. 'Occasionally,' remarked Harold Heard, 'I have a day out – usually for a farm sale.'

The tenant farmers close ranks among themselves, and with the Hall, in time of stress. This is so however heated the arguments may be between landlord and tenant at each three-year rent review, when both sides traditionally claim to be heading for ruin if the other doesn't give way.

Harold Heard recalled clearly the most recent example of landlord and tenant standing together. 'A motorway was to go right through the middle of the estate. We had television and the local Member of Parliament down. There was quite a strong case put for not having a motorway in this area. Lord Hertford had a meeting at Ragley Hall and we all gave him our support. Most of the tenants and the forestry department of Ragley Hall were there. We all explained how it would affect us. It never got as far as the local enquiry, although the tenants would have supported Lord Hertford if it had. It was all the agricultural side against those who wanted to put the motorway there. The motorway was either cancelled or shelved.'

The tenants immediately close ranks, too, when the estate is faced with damage to property caused by the occasional irresponsible lout from the towns.

'We regularly have walking parties organized through a ramblers' club in Birmingham, and they are always in touch with us before they come out for a walk,' said Harold Heard. 'But we do get a bit of trouble with people on horseback going where they shouldn't, and we get a small amount of vandalism – normally by children in outlying buildings. They smash roofs and they have been known, on one occasion, to tip someone's beehives over, and to pelt cattle with pieces of wood. But we do have schoolchildren from the local schools to look at our lambs quite often, and we don't have anything against townspeople. We just expect to receive from them, when they are in the countryside, the respect that we expect in the town.'

Did it make much difference to country living if the estate was a stately one? Harold Heard said he didn't have much to do with the landlord. They were friendly, but 'didn't visit daily'. Lord Hertford called him by his Christian name and he addressed his landlord as Lord Hertford. They more or less went their own ways. If he wanted to do anything structural to the farmhouse or the farm buildings, or make any large-scale changes of any sort, he always went to the landlord first and obtained his permission. Lord Hertford preferred them to carry out their own improvements. The two most recent were a drainage scheme covering about 10 acres on a field, and improvements to a building that was put up by his own father rather than by the landlord. Between his father's tenancy and his own, the buildings put up by his father had become legally part of the Ragley estate, as was the custom when one tenant left and another took over, or the landlord took the land in hand himself.

One occasion when landlord and tenant invariably meet is rent review time, once every three years. The form – understandably – is that Lord Hertford rings the tenants rather than the other way round. Harold Heard underlined why. 'They call it a review, but it is in effect an increase. We have professional advice: there are people who handle these sort of things. Lord Hertford will come and we will sit in the kitchen or the living room and talk about it. Even though it may be a time of recession, the rent still rises. Lord Hertford has a business to run. So have we.'

As it happened, I made a call on Harold Heard just as the rent review was about to begin. At first this made him somewhat cagey with me – a man he hadn't met before, who was now asking him questions about his farm. He tended to emphasize how many improvements he had carried out himself, and other matters material to his financial case in the rent review. It was only when he finally accepted that I was not a landlord's nark that he opened up a bit, and showed me over the farmhouse. At the same time, he told me something about his way of life in it.

To a townsman – especially on a sunny summer's day – the house looked very desirable. There was the cider cellar and the cheese room – amenities without which most townsmen manage to survive in the twentieth century. There was a sitting room (the term 'lounge' tends to be regarded as slick in the country, and the term 'living room' rather plebeian) that would have passed happily in a new town dwelling. Almost as large was the games room, equipped with a billiards table and a darts board.

Harold Heard saw me looking at the head of a deer, mounted on a wall plaque. I asked him whether this was a hunting trophy, and discovered that it wasn't. 'We didn't shoot it. I don't approve of shooting. Everyone wants to go round shooting everything that moves. I don't. It isn't in my nature.' Apparently the beast died of old age.

Next door to the games room was a dining room that would seat eight or more comfortably. Admittedly, this was hardly up to the standards of the Hall, but few townsmen would grumble at it. And, as the dining room is used for family or friends only once a month on average (so busy is the tenant farmer's life) it does not greatly matter.

116

Upstairs in the biggest bedroom – a real barn of a place with a dormer ceiling – Harold Heard pointed out that the paper tended to come off the ceiling because of the damp in winter. It was in this room that he remembered seeing ice on his bedside water glass in the morning. 'Though,' he insisted, not wishing to run his own home down, 'not very often.'

His daughter's bedroom, like the sitting room, could have been straight out of a city home. His daughter is a hairdresser. Unlike boys, girls are still *not* expected to take an hereditary interest in their parents' tenanted farms, and can seek out the city lights without family reproach.

The bedroom of his nineteen-year-old son Adrian, on the floor above, was rather different. Here there was a feature wall pasted with beermats, and a large stereo cassette radio. But there were also models of agricultural machinery. It was Adrian's gesture to his future. 'If I stay on here, I would have to get much more interested in machinery,' said Adrian. 'I am a country boy, and I would rather live in the country. I suppose it is rather more difficult to meet people, but I have got a few friends. Occasionally we will go out for a drink or to a disco. But I'm not fussed. If we have work to do, that gets done first. I'm often up by myself half the night, but it doesn't bother me. I'm not one who has to go out every night. I don't think I could adjust to life in the city. If there is a job here to be done, it doesn't matter what day, or what time of day, it is. It has got to be done *then*. If we especially want a day out in the middle of the week, we go in the middle of the week, but we don't make a habit of that.'

Then I saw the venerable barns and the historic cowshed. They made me wonder whether the pure tenant farmer, like Harold and the other Heards, didn't sometimes sigh to be his own landlord, so that any improvements didn't automatically become the property of the estate – an arrangement that inevitably makes both landlord and tenant wary of expensive schemes, however productive they might promise to be.

Harold Heard acknowledged that there were often enough ordinary expenses to be faced without thinking about major improvements. 'This house is 'L'-shaped and cold in winter. It also has a lot of paintwork. We have had an estimate to paint the exterior and it will be £500-plus. That was by far the cheapest estimate, and we have to have that done every four or five years.'

Sometimes, admitted the doughty tenant farmer, he thought it would be nice to own his own land. But you had to finance it from somewhere, didn't you? The owner-occupier was usually in a quite different position, socially and financially. 'As land values are at the moment, just the income from the land doesn't produce enough finance to start to buy land. The price of land is greatly inflated when compared with its production value. Recently agricultural land has fetched about £2,000 an acre. At present-day bank interest rates, you'd have to work hard just to pay the interest on the purchase money, let alone repay the capital.'

Tenant farmers like Harold Heard are therefore, in effect, not only tied to the land, but tied on the same terms that have applied for centuries. It may seem strange that intelligent sons like Adrian should want to carry on the tradition. But they do.

They are not even perturbed by the fact that the reputation they enjoy as farmers will be dictated – at least at first – not so much by their own abilities as by the abilities of their fathers, grandfathers and even great-grandfathers. If all or any of these ancestors had fumbled his farming, it would definitely not improve Adrian's chances of taking over the tenancy on his father's retirement.

Harold Heard explained. 'If grandfather and dad had been roughish farmers, and I had been a roughish farmer too, it would affect Adrian's chances of taking on the tenancy. My son would have more difficulty in proving he could mend *his* ways after fifty years of bad farming. That is the way it goes.'

Some city dwellers might well conclude that if that is the way the life of the tenant farmer goes, it is a wonder it hasn't gone sooner. The tenant farmers themselves do not see it that way. Nor do many of their sons, including Adrian Heard. His thick studious spectacles might type-cast him as a technician from a Birmingham or Manchester polytechnic rather than a keeper of the Ragley tradition. Nevertheless, he said: 'If the opportunity arises, I would be very interested in becoming the next tenant of Alcester Park Farm.' And his father, though still thinking it would be nice if the Heards owned land of their own, encouraged him with: 'If the past is anything to go by, I don't see why we shouldn't continue until the year 2000 or more.' The life of the tenant farmer is a tied one and a hard one; but, given current social and economic trends in Britain, it is not likely to become less popular, as might have been predicted thirty years ago at a time when the industrial sector of the economy was relatively healthy.

Not all the tenant farmers of Ragley are now purely tenants. Some have shrewdly hedged their bets, and perhaps advanced a rung on the social ladder, by buying land of their own – usually about the same acreage as they rent from the estate. This way, if economic or political conditions favour landlords at the expense of tenants, or vice versa, they are covered.

This newer breed of tenant farmer is usually a blend of country and town. As countrymen, they 'know how many beans make five' and how to make them grow. As townsmen, their accustomed reading matter includes balance sheets as well as letters from the Hall.

I found a prime example of the new tenant farmer at Ragley, wearing an impeccably tailored grey herringbone jacket and sitting in an office which might have been that of an architect in Knightsbridge. It was, in fact, the farm office of Robert Hiller, at Dunnington Heath Farm. This is the 'home' farm of Ragley – the one nearest the Hall – and Robert Hiller is its tenant. He is also a businessman, quite able to cope in London (as he has done), and the owner of about 400 acres of land – rather more than the 330 acres he rents from the Ragley estate.

It would be quite impossible to visualize Robert Hiller in a feudal setting. His type has been bred of several generations of slow social and technical revolution. I found a rather powerfully-built man of middle height with metal spectacles and a disciplined mane of steel grey hair. He could have been the captain of a liner or a Birmingham industrialist in his Saturday clothes. Asked to guess his natural habitat, I would not automatically have conjured up the square of red brick farm buildings, their floors and walls uneven with age, and their ancient roof tiles damaged, though still somehow able to keep the rain off the animals or the farm produce within. His voice was too modulated, his knowledge of his land and the agreements that affected it too precise, his confidence too buttressed by occasional shafts of sardonic humour, especially visible when he was talking about what was considered 'right and proper' in his father's day.

Robert Hiller and his partner Richard Beach are purely fruit and vegetable farmers. Dunnington Heath Farm itself is on the south side of the estate, and displays road signs advertising a 'pick-it-yourself' service that has become a weekend social mecca for the people of the Midlands. Robert Hiller says drily that his own father thought his son was making the farm too big, and Lord Hertford thought the self-service signs might be a bit vulgar. Both, one gathers, received very polite reminders of the economic constraints facing the tenant farmer in a greatly changed world. Robert Hiller, nevertheless, almost certainly dines with Lord Hertford more frequently than any of the other tenants. It is a tribute to both men – particularly to their realism.

Robert Hiller's father was the tenant of Dunnington Heath Farm from 1918, after the farm had been used for intensive vegetable growing in the First World War. During the recession in the 1930s, he asked the trustees then in charge of the estate for permission to widen the range of crops he could produce as a way of insuring himself against the economic depression and an erratic market. He asked them for what is known as an Evesham Agreement. This standard agreement was named after the town in the middle of the biggest and most noted fruit-growing area of Britain. It set out the terms under which farmers could grow fruit trees, something that tenant farmers had not previously felt able to do to any great extent. The reason was simple. It originated in the landlord's divine right to take practically everything except goods and chattels at the end of a tenancy – certainly including any trees planted – and without compensation to the tenant. The Evesham Agreement, or Custom, as it is sometimes known, came into being to overcome this inhibition to production. It provided that if the landlord gave the tenant notice, then both parties should agree on the value of the growing crop, including fruit trees, and the landlord should pay the tenant that sum. If they could not agree on a sum, then the matter went to arbitration. If the tenant gave the landlord notice, then it was up to the existing tenant to find his own successor, who would pay him what he considered the crops were worth. The landlord was given one month to decide whether or not to accept the suggested new tenant. If he declined, then he was expected to take the farm in hand himself at the same figure the sitting tenant had agreed with his would-be replacement. The agreement had been in force for several years when Robert Hiller's father took advantage of it in the 1930s' depression, and began to plant fruit trees.

Mr Hiller senior was the son of an engineer who became general manager of the National Boiler Insurance Company. Robert Hiller's father didn't fancy a business career. Instead he trained in horticulture, bought 38 acres in Evesham and went into partnership with a merchant. They took over Dunnington Heath Farm on the Ragley estate as White and Hiller in 1918 and stayed on until 1934 as a team. Then they broke up. Mr Hiller senior farmed on his own until his son joined him at the age of eighteen, becoming a partner when he was legally of age three years later.

'I was born in this house,' Robert Hiller told me. 'And it was an interesting place in which to be born.'

It is indeed an interesting house. It is built in three parts, each of a different epoch. The first and central section of the house, including what is now Robert Hiller's very modern office, probably dates back to Tudor times. Two rooms were added at a later stage. Later still, in Georgian times, the front part of the house, the one most visible from the main road, was built. This has a noted pedigree, apocryphal or not. It is said that it was built for an illegitimate child of King George IV after he had paid a visit to the then Marquess of Hertford at Ragley.

The owners of the farm, or its tenants, had obviously found Royal favour well before that. 'This is not called Dunnington *Heath* farm for nothing,' said Robert Hiller. The land was originally heathland, probably used by a shepherd or pig keeper who grazed and kept his animals on the common land. Then came the Act of Enclosure, which enabled the favourites of the King and the nobility to enclose (fence off) the common land and assume rights over it. When the Act of Enclosure was enforced, all the common grazing land was divided up into holdings, and Dunnington Heath Farm was one of them. Probably at this time a more substantial farm house was built and some, but not all, of the farm buildings were put up. Most of them would have fallen down and been replaced long since; but even those that do remain appear to have had the extensive weathering of several centuries.

It was almost jarring when Robert Hiller said, 'Where we are now sitting is a *business* office rather than a *farm* office. We use modern techniques suggested by our business advisers and we consult financial as well as technical advisers.' It was he who brought in specialist growers, of whom his partner Richard Beach is one.

I asked Robert Hiller if he considered himself to be a businessman rather than a farmer.

'You are quite right,' he agreed immediately.

What happened was that Robert Hiller, as a school-leaver, had been offered a job by the Alliance Assurance Company, which had taken over the National Boiler Insurance Company. But his health as a boy had not been good. His parents were told by the doctors he would be better off leading an open-air life. He therefore went to agricultural college and returned to Dunnington Heath Farm just before the Second World War broke out.

The Navy broadened his view of the world – for a little while. 'I lost an eye as a child. But I had such a good glass eye that the military doctors didn't notice it. I served for about three months in the invasion of Europe. Then someone discovered I had only one eye. When I pointed out that Nelson had only one eye, they were not amused. I was chucked out very quickly.'

They told him he could go into the Naval Postal Service, or become a farmer, which was a 'reserved occupation' – one that would have exempted him from military duty because it had such high national priority. The thought of the Naval Postal Service, albeit a thoroughly worthy and necessary institution, failed to stir his blood. So he went back to Dunnington Heath Farm and in 1965, twenty years after the war ended, he became managing director of the operating company on the retirement of his father.

Robert Hiller said that this was when he really 'took off'. The phrase was well chosen.

He began to *buy* land in the locality. His father was alarmed, and counselled caution – why not play safe, as a simple tenant farmer of Ragley? But a man who has joined the Navy, seen the world through his one good eye, fooled the doctors for a long period, and been cheated of a career in business through ill-health, is not the most likely automatically to assume that 'They' know best. Robert Hiller began to buy land two years after he became managing director, and continued to do so, despite all well-meaning advice.

'I was terribly lucky. I bought a small farm 4 miles from here and – dash me – if another small parcel of land didn't become available about a year later! Three years after that, a further 180 acres became available on our borders. I instructed a firm of London land agents to buy for me, because I didn't want people to know I was involved.'

Canny Mr Hiller. Certainly an altogether different man from the archetypal tenant farmer of pre-war days.

'Oh yes, things were terribly different in those days. Tenants were expected to go to church on Sundays, and all that sort of business. Because this was the home farm of Ragley and the Hall was closed down, if any of the trustees came down for any purpose naturally they were always put up here. My mother and father had to invite them as guests. Nothing of that applies today, thank goodness. I don't even remember it, actually, though I think it continued until Lord Henry Seymour – Lord Hertford's father – went to Park Hill Farm, where he had his private residence, and then did all the entertaining from there. Our relations with Lord Hertford are completely different, but even I can remember when tenants were definitely inferior products of society.'

In those comparatively recent days, the tenants took their rents twice a year, in sovereigns, to the Hall. They were then given a lunch. When Ragley Hall was temporarily closed down and the present Lord Hertford was still too young to put his own plans into action, it was not possible to have the lunch. So each tenant was handed back five shillings from his rent to compensate him for the lunch he had missed. At the price levels of the period, it must have been some lunch.

When Robert Hiller's mother and father were tenants of Dunnington Heath, it was considered right and proper that they be entertained every so often, either at Ragley Hall or at Park Hill Farm.

'Their social status,' said Robert Hiller, 'was not such that they were invited to dinner at night. Now all that has changed. Lord Hertford is still very much the landlord, but he is very much the businessman too. He is what you could call a business-landlord. I don't think we could say we are close friends, but we are on friendly terms. We have dined there. I don't think he has ever dined here, but he has lunched and drunk here on many occasions, and we know each other by our Christian names. It is a very businesslike relationship, whereas in the old days the relationship between landlord and tenant was very much a relationship between two different social strata. That really changed between the two world wars.'

There were amusing incidents in the days when 'Those Above Stairs' were thought to live in a totally different world to the hoi-polloi, but were sometimes painfully reminded that times were changing. At least, Robert Hiller's father found such incidents amusing.

On one occasion, his grandfather rang up his father. 'Look, I am going to come down tomorrow with one of my insurance inspectors. Could you arrange for a room at one of the local pubs? We are insuring the Ragley boilers.' The inspector duly took a look at the boilers, and reported back to Robert Hiller's grandfather that they were in a very bad state indeed and definitely uninsurable until they were seen to. The result was that the next day, Robert Hiller's grandfather motored up to Ragley Hall, decreed that on no account must the boilers be lit, and made it plain that it was an order. 'It amused my father terribly,' said Robert Hiller.

This was at about the time that the family at the Hall were accepting that the cost of maintaining the place was becoming prohibitive – a theory that the 8th Marquess himself has never accepted. But it was also still the era when the landlord at the Hall was able to tell the tenant farmers what they could and could not do on their farms.

Hay? The tenant farmer might have some to spare, but he could not sell it. That would have indicated that he wasn't sufficiently stocked with cattle, or that he wasn't keeping enough horses to plough his land. It could, in short, have been taken as an indication that the farmer was not a good one – in which case he could be turfed out by the landlord and the land taken in hand or rented to a new tenant. Straw? The tenant had to provide his own if his roof needed rethatching, though the work had to be done by the estate thatcher. Gates? The tenant could not choose his own. They had to be bought from the landlord at ten shillings (50p) each. Gateposts? No choice there either. The tenant had to buy them from the landlord at two shillings and sixpence (12½p).

In the hedgerows, which were then cut by hand, a self-seeded tree had to be left alone, however inconvenient a position it had assumed. The hedge could be cut – indeed it *had* to be cut – but the tree had to be left in order that it could be used eventually as timber. Machine-cutting made this regulation difficult to enforce.

'But it has been a very touchy point with landlords,' Robert Hiller told me. 'The number of landlords who have enforced that legislation, or tried to enforce it, even to this day, is surprising.'

Robert Hiller has been in a good position to evaluate just how much times have changed, even in the depths of the country. He himself sits on Land Tribunals and hears disputes between landlords and tenants. He is a man of influence: definitely the sort of man to have to dinner.

He is also a man of business in a world in which wares cannot always be sold by the soft-sell. His produce shop, situated directly on the public road that rings the perimeter of the Ragley estate, originally caused something of a conflict between traditional values and modern needs. The building was constructed in Georgian times, and Robert Hiller claimed that the farm had always sold 'at the garden gate', as the expression has it, and that the shop building was then used as a temporary store for small quantities of produce. People would call at the gate and ask 'Can I buy a box of apples and 12 pounds of strawberries?' and a small quantity would be produced from the storeroom. Robert Hiller claimed that this in fact made the building a 'retail outlet'.

In the early 1970s, the farm began developing large-scale direct selling to the public, with a unit of 200 acres on the other side of the public road.

At first the public were even invited to come in and cut their own cauliflowers, but that soon stopped. The customers were cutting them too small, meaning that the farmer was left with too much unpaid-for waste. But direct tomato selling became very popular indeed; so much so that the farm started having a stall on the pick-it-yourself side of the road, from which it sold all sorts of produce. The shop itself reverted to its former use – selling only apples direct to the public. But when it was obvious that buyers wanted every sort of fruit and vegetable and not just apples, Robert Hiller put in a planning application for a full-blown retail shop, in addition to the stall on the other side of the road.

The planners at first maintained that the site was agricultural and that there could not be a change of usage to the retail trade. 'We shot that one down,' recalled Robert Hiller, 'by saying that we had been using it as a retail outlet for many, many years, so there was no change of usage. It was just that we wanted to use it for imported fruit and vegetables as well as our own.'

Lord Hertford, as landlord, also had some reservations, seeing it as a break with tradition and with the tenancy agreement which said that the premises were for 'agricultural' use. Robert Hiller countered this with the argument that landlords charging high rents made it necessary for tenants to make high profits in order that they could pay their way. Lord Hertford accepted this business logic.

It was hardly a surprise to be told that in his younger days, both business and trade politics took Robert Hiller to London fairly frequently. Between 1960 and 1978 he was up and down on National Farmers Union business. His life as a commuter, two or three days a week, was then a demanding one. He had acquired a stand at Covent Garden Market which had been in financial difficulties; he appointed a new manager and made it successful once again. He also had a stand on Brentford Market and his routine on a busy travelling day was to go up to Reading by fast train, jump on the London Airport bus, get off it at the entrance to London Airport and catch an ordinary bus to Brentford Market, where he would have a session at his stand. He then got into the car that had been sent for him from Agriculture House to take him back there to attend to his National Farmers Union business. He would work there for the rest of the day, and return by ordinary train via Paddington station in the evening. Or he would stay at the Anglo-Belgian Club in Belgrave Square – he was friendly with the Belgian Agricultural Attaché at the time.

By his late fifties, he found this heavy schedule was becoming a bore. Brentford Market was closed; he did not fancy moving from the old Covent Garden to the new Nine Elms fruit and vegetable market in Battersea; and he had been the fruit industry's chief negotiator with the Government for ten years. Trade politics seemed less vital once his own business interests were no longer centred in London. With Britain's entry to the European Economic Community, he was commuting to and fro between Brussels and London. 'And Brussels is a ghastly town at the best of times. I was spending all my time there or on an aeroplane.'

It was hardly the average townsman's idea of the life of a tenant farmer on a country estate; and at the age of sixty he found it wasn't his idea either. It was time for a change. He gave the routine up, resigned as managing director of the firm in favour of Richard Beach, and assumed the office of chairman, working part-time.

Richard Beach, rather than any child of Robert Hiller's, is now the heir apparent to the tenancy of the farm – having come from a family in which a plethora of sons made his own chances of inheritance somewhat unlikely. And Beach has two sons who might in their turn take over the farms.

What did that mean to Robert Hiller in sentimental terms? 'I am afraid,' was the answer, 'that I am *not* sentimental. I regard the farm as being a business just like any other. And this, where we are now, is *not* my home. These are my business premises. My home is a place on the foothills of Dartmoor in South Devon. I spend about half my time here and half my time there. It was fortunate I bought this particular house in Devon, because to get there I have only twenty-two miles of driving which is not on the dual carriageway.'

Altogether, I found that the mystical appeal of the countryside, so potent to townsmen who spend little time in it, did not figure greatly in the thoughts of Robert Hiller. Nor did the apparent advantages gained by tenants at the expense of the landlord during the social revolution of the twentieth century. He did not crow about these; indeed, he was quite coldly objective.

He actually thought that the rules had swung *too far* in favour of the tenant – i.e. himself and his counterparts. 'Oh yes, very much so,' he insisted, as my face suggested doubt of his steely objectivity. 'In my view, too much so, certainly. It may sound funny for a tenant to say so. Of course, at one time it *was* too much in the hands of the landlord. It was extremely difficult to develop a tenanted farm, unless you had got a very far-sighted landlord, because as soon as one generation had passed, the tenancy went into other hands, or could very well do so. So tenants weren't encouraged to invest in land. Now I think legislation has probably swung too much the other way. I mean the fact that you have security of tenure for three generations for example, which is an awfully long time.'

The fact that the law was now in favour of the tenant could actually be a disadvantage to the tenant farmer, in Robert Hiller's view. When land became vacant, landlords became cautious about reletting it and were tempted to take it in hand themselves and appoint a manager to run it for them even if – unlike Lord Hertford – they were not especially interested in managing land themselves. At Ragley, there were now only half the dozen tenant farmers there once were. Robert Hiller believed there might have been more if Lord Hertford had known that on the death of a tenant farmer – or at a date twenty years from the start of his tenancy, whichever was the longer – the landlord could regain possession of his farms.

But, in Robert Hiller's view, the legal balance in favour of the tenant had not raised his *social* position in the eyes of the landlord. Sometimes it might even sour relations. The conduct of business negotiations between a landlord and a tenant farmer could do that, and he himself was very careful to ensure that this didn't happen.

'I don't think it affects our social relationship at all,' he said. 'So far as the financial side is concerned, I never negotiate rents myself. It is not good for our friendship, which I regard as important. You have got to understand the landlord's thinking, and therefore you have got to get to know him. I always appoint a negotiator, and he does the same. In the last ten to twelve years, when the rent has been reviewed, Willis has been appointed to represent Lord Hertford and Mumford has represented Richard Beach and myself. They argue for about a fortnight and eventually reach agreement on what the rent should be. On some occasions – not so much with Lord Hertford, who is a businessman in his own right, but with some landlords – you will find their social station very much influences their business thinking. I know, from sitting on a Land Tribunal myself, that very often you will find antagonism has built up because the landlord is a keen hunter while the tenant is a keen shot. He shoots all the foxes, and the landlord therefore has a low opinion of him. You very often get this detrimental type of relationship; and it is very important that it should *not* exist.

Lord Hertford and Robert Hiller are each aware of the other's feelings on such matters. They socialize enough for that. Lord Hertford hunts, but with regard for the views of the tenants of his farms. Robert Hiller likes 'to leave nature alone'; he is a keen naturalist, but runs the financial side of the syndicated shoot which operates around the Ragley estate at £2,000 per gun per year – an activity that only tenant farmers and well-heeled Birmingham businessmen can afford these days. Lord Hertford himself does not belong to the Syndicate, but has Cold Comfort Farm – one of Ragley's – in hand for shooting purposes. Robert Hiller thought that a mistake; it would be better if the landlord had one gun in his own shoot and one gun in the Syndicate's – which was one of the best shoots in England, over 3,000 game-strewn acres – even if it did cost £2,000 a gun for ordinary running expenses, plus the actual costs of shooting on the day. So far Lord Hertford has remained elusive in the face of such blandishments, though a lot of members of the Syndicate have compromised with hard necessity by sharing the cost of a gun between two people. Richard Beach in fact does so. At the time Robert Hiller was explaining how the syndicated shoot operated, the Earl of Yarmouth, Lord Hertford's son, was not a member of the Syndicate. 'He doesn't concentrate hard enough at present,' explained Robert Hiller. Lord Yarmouth, I knew, had more urgent bread and butter issues on hand, like the care of the sheep for which he was responsible.

The operation of the syndicated shoot within the Ragley estate shows how much things have changed, even in this country, during this century.

'Shooting at one time played an important role at Ragley,' said Robert Hiller. 'They had goodness knows how many keepers. Heaven help the poacher who got caught! With modern taxation and the cost of living, Lord Hertford simply could not afford to keep two shoots; the situation is very different today. There was a certain amount of trouble with Birmingham people who didn't know how to behave in the country. But now it is a most amicable arrangement. Certainly any of the farmers who can afford it and can shoot would be welcome, but there aren't many tenants now – we definitely couldn't raise eight guns at £2,000 a gun from tenants, even if there were eight tenants, which there aren't.'

It would be understandable, in a situation that has given a lot of sway to Birmingham businessmen and to tenant farmers as compared with landlords, if the noble landlord were to respond by condescending to everyone socially. Robert Hiller maintained he saw no signs of it as far as he himself was concerned. 'I don't feel *patronized*,' he insisted. He paused for thought and then added, 'I have, however, felt myself on occasions under certain obligations to Lord Hertford where I have taken a line of action which I might not have taken had I not been his tenant.'

The proposed motorway was a case in point. Lord Hertford had 'fought it like a tomcat' and had invited Robert Hiller's assistance, which was given. 'Frankly, I could not have cared less whether the motorway was built or not, and in some ways I would rather have liked to see it being built, because it would have been convenient. But he felt so strongly about it, so I supported him. . . . But I don't think the Lord thing came into it at all. He used his title to fight the Ministry of Transport, and that is fair enough. That is no business of mine; but as far as I am concerned, he could have been plain Mr, or he could have been the Prince of Wales, it would not have made any difference. I would have treated him as my landlord, and I would have decided on the arguments whether or not to support him. In the case of the motorway, I was very much in two minds. I would have supported him if he had been Mr Hertford; whether I would have supported him if he hadn't been my landlord, I'm not sure. There is no feeling now that one is in a sort of feudal relationship, none at all. Now, to all intents and purposes, I don't think there is any feeling of social difference as such. Lord Hertford has his own circle of friends and I have mine and sometimes we have mutual friends. Our relationship is very much on a business footing although when we meet socially we get along well. I am probably the tenant who is friendliest at all with Lord Hertford. This is the home farm and I think it is the most prosperous of his farms.'

With some modern tenant farmers, family pride in agricultural skills runs as strongly as in the aristocratic landlord, and the personal influence they hold in today's revolutionized world, even in the country, may make any image of the cap-touching tenant farmer quite out-dated. In the old days, the positions of the aristocratic landlord and the humble tenant farmer may have been unfair, but at least both sides knew what they *were*. Nowadays the tenant farmer transcends the borders of class and public influence in a way which must make both sides a bit hesitant – Robert Hiller as a successful businessman and landowner and Mrs Pat Bomford as chairman of the local magistrates are good examples of tenant farmers who have broken through the social barriers. Mrs Bomford has a position of undoubted influence and stature in the community, not lessened by the fact that Lord Hertford himself has never been appointed a magistrate.

Pat Bomford told me she rented slightly under half her farmland from the Ragley estate – some 300 acres. She rented another 150 acres from her nephew and the rest of the 700 acres was her own.

She lives adjacent to her own farm in The Old Granary, Rushford, Iron Cross, which commands a fine view of hills on a clear day. It is an altogether charming, modernized old granary building with the benefits both of genuine old beams and a new glazed patio where, when I visited her, sparrows were nesting, meaning that she felt she had to keep the door permanently open so the mother could get in and out with food for her babies.

'I haven't got the heart to cut the babies off from their food,' she admitted.

Very sentimental. But a soft heart can accompany a hard head, an attribute Pat Bomford evidently shared with her in-laws. The Bomford family had farmed land on Ragley from 'time immemorial', she said. 'It was certainly farmed by my father-in-law and, as far as I know, by his father as well, going right back to old Benjamin Bomford, who was a very famous agriculturalist.'

Old Benjamin was a pioneer of steam tackle, the successor of oxen and horses in the ploughing of fields. Steam engines would be put on both sides of a field, and used to pull plough-shares through the soil by means of chains. Old Benjamin had two sons, Raymond and Benjamin Junior, and they jointly farmed at Ragley, ploughing up some scrubland called Bevington Waste in the First World War to produce badly-needed cornfields. Raymond's four sons inherited some of the farms, Dick going to Rushford and later selling it to Pat Bomford's husband, who died prematurely in the early 1960s.

Pat Bomford took over the farm. She was not a country girl. She was a Brummie – a citizen of Birmingham – and unused to the ways of the land until she met her husband. She came out from the city to the country as a relief secretary to Bomford Brothers when their regular secretary had a nervous breakdown. She came in the first instance for a month, and six months later she and her employer decided to get married. They started married life at Rushford Farm and it was not until five years after her husband's death that Pat Bomford decided to modernize The Old Granary. It was a building in which she remembered playing as a young girl. Where the living room is now was a lorry-loading ramp for the delivery of bags of grain. Above it was the granary where grain was stored. She took away the outside steps and created the sort of home which any middle-class townsman would fall in love with immediately.

To me, Pat Bomford had an aura of her own, and it was certainly *not* that of a cap-touching yokel: 'I was thoroughly spoiled by my husband, who regarded me as a city girl who couldn't possibly milk a cow or pluck a chicken, which I suppose I traded on. I have always managed to find someone to do the work for me . . . I tell my farm manager he keeps me in idle luxury!'

This was drollery. Pat Bomford watches the progress of her business carefully and signs all cheques. She is very prominent in public life. Apart from the chairmanship of the local magistrates she was, at the time I encountered her, running an Over-60s' Club for old people, acting as treasurer of the Women's Institute market, which the local branch holds at Alcester every Friday, and, at various times, doing many other jobs for the Women's Institute. She became county chairman soon after her husband died, deliberately throwing herself into the work to contain her grief.

'It was a lifeline,' she admitted to me. 'I was just coming up to be chairman and I decided I would go on with it. I am very grateful to them.'

I asked Pat Bomford to what extent she felt part and parcel of the great estate of Ragley.

Not much, apparently. 'I am a tenant farmer and, as such, below the salt, if you see what I mean. I am not on visiting terms with Lord Hertford except when he has a tenants' "do", but I am not worried about that. I am not landed gentry nor anything like that. This slightly narks me, although it doesn't worry me, because I have no desire to be considered one of his friends. My father used to shoot a lot with his father, Lord Henry, but I don't think I have ever been accepted socially – put it like that – mainly because I am a tenant farmer. Don't get me wrong, it doesn't bother me. I get on very well with Lord Hertford. When his son Harry was twenty-one, there were great celebrations around for every sort of person on the estate and we had a super dinner in the dining room and I made a speech and Lady Hertford was very charming. I couldn't complain about my treatment.'

Perhaps any aristocrat at the Hall may today be pardoned if he keeps himself slightly distant, mixing only with his own friends and generally presenting as small a target as possible to people and influences which could be in the slightest degree unfriendly? Pat Bomford said there could be something in that theory. She was also candid enough to add that she felt she might have been a bit of an inverted snob over the situation and have mentally said to herself, 'They are nothing to do with me.'

'It is probably fifty-fifty,' she said.

The ambiguities in relationships between the modern Hall and the modern tenant farmer, complicated by the pullings and tuggings of more general social forces, may have left all parties feeling that business is business, and best not compromised too much by personal feeling.

'I wouldn't say I am exactly sentimental about my farms, no,' said Pat Bomford, 'but it is a marvellous life here for me. I don't have any of the worries, my farm manager does all the day-to-day work and I sign the cheques. We have discussions on major policy. If we want an expensive new machine, we will talk about it. I know exactly what is going on around me. I have a nice house with a pleasant garden. One big sitting room and an open plan hall, a small dining room and a kitchen. I have three bathrooms and *four* loos. I have built an extension downstairs, with a bedroom and bathroom, ready for my old age. We shall go on farming until I die. I don't think I would change places with Lord Hertford. He must have an awful problem as landlord. It isn't an easy job. We have got ten or twelve cottages ourselves, and I know what a game it is to keep them in good repair. They are a drain – you don't make any money out of them, you just house your workers as best you can. Lord Hertford has these sort of problems multiplied I don't know how many times over. I certainly would have no ambitions to live at a place like the Hall, no ambitions at all. I am very happy as I am.'

Does that apply equally to the employees of tenant farmers? Many of them certainly do seem happy as they are – perhaps strangely so in an era of increasing household expenses and rare or non-existent public transport.

One mid-day I found Dan and Jill Bryan working on Robert Hiller's 'pick-it-yourself' fruit farm at Dunnington Heath. To be more precise, Dan – the farm manager – was sitting in one of the twenty-two polythene tunnels used for growing, storing and weighing the crops. He was having a sandwich lunch and his wife was weighing up some tomatoes a customer had just selected.

'It's nice, being able to work in a job with your husband,' said Jill Bryan, who managed the shop as well as helping out on the opposite side of the road, with the self-pick operation. 'I do it on a part-time basis. In the country the atmosphere is leisurely, except on Saturdays and Sundays, when we get a lot of people in from Alcester, Redditch, and further afield. We see them every weekend, yet there's no time to chat. But we can chat to the others on weekdays.'

Self-service tomatoes had been a very successful enterprise, Dan Bryan thought, because people didn't know when to stop picking and so ended up with more than they really wanted. 'The weekday trade is far more discriminating,' said his wife. 'Ladies from Solihull, which is the posh stockbroker belt of Birmingham, come to stock up their freezers. They know *exactly* what they want. We have the Rolls Royces in – we get everything from the Rolls Royces to push bikes and tandems.'

The couple outbid one another in their eagerness to describe the interesting nature of the job. 'We get all classes,' said Dan Bryan. 'The recession hasn't made any difference. We thought the petrol costs would make a big difference, but no!'

'The majority feel it's a day out. Isn't that right, Dan?'

'They have a picnic. Refreshments are available in that garden up there, and there are lavatories, flush loos – portable. Four portable loos for the ladies, plus the Gents in brick. And a washbasin for the pickers.'

'It is very much the social scene. They will pick in rain, hail or snow. Yesterday you could not move for people. All the four tables were used for weighing up. They were mostly Birmingham people, all colours and nationalities – it is particularly like that at weekends. In the week it is primarily elderly people, mothers with small children, holidaymakers, isn't that right, Dan? We even get disabled groups on their days out.'

Pastoral good nature, indeed. It is surprising to a townsman to find it can still exist in the community adjacent to the Hall, despite all the conflicting social pressures.

It is less surprising to find that the old, and now retired, employees of the tenant farmers see their own lives in an even more rosy light. They look back on their relationship with their employers through very kind eyes, even if they think the times themselves were hard.

I found Joe Cresswell, at the age of seventy-seven, enjoying his retirement in a cottage at Dunnington Heath, near his ex-employer's house. He used to be Dunnington Heath's foreman. He was in the job for over thirty years, starting work during the depression of the late 1920s. 'I suppose I got a bit big-headed. There was a great gerfuffle about setting up your own smallholding and I was one of the mugs. I fell for it. The slump hit us for six and we were just struggling along. Mr Hiller offered me the job of farm foreman – today it would be called farm manager – and I have been here ever since.'

Joe Cresswell had been pointed out to me as 'a man who might take to you and might not, and you'll know if he doesn't.' In fact he was invariably helpful and informative. 'It's nice to find someone who's interested in how it used to be compared with what it's like today,' he said more than once. 'I was treated very good and I think that was pretty general. The farmers themselves were literally scratching for every penny – they were as hard up as the workers. Things are a thousand times better today. They can talk about the good old days! It's a pity every generation didn't have some of what we had in the 1920s and the early 1930s. I hope to God they never will, because we all had to watch every penny. But there were very few cases of employees hating their employers – not on farms. Between the average farm worker and the average employer there is a bond of friendship and unity. I am sure it's true that the workers *still* regard themselves as part and parcel of the farm – they don't just regard it as being a way to get the last penny.'

Hence he'd never come across any farm worker in his experience who smashed up new machinery, as the Luddites and others had done in towns when they thought their livelihood was threatened by it. In his experience, the farm worker always welcomed the advent of new technology: 'Anything to make life easier and pleasanter! A farm worker has too much sense to maul his guts out with a pitch fork when he can switch on a machine to do it. It's as simple as that.'

No doubt Joe Cresswell's background influenced his thinking. He first came to the Ragley estate a few weeks before his twelfth birthday. This was during the First World War. He had been 'turfed out' of school and out onto the land, to produce urgently-needed food. When Mr Hiller senior took over in the autumn of 1918, having been invalided out of the Army, Joe Cresswell made his dash to go-it-alone as a smallholder, then came back again to live and work at Dunnington Heath permanently. In 1934, he moved into the cottage in which I found him nearly fifty years later and he was still growing vegetables for visiting relatives and other social callers in its half-acre garden.

'I get my pleasure out of helping other people,' he explained.

I believed him. It is an attitude of mind more often found in those who live or work on the tenanted farms of Ragley than it is in people who spend their lives in towns – or perhaps even in those people who work on the farms kept in hand by the landlord, a figure who is inevitably more removed from them socially.

It may make for a more harmonious and prolonged life. At any rate, Joe Cresswell, at seventy-seven, was still driving his thirty-three-year-old Rover at the time I visited him. It almost suggested that the country air might be as good for automobiles as it was for their owners. Like most elderly gentlemen who are hale and hearty, he had his own explanation of why he was so fit after a life of often backbreaking toil. 'Mainly good luck – I have always made a good, substantial living. I am an outdoor man. Frankly, even in my young days I never liked going to the cinema or the theatre. Never appealed to me or interested me in the least. I've had a good life. At one time there were twenty people on this farm and the employers were on Christian name terms with all of them. We were never treated as inferior beings. They never regarded their workers as nitwits. I think you will find that, generally speaking, there is still a bond between master and man. It has come down the ages and still applies today.'

There is thus a considerable irony in the lives both of the tenant farmers and their workers on estates like Ragley. Lord Hertford would like to repossess as many of his own farms as possible, because he could make more money by farming them than by renting them out; but his tenants and their employees still draw a sense of personal continuity and security from their jobs. They do not like their work because it is easy – on the contrary, it is demanding and gritty – but perhaps because it has the aura of permanency in an alarmingly shifting world. The reality of that permanency may be vulnerable, but the *atmosphere* is still very firmly there.

I came to the conclusion that the 'bond between master and man' spoken of by Joe Cresswell applied in some measure to all the farms at Ragley, whether they were tenanted or farmed by the 8th Marquess. The reason? It could be a shared interest in the new techniques of the trade. It could be a sense of being allies against the encroachment of the towns. Or, as every harvest proves, it could be the very stark knowledge that, without a very great deal of mutual give-and-take and co-operation, there could easily be an expensive disaster that would be damaging for them all – master and man.

11
Harvest
Help

*I*T WAS HALF-PAST-FIVE in the morning when Percy Harris got out of bed, seven when he went to work in the hayfield and over thirteen hours later before he finally finished his working day.

At the age of seventy-one, he was helping to turn and dry the newly-cut grass in some of Ragley's fields. It was harvest time. At this time of the year, from July to October, even septuagenarians put in a working day that would leave many townsmen half their age pale, gasping and looking for alternative employment.

In Ragley's heyday, a century ago, there would probably have been at least thirty full-time workers on the estate to cope with the harvest. They would have been a community; drinking their cider at nightfall and comparing notes before going on to work on the lamp-lit threshing. Today, harvest time at Ragley is a rather more improvised affair. There are no more than half-a-dozen full-time estate workers, but at harvest time they are assisted by a temporary workforce made up of independent contractors, tenant farmers and their workers, and their sons, brothers, fathers and cousins.

Hence Percy Harris's presence in one of the fields behind the stables of Ragley, where grass seed and hay were being harvested. It was a baking hot day and on his head he was wearing a handkerchief with a knot tied at each corner – a device more widely utilized by Victorian seaside paddlers than present-day farmers. To fully understand his role in the proceedings, one would need a family tree and infinite patience. In short, when I met him Percy Harris was the tenant farmer of Holly Bush Farm

Lord Hertford's dilligent secretary, Mrs Maureen Lawrence (*below*), attends to everything from preparing quotations for, and arranging, large commercial functions to running personal errands for the family. Fobbester the butler and 'Mrs Fobb' the cook (*right*) are as much a part of Ragley as its famous portico. Today they cope with a wide variety of jobs virtually alone, whereas in the past they would have had many under-servants. Mrs Marian Crabtree (*bottom*) handles the accounts of the Hall and the estate, as well as helping her husband Peter at the farm office.

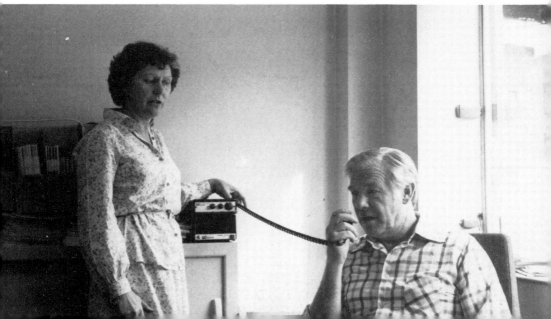

John Lindsey, the head gardener (*top left*), a refugee from industry, thoroughly enjoys his stately existence a with great diplomacy and expertise has helped the forthright Lady Hertford to transform the Ragley garde into a blaze of colour. The Earl of Yarmouth (*above*), heir to Ragley and no lover of nightclubs, concerns hims with more utilitarian matter ensuring that Ragley's flock of sheep contribute substantially to the estate revenues. Tenant farmers lik Harold Heard (*left*) have an arduous lifestyle that city dwellers might nevertheless envy because of the security gives not only to the farmer himself, but possibly also to his sons and grandsons. The Heards' farmhouse (*bottom*) certainly picturesque, but in winter glasses of water at th bedside have been known t freeze overnight.

The Princess Alphonse de Chimay, Lord Hertford's mother-in-law, and her dog Winky (*top left*) live in an imaginatively renovated house in Ragley Park, with paintings of ancestors adorning the walls. After a riding accident in the family, the Princess persuaded her daughter against using a saddle and Lady Hertford now almost always rides bareback around the estate (*top right*). One of Ragley's most striking features is the stables (*above left*), designed by James Wyatt in 1780. Phil Roberts, the groom (*above right*), is now in solitary charge of Ragley's horses, and receives extra help only for the hunting.

Harry Green, the local farrier (*top left*), still shoes Ragley's horses and supplements his income with general blacksmithing. The gamekeeper, Ken Ward, is now employed by a local shooting syndicate, but continues to cull deer for Lord Hertford. Colin Bindley, the head forester (*middle left*),believes that each of the Ragley woods has its own personality and commercial potential. The Rev. Arthur Stally (*middle centre*) follows the tradition of taking harvest parcels to old people in the area, many of whom, like Miss Marjorie Crick (*middle right*), Alf Goddard (*bottom left*), Albert Richards (*bottom centre*) and Bertie Brass (*bottom right*), are former estate workers or their relatives still living in houses on the estate.

on the Ragley estate, a tenancy his father before him took over in 1910. But on this particular occasion (such are the wheels-within-wheels at a Ragley harvest) he was assisting his son, George Harris, who now virtually runs Holly Bush Farm, but who on *this* particular harvest was acting as an independent contractor, bailing up and taking away the hay from the fields to be sold all over the country.

Percy Harris was clearly a farmer of an earlier age. He was born at about the time *his* father was taking over the tenancy of Holly Bush Farm. Apart from spending twelve months farming in Canada when he was nineteen, for people of Scottish descent – who would 'give you anything but money, plenty of food, but only $30 a month when a dollar was 4s 2d, plus keep' – he had spent all his life at Ragley. He liked cricket, didn't mind the town, but didn't go there more often than he needed to, and now lived in a small cottage on Holly Bush Farm, while his son George, in his mid-forties, occupied the main farmhouse.

George Harris was cast in a different mould, and one which would not have really conformed to the restrictions of semi-feudalism. He was a portly man with a hearty and persistent laugh, a very shrewd eye for how to market hay in the depth of winter, when supplies tended to be leanest and profits largest, and an unusual hobby (for a tenant farmer): building and driving one-man racing cars.

Temporarily doffing his flame-red greasy cap which advertised a make of sparking plug, the younger Harris took time off from bailing his hay and packing it onto a tractor to explain how he had got himself involved in a pattern of life rather different from most of the Ragley farming circle.

'Most of my racing friends were Battle of Britain pilots, and they can all drive well. You only drive for about thirty seconds on most of the runs, which is about a mile or something like that, but most of the older chaps can't breathe at the end,' he guffawed. 'It is a young man's activity. One of my friends is sixty-five and he once told me he was too old for women and racing cars. But recently I saw him racing. I don't really know at what age you *should* pack it in.'

Such events are only diversions and quite out of the question at harvest time; but they are, albeit subconsciously, almost certainly an assertion of independence against the 'set form' of Ragley life, which has sometimes in the past taken on a distinctly puritanical tone. The three-bedroomed detached farmhouse that George Harris lives in was once the Holly Bush Inn. When his grandfather first took over Holly Bush Farm, the then

Marquess was in the process of closing the pub because there was so much alcoholic merriment on Sundays. George Harris's grandfather went to a sale at which the Holly Bush Inn sign was sold for one shilling (5p). He wished later that he had obtained this trophy for his family. Perhaps he feared that the public purchase of the sign of the 'undesirable' inn would be interpreted as an act of disrespect and rebellion. What the then Marquess would have thought of it had he been faced with a tenant farmer who indulged in motor racing is scarcely imaginable.

Times had indeed changed. When I saw him in the fields beyond Ragley Hall's 1780 James Wyatt stables, George Harris was firmly in charge of the collection of the hay. He had at his immediate beck and call a lorry and two trailers, plus two more lorries and three tractors which he could call on if necessary. His father was on one of the tractors, turning over the grass. It did not take much drying out as it was pretty dry to start with. It had been a good year for the grass, which put everyone into a good humour. Grass can be a temperamental crop: it usually has to be left until eight or nine in the morning before it can be cut. Before that it tends to be still damp from the dew, so it won't cut properly and often fouls the machinery into the bargain.

'First they split off the grass seed. Then we buy the hay and bail it up ourselves. We are going to sell it chiefly in South Wales and Derbyshire. Sheep feed on it,' explained George Harris, who said he farmed a Ragley market garden as well as dealing in hay and straw, together with an associate.

Trade this year had not been too good, he admitted. 'But,' he added, 'we can still sell hay anywhere if it is cheap enough. There are plenty of customers if you can take it to the right place at the right time – it has to be a winter's day when someone needs it. I can tell you how we find our customers. We put lorry loads of hay into the hay markets and hope to find customers who will then carry on trading with us if they are pleased. We go around the country doing that, but mostly in the South-West and Derbyshire because that's where the demand is, and where the money's to be found. We must handle thousands of tons a year and we sell it all the year round. It is stored in different farms around the Cotswolds.'

Such is the role of the entrepreneur in a modern harvest at Ragley. Everyone appeared to be satisfied, including the occupants of the Hall, because it undoubtedly spreads the risk. George Harris, too, was clearly a fairly satisfied man. When I asked him if he had ever had a bad year and lost his proverbial shirt by not selling his amassed hay, he gave one of his explosive laughs. 'Not really! We don't buy it until we have got it sold. If we don't think we can sell it, we don't have it, although we have had odd times that we have been to auction and haven't sold it. But very few.'

I did not find it entirely surprising that the quick-witted George Harris had also done well on the race track with the cars of his own construction. He had raced at Silverstone, and in the seven years he had been racing he had had nine wins and he had come second in a John Player Trophy.

'It makes quite a change,' he said. 'But I haven't done so much this year because I have been so busy.'

The harvest on estates like Ragley would indeed be precarious if it were not for the modern breed of independent merchant and technician, though there are, of course, still Ragley workers, and even descendants of Ragley workers, involved. Working on the same hayfield, driving a tractor which was hauling a trailer, was Philip Gosney, sixteen-year-old son of Frank Gosney, Lord Hertford's longest-serving farm worker. Young Gosney had been working five days in the field – not for Lord Hertford, but as part of a Government work experience scheme for school leavers who would otherwise be unemployed. He had been working for three months under the scheme, earning a small wage, and it was certainly teaching him something about the frustrations of harvest time. Three out of the five days Philip Gosney had spent on the seed and hay harvesting had been wet ones. This had delayed work badly. He was also finding out something about the euphoria that grips the countryman when at last the weather lifts, work can proceed swiftly, and there is a feeling that even God is on one's side.

A large combine harvester was being driven over the fields, stopping after four runs to tip its load of grass into Gosney's trailer. It was being driven by yet another of those independent entrepreneurs on whom the landed aristocrat now depends to a marked extent.

Tony Suffield had been involved in the Ragley harvest for four years when I spoke to him as he was battling with Lord Hertford's grass seed and hay. He had begun this year's harvest a fortnight previously at the usual starting point at Ragley: the oil seed rape, the most delicate and temperamental of all the crops, not excepting the wheat and the winter barley.

A sprightly man in his middle fifties but looking younger, he pointed out that the year itself had been somewhat temperamental. They had started on the oil seed rape; moved on to the grass, found conditions too wet and so moved back to reseeding with oil seed rape, and then finally moved back to grass again.

'When we get to the cereals,' he said, 'you can't start until about nine-thirty in the morning. You have to wait for the dew to come off. It is impossible to say how many hours we put in altogether. You can work until midnight or one, two, three in the morning – and we have done. I was up at four-thirty this morning to move one of our four combines. There were roadworks on the way. That was all we needed!'

The Suffield's is a family firm and Tony Suffield said that he had always worked for himself. The firm was based some 4 or 5 miles from Ragley; it involved many hours of hard work, and was, in fact, a total way of life.

'It's not *easy*,' said Suffield, taking a momentary break from his combine. 'But I prefer it to working for a boss. When I was nineteen I did work for someone else, but that's about the only time. We don't employ any labour. We have three sons working for us – John, who is twenty-nine, Ricky, who is twenty-four and Nigel, who is twenty-one.'

Tony Suffield, though he now runs four modern combines as an independent operator, has ancestral roots in the land. His father was a farmer in the Midlands – at Daventry and Aston Cantelow, where he had seventy acres, mostly devoted to dairying. Tony first set up in business on his own account in the late 1950s, and his combine harvesters were now heavily called upon throughout the district at harvest time.

Unfortunately, after the lucrative harvest-time contracts, comes the lean winter. This is when necessary work, like the upkeep of machinery, absorbs a lot of time without bringing in any revenue. Tony Suffield and his kind are always on the alert for new sorts of winter work – some of which would have been incomprehensible to his grandfather. At the time we spoke, he had just started ammonia injection on fields, using aqua-ammonia, a fertilizer which is injected into the ground in winter. As soon as the ground temperature begins to rise with the coming of spring, nitrogen is progressively released. This fertilizes the soil – a sort of fertilization by time-warp that is used mainly by dairy farmers. Tony Suffield's firm also made a practice of taking on the winter repair of other farmers' machinery. This brought in some income during the lean winter.

At Ragley, Tony Suffield has been in the habit of helping with drilling the new crop after harvesting the old. He was thus as much affected by the bad weather as Ragley's own workers. When I saw him he was jubilant because he felt drilling might be over by the end of September, whereas he could remember years when it was November before the work was all done. As Tony Suffield was also a farmer in his own right – operating Homelea Farm at Aston Cantelow – I could well understand that balancing the needs of his own farm with the needs of his contractual customers like Ragley, often took some fine political juggling. But Tony Suffield maintained that his principle was clear: 'Our main business is contracting. We run the farm as well as we can, but that comes second. I like to go and look at my own corn when I can, but if anyone else wants a combine before we use it, then they have it.'

Though this philosophy represents a clear break with that of the old-time farmer (who would regard neglecting his own land, albeit temporarily, as sacrilege), Tony Suffield came across as a man who was as wedded to the country life as his father and grandfather before him. When I asked him if he had ever wanted a life in a town, where he might get a greater return on his investment, he laughed dismissively. 'This is my way of life. Farming on the land as we do *is* life. Tonight we will pack up at eight-thirty. On cereals, it will be more like eleven at night. But it is not money we are concerned with, it is the quality of life.'

The harvest itself is far from being the *only* busy time for Dick Cookes, Ragley's farms foreman, a man in his late thirties who came to Ragley in 1973 as a tractor driver. When Ragley's farms were expanded in 1978, by taking over farms up till then let to tenants, Dick Cookes was given the foreman's job as a result of Frank Gosney's firm refusal to accept 'worrying promotion'.

Long before the harvest, usually as early as April, Dick Cookes has begun what he calls his 'corn-walking'. This meant, he said, that he walked around all the fields on the estate, seeing how the crop was progressing and estimating when it would be ready for harvesting.

'I do a lot of corn-walking in the afternoons,' he explained. 'The fields haven't all got a public approach road. I have to walk at least 150 acres a day and perhaps as much as 200 acres, so that I see each field at least once a week. A large amount of this I do out of working hours.'

But Dick Cookes always knew that, with labour in such short supply, everyone would be working valiantly by harvest time itself. When I spoke to him, having traced his whereabouts with the aid of the radio telephone he had installed in his farm van, he was watching hay being brought into Weethley Farm (Ragley's dairy farm) from surrounding fields.

'We grow different types of crops to spread the harvest load,' he said. 'There are seven people from the Ragley farms now engaged on the harvest and we would not have more than ten people working on it ourselves. Before the coming of machinery, a 200-acre farm would carry at least twenty men, probably twenty-five. We are approaching 3,000 acres and we have got only six full-time tractor drivers; whereas in the days of binders and sheavers just after the war, there used to be a man for roughly every 100 acres. Before the First World War, when it was horse and cart, it would be a man to forty or fifty acres – or sixty men to a farm of this size. There would be a terrific number of people compared with today.'

Dick Cookes might be right in saying that most modern tractor drivers at harvest time don't mind their lonely lives as they run over the harvest fields, two to a field, and usually well away from one another. The social life of the harvest field might have gone but, in his view, today's tractor driver is usually a man who enjoys being on his own and can reason out for himself what to do next. He does not mind working in the fields for twelve hours a day, exchanging hardly more than a few words with his co-workers.

Now all this might be quite true; but the fact remains that, with fewer men, faultless organization is more important. There is no slack in the labour pool which can be called upon in the event of a miscalculation.

Hence Dick Cookes' emphasis on his corn-walking, and also on the need constantly to look for traces of disease and pests in growing crops. The first crop that he reckoned to keep a special eye on at harvest time was usually the oil seed rape. Generally, more spraying is done these days than in former times, primarily to kill off disease and pests. But the oil seed rape might ripen unevenly and has to be sprayed with chemicals to defoliate it and retard the ripening process. Alternatively, it can be cut off at the roots and left to ripen in what is called a swath – a piled-up row.

On the sunny day I met him, the first 38 acres of oil seed rape at Alcester Lodge Farm on the estate had been swathed, though it was still only the middle of July. It was done overnight. The next day the entire crop at the same farm was carefully looked at and Dick Cookes decided to desiccate (spray) half of it and swath the other half. The whole of the oil seed rape had been combined by the end of July, to everyone's great relief.

The next decision should have been almost automatic: to move into harvesting the grass seed. But decisions in the countryside are rarely that simple in practice. The grass was late in coming to ripeness, so the work-force turned to the winter barley. That wasn't quite ripe enough either. It had 18 per cent moisture, when ideally barley should be combined when it has moisture of only 14 or 15 per cent. In that state, it can be stored straightaway. At 18 per cent moisture it has to be dried in store, which in this case meant paying the co-operative farm store at Stratford-upon-Avon more money than they would normally be paid merely for storage. But unless the winter barley *was* cut, the labour force and the machinery would be standing idle with no work to do. So, in consultation with the farms manager, Peter Crabtree, Dick Cookes decided that the barley would have to be cut, too moist or not. Decisions at harvest time tend to be uneasy compromises – and they usually have to be taken on the spur of the moment and not at leisure.

'It is the first year we have had difficulty in finding anything that is ripe. We have been darting about from one crop to another,' Dick Cookes complained. Unlike his industrial counterparts, he has never found it possible to blame a mysterious 'they' for his troubles, but has been able to blame only the weather, against which no discipline or sanctions are possible.

'The whole thing,' he continued, 'is more complicated because you have to go for the crop you feel to be most at risk. Oil seed rape is very delicate; you can lose a tremendous amount of the crop. The winter barley will stand a certain amount of leaving, though the combiner tends to knock the ears off it if it is too ripe.'

The Ragley philosophy when it comes to harvests is very typical of its plan for survival as a whole: look to the future rather than brood over the past. Dick Cookes thought that many farmers were wrong in thinking the harvest was *the* most important thing in the summer. In his view, the *most* important thing was to get the next year's crop planted: 'The faster I can do that, the better. We can't, now, do any more to last year's crop. What I am looking to do is to get this year's harvest in as quickly as possible, to enable me to get started on next year's growing period. That is the way you have to think. Forwards.'

Drilling the oil seed rape at Ragley usually begins in the third week of

August and lasts until the first week in September. Drilling with grass seed will start at the beginning of August and also go through to the first week in September. The winter barley starts going in early in September and the whole drilling process is over by the end of October, or the beginning of November at the very latest.

I asked Dick Cookes a rather naïve townsman's question: did he then relax?

In answer he gave me a wry smile. 'I would say we ease up a little. At the peak, I get up at six-thirty and am into work around seven-thirty, deciding where people have to get out to that day. I have had this van with the radio telephone for eighteen months. And I need it, believe me. In the evening at this time of the year, I pack up at about ten-thirty at night. I go on with these sort of hours – with some breaks, possibly – from May till October. We work until dusk – we don't very often drill in the dark. We do sometimes work in the dark, but not much. Going on like this, the last of the winter wheat is drilled by 7 November. You have to do everything before the weather breaks. By the middle of October the ground rarely dries again, it just gets wetter and wetter. We are controlled a lot by the weather. When the weather is good we try to do the maximum amount.'

They were certainly doing the maximum amount at Ragley in the sunny August week I watched them at work. It was pleasant to see hard work and gratified smiles going together – I rather suspect that this may not always be the case on the production lines of the factories only a few miles away. Fresh air and a shared sense of responsibility seem to breed sense and sanity, or a socially passable impersonation of it.

12
The Princess at Home

THE PRINCESS ALPHONSE DE CHIMAY, Lord Hertford's mother-in-law, had been house-hunting for some time when her husband, Lieutenant Colonel Prince Alphonse de Chimay, told her, 'I have just seen exactly the place you want.' It was, he said, in Ragley Park itself.

'Nonsense,' replied his wife, never a lady to mince her words or express herself in half-tones. 'You can't possibly live so near to your relations.'

The Princess, having now lived in the Kitchen Garden House, encircled by its own brick wall in Ragley Park, for over twenty years, remained of the same general opinion, but she was prepared to admit that there were exceptions to the rule, one of which was her own situation. She always made a point, she said, of not living on their doorstep and never imposing.

The problems of the aristocracy overseas are often even more extreme than those of their British counterparts. Prince Alphonse de Chimay's home, the Chateau de Beauchamp, near Chimay in Belgium, was destroyed in the Second World War. The Prince's family evacuated it in the First World War, and came back to find it heavily looted. In the Second World War it received even worse treatment and the family came back to the house to find it beyond repair.

The Prince, soldier and businessman, had fought in both world wars (fiddling his age for the privilege on both occasions). After the end of the second war, his career as a soldier was obviously over and when he eventually retired he was a businessman, living in London. His only daughter was married to Lord Hertford and helping him to renovate Ragley Hall. Hence the Prince and his wife felt a tug of attraction towards

Warwickshire. The sheer lure of making something out of dereliction may have appealed to them too. It is more than possible that the Prince might have fared better in arousing his wife's interest in the Kitchen Garden House if, from the outset, he had put less emphasis on its proximity to Ragley Hall and more on its utterly derelict state. The Princess, I soon came to realize, enjoyed a challenge even more than she enjoyed comfort.

It was on the grassed terrace at the rear of Ragley Hall that I first met the Princess. She then admitted to the age of eighty-three, although there were admiring members of the staff of the Hall who pointed out that she had admitted to being eighty-three two years previously. I saw a poker-backed lady who looked perhaps sixty, entertaining two friends to coffee. She had just treated them to lunch in Ragley's new and improved restaurant, being temporarily between house-keeping couples at her own home. Also she was probably glad to give her son-in-law a boost by showing off his new and improved restaurant.

How does one address a Belgian Princess? The staff advised me that 'Princess' was passable, though they preferred to be on the safe side and say, 'Ma'am'. All such questions fell by the wayside when I encountered the energetic lady herself. Her features were those of the classic aristocrat, but her manner was as businesslike as a builder's or a market gardener's as she described how she and her husband had first come across the Kitchen Garden House and then licked it into shape.

'We lived in London then and we used to come down at weekends and work on it. There was this enormous 4-acre walled garden, plus 2 acres outside it. Then there was this darling little house, the same age as Ragley, plus a cottage next door. We became tenants. It was absolutely derelict: no one had lived in it for ten years. Utterly fantastic. There were fourteen greenhouses beside the house and nettles were growing out of the roofs. The first thing we had to do was to dig out the house, which had silted up over the centuries. We worked outwards from the house, towards the enormous 52-foot pond in the middle of the garden. There was a positive *wood* in the middle of this pond and when we went into it, two snipe flew up. We re-created it and filled it with water lily. I can't actually say I laid the concrete, but I did all the designing.'

She also helped her daughter and son-in-law with the renovation of Ragley Hall: 'We used to scrape the floor itself in the ghastly early days before they got help and became established. In those days one made the curtains, scraped the floors and polished the furniture to get it straight. It was seven years before they got any help at all. They started off living in just two rooms.'

More or less simultaneously, she and her husband were practically rebuilding the Kitchen Garden House.

I said I suspected that she had rather enjoyed all this. 'Nothing I enjoy more! I enjoy it enormously. And it will be disappointing when the whole thing is perfect and there's nothing left to do. I sometimes think I have created an enormous garden for nothing at all, which is overwhelming me. I must start cutting it down again to get it in order. But you must come down to see the house.'

At this point, out of courtesy to her guests (and to the relief of my note-taking hand) our conversation was adjourned. Later I drove down the winding drive of Ragley to look over her house.

The Kitchen Garden House stands nearly at the bottom of the main drive of Ragley Park, and to the north of it. In the wall, visible from the driveway, are French black iron gates by Tijou, brought down from Ragley itself by Capability Brown when he redesigned Ragley's gardens. There was a sort of cart-track leading off the main drive to the back of the house, where I found the door now used as the main entrance. The first thing any visitor encounters is a notice warning him against 'ferocious dogs', though the only dog I actually saw was Tiddlywinks, a lap dog affectionately known as Winky who, I was assured, wouldn't bite me if I minded my manners and didn't touch him.

The house, as it now stands, has a great deal of charm. Indeed, when many less privileged people dream of their ideal home, it is likely to bear more resemblance to the Kitchen Garden House, as renovated by the Princess de Chimay, than to the more grand Ragley Hall itself; the real appeal of which lies in the fact that it is representative of a totally different way of life. The Kitchen Garden House has the attraction of approachability.

Before she showed me round, the Princess talked to me in the smallish sitting room, now panelled in a medium shade oak but due, she said briskly, to be painted apricot. 'If I want to write in here at present, I have to put the light on,' complained the Princess, ever the innovator. 'Otherwise I have to go into the writing room next door. It used to be the potting shed, until we incorporated it into the house.'

From the house that I saw, it was difficult to visualize its derelict condition when Prince Alphonse and his wife first took over. Apparently, in the attics the ceilings had collapsed onto the floors. The rooms were redecorated with the help of a Mr La Resche of Alcester: 'Perfect workmanship and good taste and never did things without asking me.' Three bathrooms were put in, one above the other, on each of the three floors. The major work took about three years and then the potting shed was incorporated into the house as the rather restful writing room. It was given pale green walls and 'Eye of the Bull' circular windows were installed, with embellished circular shutters painted by an artistic friend in Chelsea.

The interior work included remodelling all the existing rooms. But the aristocratic innovators had an eye to economy. The small dining room, next to the hall, with the kitchen on the far side, did not, I noticed, have what the Princess called the 'usual mahogany tables'. 'They are *boring*,' she maintained. 'I got someone to marbleize them in green. It is pretty, gay and amusing. The corner cupboard is Country Chippendale – we found it in pieces on the floor. All the side tables were bought at sales and all are the right size for this neat, compact little house. I said, "I am not going to pay more than £5 for anything." The hall table we saw went over the £5, and afterwards I thought, "What an idiot to have lost it!" But when I went back, it had been unsold. I got it for £4 10s.'

In the kitchen the original old beams were allowed to remain. So were two boilers: an electric one for use in summer and a central heating and hot water system for the winter. Because of the thickness of the walls, the serving hatch from the kitchen to the dining room had to be about four feet deep; and so dishes are passed from one room to another through what is a virtual tunnel.

There are enough paintings in the de Chimay family to cover every available square inch of the walls of the house. In the sitting room the Princess put an oil of Prince Alphonse de Chimay (grandfather of the Princess's husband) fighting for the King of Holland. 'They were all called Alphonse,' pointed out the Princess. 'They said if I had a son, he would have to be Alphonse. Fortunately I had a daughter – Alphonse is *not* my favourite name.' She showed me a painting by Landseer of her grandmother, the Duchess of Abercorn, a lady who had fourteen children, only one of whom died young, and who herself lived to be ninety-four. It showed a beautiful young lady in Spanish costume – presumably fancy dress worn for some social occasion, or specifically for the artist. There were also photographs of the Princess's husband. They showed a handsome smiling man, who was very believably once the boy who ran away from

Eton to enlist at seventeen in the First World War, when, of course, he was too young. He also enlisted in the Second World War when he was really too old, but survived the Italian campaign with some elan. 'He simply loved every minute of it,' recalled his widow. 'He looked fifteen years younger when he came home.'

Showing me around the outside of the house, the Princess put on a broad-brimmed straw hat with the crown missing; 'I should like to take the credit for that idea – I'm full of ideas – and it does help to keep the head cool, but I'm afraid Winky did that. He'll chew anything. However, I have done many things – for example every single thing in this garden I planted with my own hands.'

The Conway crest on the gates and the four Seymour stone heads on the parapet were immediately noticeable. The heads were now getting weatherbeaten, though the ear-rings worn by the Seymours were still visible. The lead statue in the middle of the lake was attractive, but the pool itself was continuing to leak and the Princess knew that she would have to have something done about it.

But she was more interested at that point in showing me the terrace, created at the front of the house by demolishing all the fourteen green-houses, together with their protruding nettles. And she was very proud of the cottage adjoining the house, which had also been stripped of intrusive growths and faced with Portuguese laurel bushes which had now grown so large they must be pruned in order that the housekeeping staff in the cottage might see out of their own windows.

At one extreme end of the garden, opposite the very end of the cottage which is built alongside the house, red maize and lilac had been planted and were now rather dominant; but the Princess claimed that fortunately they were never seen, because people never gravitated that far – they just had a cool drink and flopped into a seat by the house. 'I will get it into better shape eventually,' predicted the energetic octogenarian, who herself plainly had little liking for flopping, with or without a cool drink.

Asked how she spends her time in her mid-eighties, the Princess has been apt to say: 'I am the gardener here; that's my job.'

What was formerly a small mountain of stones, weeds and rubbish taken from the greenhouses, is now a flower bed, and a testimony to her words on the occasion I spoke to her. The Princess smiled at the thought that she now spent a lot of time taking *out* the stones that she once spent so much time throwing *in*. The work had been largely in her hands rather than her husband's, she explained, because he didn't know about gardens. The French and Belgians didn't take any interest and pride in gardens – something to do with the nature of the soil over there, perhaps. Her husband had once asked, 'What are those white things in the hedge?' She had told him they were snowdrops, one of the commonest of flowers.

The Princess evidently believed that her efforts had been thoroughly worthwhile. 'Looking at it all used to be so awful. Now my garden is absolutely famous. It's been featured in all the *Vogues* and the *Harper's Bazaars*.'

It had also served its purpose as a local attraction for charity. 'I do everything they ask me,' said the Princess of her outside activities. 'We had the garden open two times last week, for instance; once for the Ladies Luncheon Club, the other time for the church, and we have had eighty people each time. I will do everything for Arrow or Alcester, nothing for Bangla Desh or the Middle East. Charity begins at home as far as I am concerned. I do the church flowers once a month. Endless bring and buys. I think they have forgotten about me being a Princess now. They accept me. They were a bit stunned at first; now I am one of the Alcesterites. It has never occurred to me to involve myself in general social activities.'

Insularity or concentration of effort? Perhaps a bit of both; and both understandable in a Princess of eighty-three.

In any case, her garden and her frequent trips to London kept her busy, she said. She always drove herself to London. In fact she drove herself everywhere, hadn't been on a train for years. She loved driving and she loved seeing her 'chums' in London.

'I am eighty-three,' she said, paused and added, 'I think. I don't mind ages – great mistake. I take the dog for two walks a day because I like walking. I work in the garden most of the time. Never think about age. Some people do think about it a lot – especially men. Mistake. They think of their ages and they *believe* it. Wrong! They are always thinking about the age they will be next birthday, and they *become* it. It is a great mistake – keep healthy! Yes, I have got people to cut the grass, but I have created the garden completely. There are four acres of grass to cut, and so a man spends his time cutting grass. We have got every sort of machine, all of which are breaking down. I never stop pulling at weeds. But I have already made the garden and it is rather boring now. The exciting part is planning and creating it; I live for nothing else really. Then it is finished and I am rather bored with it.' She paused and then brightened up. 'I have got to cut down a lot of things I have planted because it is getting overgrown. I think, "How can I eliminate work?" But things grow. I have now got to cut down a lot of trees I have planted.' She sounded quite cheerful again.

The bushes in front of the cottage windows, she said happily, would have to be cut back for sure. She told herself she didn't want to spend her life 'upside down in a garden'. But in practice she was always working on something.

With frequent visits from her grandchildren, parties at the Kitchen Garden House, and her shifts as a guide at Ragley Hall on Bank Holidays, the Princess still lived a full life: an aristocrat of the past on good working terms with the present. When I noticed that she always kept her back door locked, though the whole garden stood within the high estate walls, I wondered if she felt the outside world to be hostile. 'No. It was just that Winky got out once for five weeks in Badger's Wood, so I always keep the door locked now so no one can open it and let her out again by accident.'

The future of the big Halls like Ragley was one subject that tended to make the Princess momentarily pensive.

'Let's not think,' she said emphatically, showing me out, 'beyond next week. It is so appalling. Better not think about it. I admire my son-in-law enormously. Whatever happens, he never gives up, he is always cheerful. Whatever it is – rates, bills – he believes he will get through it. And if you think like that, you *do*, you *do*.'

On the whole, the Princess has been proved right. But there have been some bright schemes for the rejuvenation of Ragley that have never borne fruit.

13
The Very
Idea

THE PLANS for a great international sporting centre beside Ragley lake, financed with American cash, never did become reality, but the people of Ragley and its neighbourhood were well able to contain their disappointment.

The complex was to have included two 18-hole golf courses. There would have been an enormous club house with a hundred bedrooms, and members and their jet-set guests would have had the benefit of an expensive swimming pool, twelve tennis courts and sixteen squash courts.

Though undoubtedly one of the most radical cash-raising ideas to have surfaced in Ragley's battle for survival, it never materialized, because at the eleventh hour the would-be financial backers decided their money would be better spent elsewhere.

'I think rightly so,' Lord Hertford will say today with the benefit of hindsight. 'I was slightly sad at the time from a financial point of view, because it would have made us enormously rich. But I think, looking back on it, that I am extremely glad we haven't got it. It would have spoiled the place to a great extent.'

An aristocrat with a hall and estate he wants to preserve must always be on the look out for new ideas that will bring in large sums of money. But he must also be cautious about changing the character of his estate, for it is in order to preserve it as it is that he really needs the money – and it is the character of the place which so fascinates the ticket-buying public.

Visitors to Ragley all appeared to like the Hall because it was 'lived in' or 'the real thing'. It is doubtful whether they would have responded so well to a Lord who had become in effect nothing more than a superior sort of fairground barker.

The magnificent sporting centre that never materialized was an idea that took seed in the 1960s, when London in particular, and Britain in general, was 'swinging' for the benefit of foreign visitors, who regarded it as the height of international chic. The centre would not actually have been visible from any window of Ragley Hall – Lord Hertford saw to that – and at the time there were other factors which made a deal look distinctly possible. The would-be investors were a subsidiary of an international shipping line and quite reputable. They had just sold a ship and wanted to invest the money elsewhere. The money was actually ready and available. Yet today Lord Hertford will cheerfully admit that the thought of all those jet-set amenities at Ragley filled him with horror.

'But they offered me such an enormous amount for the Park that it would have been silly to say no to it,' he admitted.

In the end he didn't have to say no. The would-be backers decided that their money would show a greater return if it were invested in a large private hospital in London. They went ahead with this, while Lord Hertford sincerely assured them that there were absolutely no hard feelings.

Less revolutionary ideas have been considered in continuous procession. 'I always look at everything,' Lord Hertford told me.

Ideas for raising cash that do not entail wholesale alterations are especially favoured. Letting out the Great Hall for events, either organized by outside bodies or self-generated, is a particular favourite. One of the most successful exhibitions in the enormous, yet somehow warmly intimate, Great Hall was the exhibition of copies of royal jewels from all over the world. An American had put together the collection, called Crown Jewels of the World, over many years. It included almost everything from replicas of the British Crown Jewels to the Shah of Persia's Crown. The public flocked to Ragley to see it. Picture exhibitions in the Great Hall have not been quite so successful. One, at which visitors were offered champagne as well as a view of the pictures for £10, was described by Lord Hertford as 'a big flop'. In retrospect, he thought a meal should have been provided too. Ragley continues to be the venue for art shows and once, when I was visiting, preparations were being made in the Great Hall for an exhibition of pictures by people in prison, put on by the charitable Burnbake Trust in whose work Lord Hertford has taken an interest. There are concerts, readings, dinners and dances. Judi Dench and six other actors once gave a

Shakespearean evening in aid of a cancer appeal. Then there was a concert of music thought to be appropriate to a stately home designed in 1680. This pleased the customers, though the feelings of the proprietor himself were mixed: 'I think Mozart is perfection. I don't really recognize music as being *there* before Handel. Before that, they made curious noises.' Fortunately the public did not agree.

Britannia, in the shape of a magnificent medallion by James Gibbs, circa 1750, has often looked down from the ceiling of the Great Hall upon highly commercial enterprises, though many have had a charitable element. A new motor car, produced by a local engineering firm, was given its launch there: it was an invalid car.

'If I am letting the Great Hall just for an evening, I would let it for almost anything,' said Lord Hertford. 'I mean anything that won't do any harm. The only time we have had actual damage was when we had a display of – not clog dancing, what's it called? – Morris Dancing. They stamped so hard that although there was a dance floor laid in the hall, they cracked a great many of the paving stones. Morris dancers are out! The stones are still cracked. I mended about thirty of them because a local architect, who is a friend of mine, managed to find the correct stone, which is quite rare.'

The estate as a whole offers many more venues, at least in theory, than the Great Hall and numerous ideas have been tried. In his younger days, Lord Hertford and the Cambridge University Water Skiing Team used to give displays of water skiing, until the 8th Marquess came to the conclusion that (a) he was getting older and (b) everyone in the Midlands who wanted to see him fall into his own lake had already done so. 'It had ceased,' he recalled, expressing the nub of his perennial problem, 'to be *new*.'

The idea of polo was not tried until 1982. Lord Hertford had not been terribly keen, doubting that it would prove a sufficiently popular attraction: 'If you got the Prince of Wales, it would be attractive and if you didn't, it wouldn't.' Freefall parachuting has been tried several times and so have hot air balloons – 'a most awful bore, because they take so long to go up.' Donkey derbies and pig roasts (oxen take rather too long to cook) have been held too. Pony rides did not attract enough daring customers. Several horse shows had varying responses, largely depending on the weather, and took too much organization. The Ragley Horse Trials, organized by the local hunt in April or May, emerged as the one regular equine feature of Ragley. As for the motor cycle scrambles in the corner of the Park, they were a much bigger success with the public than they were with the neighbours. Though there weren't any neighbours within half a mile, those who were within earshot at greater range complained that their Sunday afternoon peace and quiet was being ruined. The motor cycle scrambles were discontinued to pacify the neighbours at nearby Wixford.

What about a pop concert? Theoretically a very large crowd of young people could be absorbed in the mile-wide stretch of land that lies between Ragley Hall and the main gates; but the idea has not met with aristocratic approval. 'I have slightly avoided pop groups. I am afraid of getting windows broken, or something. Ten thousand young people camping in the garden would not leave it looking very good. But apart from that, there is nothing I would not do if I thought it was leading to the making of money and would leave the place looking respectable the next day.'

I felt I had to challenge this sweeping blueprint for survival: what about a Nazi rally, for instance?

'Ah! I think I am covered there, because the place would *not* look the same the next day! A lot of people who feel as I do would come and break the place up. I would prefer not to let Ragley for any political rally, but I would not mind fund-raising events for political parties, for instance.'

It is unlikely that Lord Hertford would discriminate between political parties. He is still a member of the Conservative Party, and sits on the Conservative benches in the House of Lords when he goes there on his visits to London, about twice a month. But he is hardly a fanatical ideologue.

When I tackled him on the subject, he had to rack his brains to remember the last time he had spoken in the House of Lords, and then admitted cheerfully that it was on a matter of direct relevance to Ragley. He had moved an amendment to the Heritage Bill. This was the bill that set up the National Heritage Fund, under which the Government can accept works of art in lieu of death duties (now capital transfer taxes); the fund, in effect, meeting the liability on behalf of the stately estate. The bill meant that people like Lord Hertford's heir, the Earl of Yarmouth, could agree to give the Government all the Reynoldses instead of cash; and that, unless a museum wanted them, the Minister *could* allow the paintings to stay physically where they were, though they became the property of the

Government. Lord Hertford's amendment, which amounted to another idea for keeping Ragley and other great houses viable, was that the Minister *should* (rather than merely *could*) allow the pictures to stay where they were, unless experts advised they should go to a museum. Lord Hertford, who faced a formidable museum lobby, did not get this particular liferaft to float.

One of the more large-scale ideas which has borne fruit and worked successfully is the Adventure Park, located discreetly out of the sight of the Hall behind trees. The idea is simple, cheap and popular; and, in the view of both the owner of the Hall and of the public, has not spoiled the character of Ragley.

When I first saw it, down the hill to the south of the front entrance to the Hall, Carl Couchman, the eleven-year-old son of a Birmingham telephone engineer and his wife, was just trying the seventy-five-foot walkway, twenty feet above ground. He decided it was a little too difficult for him and hesitated when it came to stepping on to splats separated by about three feet of empty air.

'If the weather is nice there is plenty for children to do here,' said his mother. 'I don't think that even this apparatus is too advanced, because they can always come down if they can't do it. Children have got their own sense. It's a good idea not to let them in without adults, but the whole thing is an ideal way of keeping children out of mischief. I like this sort of atmosphere. Ragley hasn't got too many commercial aspects; that's why we like it.'

What is has got, in the Adventure Park, is the walkway; a stockaded fort that can be stormed by cowboys or Indians of immature years; a sort of sangar or frontier-post observation tower; a rope which swings over a log; an air bed for bouncing on; a stockaded fence for climbing; a log see-saw, a rope bridge and various hollow tree trunks. There is also (for an extra admission charge) the Ragley Maze, which has a typically shrewd deal to encourage participation: one child is admitted free when accompanied by two adults, while grannies and grandads get in at half price.

The Adventure Park is virtually all constructed from Ragley's own timber, involving the estate only in the expense of cutting and installing it. When I visited the Adventure Park shop for the first time, one blazing August, Mrs Mildred Hayes was behind the counter. Mrs Hayes is the wife of Arthur Hayes, who used to be the warden of the Adventure Park before a slight heart attack forced him into semi-retirement. But his illness had not, I was to discover, entirely divorced him from the goings on at the Adventure Park.

'The place is now run by a gentleman called Mr Edwards,' said Mildred Hayes. 'We have been here for five years. We ran it for three years, up till two years ago, when my husband had his heart attack. We only work weekends now, during July and August. Otherwise Mr Edwards does it all by himself. It's only open in the afternoons, except in July and August.'

The Hayes family were recruited to the Ragley workforce in the usual way. Mrs Lawrence, Lord Hertford's alert secretary, happened to be in a pub in Evesham and she told the landlady that she was looking for someone to run the Adventure Park. 'Why don't you ask Mr Hayes?' suggested the landlady. Arthur Hayes happened to be in the pub at the right time.

'We thoroughly enjoy working here,' said Mildred Hayes. 'You couldn't ask for nicer people. I think it's absolutely super, working at a stately home. When you work for the gentry, if they are really gentry, they make you feel one of them. Lord Hertford comes every day to say, "How are you?" and to see if we want anything, and we have been invited to the parties at Christmas. He has very much got his workers at heart.'

At this point Mildred Hayes had to break off to tell her grandson, Nicholas, that he would have to find another penny for some sweets he had just bought from the shop. He must pay the full price. 'He has got to learn you have to pay for things in this life,' explained Mildred Hayes. Then she had to deal with another young helper, who reckoned he needed two pieces of sticking plaster for his fingers, because he had cut himself on the motor bikes. 'I have to teach the customers and show them what to do, don't I?' insisted the spirited ten-year-old.

This lad turned out to be Baron, the son of the man who runs the amusements side of the Adventure Park; and the motor cycles themselves were the latest idea of his father, Robert Laight. There were four machines, Japanese 50cc Yamahas made especially for children. Robert Laight's youngest son, aged five, was – his proud father maintained – fully capable of riding them.

Robert Laight, a man in his thirties, was originally a plumber. But he married the daughter of a showman. It turned his life to more flamboyant but less secure pastures. At the time I met him, he had been on the estate for five years, carrying on a family tradition. His family had been on the estate for nearly eighty years, and his father, Frank Laight, was doing general work on the estate before Robert was born. His uncle Bill was a gamekeeper on the estate in the days when it could still afford the luxury of multiple gamekeepers. When Robert's father married, he moved away from Ragley to work at a factory in Redditch, and Robert was born at a place nearby called Headless Cross.

After his own marriage to a showman's daughter, Scheherezanne, he went travelling with the family fairground. It was his first contact with show business: travelling from town to town, and site to site, with a fair.

The world of Ragley and the world of a travelling showman did indeed seem miles apart, confessed Robert Laight. 'Yes, and this has suited me better, being here at Ragley. I couldn't seem to make a go of it in a fairground. I could not seem to find good places to go to. When you marry into the fairground circle, normally your in-laws and your parents help you along. It is like a street market: people in the same line year in, year out. I, not being from the same background, didn't have anyone to give me a good grounding, so I could not make it pay. My father-in-law settled down in the plant-hire business and gave all his fairs up. We went into it blind, and we were doing it for five years.'

Then the Ragley grapevine triumphed again. Patrick Kenyon, the man who then held the Ragley concession for amusements, didn't actually have the necessary equipment to make a success of the concession. Robert Laight had a roundabout and a Lunarland amusement tent; and he had begun to feel the need to have a concession on a permenent site. Kenyon knew Laight because both men were plumbers by trade, and soon Robert Laight took over the concession himself. As a result of such machinations Ragley's Adventure Park amusements centre has now got two Lunarworlds, a roundabout, swing boats and the four motor bikes.

What is and what is not acceptable in an amusement park at a stately home is obviously a matter of fine negotiation between the presiding aristocrat and the concessionaire.

'The motor cycles were my idea. But I always consult Lord Hertford,' said Robert Laight. 'If there is anything new, I check with him first. He is normally in agreement if he thinks it will attract more people to the park. I have got a seven-year agreement with him starting next year; we are just signing it. I don't think His Lordship would like us to have all the things they have at some other stately homes. He wants to keep it more a *stately* stately home.'

Robert Laight, showman and unlikely adjunct of Ragley, thought his present life was the best of both worlds. He had a house in a nearby town 'next door to the pub', but had plenty of country air in the course of his job. Apart from his connection with Ragley, he rented out Space Invader machines to a number of public houses in the area and was on call for their repair and maintenance. This was in addition to the four Space Invader machines in his own amusements centre at Ragley. In the winters, he repaired and renovated his own machines. The winter after he brought the children's motor cycles to Ragley he spent levelling off the ground for a proper track. He did most of the work himself, he said, though his wife often helped out with the amusements generally.

'I would be content to be here for the rest of my life,' he admitted cheerfully, 'provided the living was adequate. The estate has got its hold. It is nice to feel part of it. Mind you, I enjoy the town life; I play squash and football. But I like work, I get a lot of pleasure out of it. I would sooner be down here working than sitting at home. Fortunately, my wife is as keen as I am. She enjoys looking after the Lunarlands or the paybox. She likes to be part of the estate, too, and she likes being in one place. We still do all the fêtes and galas with the Lunarland in the summer. We have the best of both worlds – some sort of security, yet we are free agents.'

And who keeps an eye on the amusements centre when Robert Laight is keeping an eye on the other areas of his life? On the first day I paid a visit it was Arthur Hayes, the husband of the lady standing-in at the shop. He was manning the desk for changing money and seeing that the visiting lads did not get too excited over the Space Invader machines.

But the Adventure Park is probably about as far as the family at the Hall will go in the direction of commercialism – though, no doubt, hopeful people will carry on suggesting more and more bright and potentially lucrative schemes.

'Ragley,' said Lord Hertford, 'has been open to the public for twenty-five years. If you want greater crowds you have to have something *extra*, some reason for them to come *this* week rather than leave it until next year. You need something new. It gets increasingly hard to think of what.'

Could he, I asked, ever follow some of his more commercially minded aristocratic friends. 'He is a very, very good organizer,' remarked Lord

Hertford of one. 'He runs his place very efficiently, but he employs three hundred and fifty people. *I* want to preserve Ragley very much as it is. But if I could find a way of making a lot of money without spoiling the place, I would.'

Ragley's owner paused pensively. 'I don't think it's impossible to find such a scheme, but I haven't come up with the right idea yet.'

Such is the buoyancy and flexibility needed by a traditionalist who hopes at least to force a draw in his contest with modern conditions. He needs continually to be open to new ideas, even if he has to reject nine out of ten with a politely repressed shudder. And, as Lord at the Hall, he has to consider how his revenue-raising schemes will affect the whole neighbour-hood, bound to it as he is by many strands of fraternity which do not exist in the same way in towns.

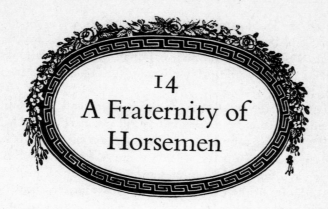

14
A Fraternity of Horsemen

I N THE TINY VILLAGE of Dunnington, one of those within the Ragley boundaries, there stands the Forge. A red brick building rather like a village school in miniature, it is set back from the road and sheltered by a line of fir trees. Villagers in the half-timbered cottages opposite can hardly see it, a fact which is symbolic.

Once the blacksmith at the Forge could have made his entire living from shoeing the horses of the Ragley estate. No more. The Forge, in modern times, has almost disappeared from view as an institution.

Harry Green, the blacksmith and farrier, supposed that today he had no more than twenty customers who wanted horses shod. 'Mostly riding schools, pony clubs and farmers,' he explained. 'There *is* a demand for shoeing, you could work at it day and night; but I have a bad back as it happens and it doesn't suit me to. I do more general ironwork now, but at one time I used to do shoeing all day.'

In Harry Green, a balding man in his early fifties, I found a veteran of an art once thought to be dying. In the 'Swinging Sixties' when jobs in industry were easy to get and wages high, young men were not especially keen to do the dirty job of beating horse shoes out of red hot metal and fastening them to the hooves of the horses with nails. Now young men are rather keener to learn the crafts of the blacksmith. But then, having learned it, they are apt to leave a forge like Dunnington's very soon after their apprenticeship, so that they can set up on their own in more prosperous areas – leaving little villages like those around Ragley still short of farriers as well as men who can do general blacksmithing work.

'There are stacks of farriers about, most of them young,' said Harry Green, whose blackened hands and grease-stained clothes are the hallmark of his trade. 'But there are not many of them who do general blacksmithing as well. I do quite a bit of that. I have just done quite a range of iron park railings.'

The lifestyle of Harry Green, farrier and general blacksmith, is not lavish. He drives around the surrounding villages in a battered Morris 1000 van, twelve years old, and with 134,000 miles on the clock. It has a portable forge in the back – a sort of safe made of firebricks, with the door always open and with a blow torch fed by a cylinder of propane.

'The economics of the business,' said Ragley's farrier, showing me this vehicle with a sort of masochistic pride, 'aren't such that you can get a new vehicle. It is a matter of enjoying your job and just ticking over financially. You will never make a fortune. I have tried working all hours, and you just lay yourself up. I used to work from six in the morning till twelve at night, every day. I didn't make a lot of money, because you're never able to charge what the job is really worth. It's the opinion people have of blacksmiths. And there's always someone around somewhere who'll cut the price down. We've never got together and fixed a price. We aren't that sort of craft. There is an association of us, but it is poorly attended. It all boils down in the end to job satisfaction. You just carry on and get a living. Some people would think I am a fool to say it, but that is how I feel.'

It is a feeling that, whatever its rights and wrongs, has served Ragley well. Harry Green has a farming background, which perhaps predisposed him to life in the vicinity of a great estate. His father worked on a farm before going into a factory and Harry, who was born at Web Heath, near Redditch, went to work on a farm when he left village school. He used to take the farm horses to the forge and that was how he became interested in farriering as a craft. Later he rented a village forge at Redditch and went to work for himself, but the building was demolished to make way for Redditch New Town. Fortunately the forge at Dunnington became vacant and he was able to rent that. 'A very picturesque building, I think –a picture in itself,' he will say proudly.

It is perhaps just as well that there are advantages other than the strictly economic. At the time I spoke to him, Harry Green was charging £10.50 for a set of shoes. To do a good job, he reckoned that a set of shoes took half an hour to make and another hour to fit, and that didn't include travelling time. Some farmers bought the shoes and simply fitted them, he said, turning down the corners of his mouth a trifle. He didn't believe in that.

'Wherever you go, every horse is different,' he maintained. 'The shoes should be made to fit.'

Horses can differ in temper as well as in the size of their feet. This is often proved on his visits to the Ragley farms, which are sometimes made as frequently as once a fortnight, though more usually once a month in winter and once every six weeks in the summer.

The same applies to the horses at Ragley Hall itself, who keep the farrier busy on his regular visits. 'That big black one, Petrello, is a bit nervous and will jump away from you. The others are more quiet,' said Harry Green. 'They all have their own personalities.'

The Dunnington farrier gets more work at Ragley Hall than he would do from many aristocratic homes, for at Ragley the horse is still king. Lord Hertford and his family build their lives around horses. They have no fewer than six horses and a pony.

Indeed, standing in the rather grand James Wyatt stables of Ragley it would almost be possible to imagine that the horse was still the dominant mode of transport. This aristocratic animal is still very much favoured on the estate, even if outside it Lord Hertford prefers his Japanese estate car and Lady Hertford her collector's-item sports car, a Triumph Stag, with a powerful exhaust which heralds its approach well in advance.

The whole of Lord Hertford's family ride: it is an activity all the family share, together with tennis and swimming. Lady Hertford brusquely dismisses the saddle as a necessary part of riding, and goes bareback. She was doing so one summer morning when I saw her about to take a morning ride with Lord Hertford (combining business with pleasure, since a horse is the best and quickest way of keeping an eye on all the operations on the estate, from the farms to the Adventure Park).

'I *prefer* riding without a saddle,' said Lady Hertford as she climbed on to Rocket, the twelve-year-old she had not ridden since the spring. 'A saddle between you and the horse is such an artificial thing. When you start to ride a horse it is better to ride like this, then you get together with the horse, rather than being part of some artificial device.'

Another reason why Lady Hertford is used to riding bareback is that her mother always made her ride bareback as a child, after a cousin got thrown from a horse.

'She was riding side-saddle,' explained Lady Hertford. 'Her horse threw her and her foot got caught in a stirrup. As horses always do, that one pulled for home with the girl being dragged along like some ghastly doll. Her head was slammed against the gatepost and she was killed. When I inherited her pony, when I was sixteen, my mother said I could ride, but could never have a saddle. So for a long time I didn't. That was why I became quite accustomed to riding without one.'

One needs to be tough for the family sport of hunting, and there is no lack of mettle in the family. Lord Hertford started riding at the age of one and claims to remember hunting when he was five years old, with the under-groom running beside his Shetland pony. 'It is something I have done almost literally all my life. I love it and my wife loves it and so do all the children. It is quite a family day out when we go out together on horses, all six of us. In theory I hunt every Saturday from October till March, but in practice not every one because other things can happen to prevent one.'

The deterrents are rarely anti-blood sports groups. Once, when there was a meeting of a Warwickshire hunt at Ragley, there was advance warning on the grapevine of some sort of demonstration.

'But,' recalled Lord Hertford, 'there was a splendid woman who stood at the gates. When a bus full of people pulled up, looking more like anti-blood sports demonstrators than sporting types, she stopped them and asked them if they had been invited to come. They looked rather surprised and said, "No." And she said, "Surely you realize Ragley Park is private property?" Fortunately they didn't observe the enormous signs saying *Open to the Public*, so they said, "Oh, sorry!" and drove meekly away. We thought it terribly funny. They were tough demonstrators armed with staves and sticks and things to make noises with. But this one splendid lady in tweeds sent them away.'

Usually the family hunt with the Warwickshire hounds, all over the county and sometimes over Ragley itself. 'Hunting people are absolutely our type,' Lord Hertford told me one morning as he set off for his usual ride, this time on the nervous Petrello, thirteen years old and known in the family as the 'spare wheel', because he is most likely to be ridden when other horses are lame or otherwise unavailable. 'Most of our friends are people we hunt with. It is a wide cross-section of Warwickshire society

– landowners, farmers and people who work in Birmingham but live in Warwickshire.'

Sometimes hunting acquaintances are not quite sure who Lord and Lady Hertford are. Lord Hertford remembers one 'splendid lady' who asked him, at the time he was a partner in a Fleet Street public relations firm, 'And what do you do?'

'I work in Fleet Street.'

'Oh, how marvellous for you to come all this way for your hunting.'

Recalling the incident, Lord Hertford will say, 'I didn't like to point out that I had reasons other than hunting for coming to Warwickshire. But I would have come up just for the hunt, as a matter of fact.'

Against such enthusiasm, the occasional fits of temperament of the horses, and the occasional spill, tend to be dismissed at the Hall with a remarkable stoicism.

'We have *all* had all sorts of falls,' reported Lord Hertford with the lightest of laughs. 'But, touch wood, we have been quite lucky as far as accidents are concerned. I broke my wrist hunting a few years ago, but it got better; and anyway I went out hunting with my right arm in a sling. That went on for a few weeks. My wife had a nasty fall and damaged her neck and spine quite badly. It put her out for a couple of months, and she had to spend a month in bed, but she thought it was just bad luck.'

What enthusiasm cannot achieve at Ragley is overcome by sheer economic logic. Once there were four or five grooms employed to train, exercise and clean the horses. Today there is only one. Few people still alive can recall the good old days.

I was able to find one man living as a retired groom in a Ragley cottage who, at eighty-three, still remembered the age when grooms were prolific. This was not at Ragley itself, however. Bertie Brass came to Ragley as a groom at the time when Lord and Lady Hertford were still scrubbing the floors themselves in their efforts to restore the Hall, and he left in 1964, before the peak of Ragley's revival. A tall man who had obviously been handsome in his youth but who was now a rather saddened widower, he was living in a half-timbered cottage in Arrow. The building was of some historic interest – the old bread oven, and the well in the front garden from which village people got their water, are still visible and shown proudly to interested visitors.

But when Bertie Brass first came to Ragley as groom, he frankly didn't think much of the place. It was not just that there were only three horses, whereas he had usually dealt with more than that in his varied career. It was the lack of staff and the general air of struggle that pervaded the place.

'It was a bit of a let-down when I came to Ragley and found no one to open the gates,' he admitted. 'In those days, when I was at the Rothschild's, you had people to open the gates for you. Up here you had to do it for yourself. If you went in with a car, you had to hang about waiting for someone to open the gates. It was like being in prison, was Ragley, at that time.'

To a man used to tending lots of horses and to the ways of the very, very comfortably rich, the tribulations of Ragley were, possibly, more noticeable.

'I've been in private service all my life,' said Bertie Brass. 'I have been in the service of Princess Mary, the Princess Royal at Goldsborough, Yorkshire; and I was with Lord Rosebery at Mentmore. I was at the Rothschild's place at Wing. I got the stables built at Mentmore. There were twenty-seven grooms there and at Princess Mary's in the winter we had twenty-seven single and eight married grooms.'

Such a background is understandably quite likely to make any groom fastidious about his future places of work. He has many stories to tell about top people, even Royalty. The Irish people gave the Princess Mary a grey horse called Portumna as a wedding present. Because crowds used to collect everywhere she went, she rode the horse rather less than Bertie Brass did. When they went out riding together they had to take to the woods in the hope of not being spotted. Then there was the then Prince of Wales, later King Edward VIII, and even later the *abdicated* King Edward VIII. He used to visit the Princess Mary, go into the local pub, start drawing pints of beer and then give them away to all and sundry. The landlord went around wringing his hands and saying, 'But who is going to pay for all this?' Possibly out of genuine apprehension and possibly to assist the joke, since someone always paid in the end, albeit not the Prince of Wales.

The Brass family had been horse fanatics for much longer than one generation. Bertie Brass's father was a trainer of steeplechasers in Yorkshire, who took his young son away from his first groom's job because, he said, he wasn't getting enough experience of riding. Bertie went to another job in Yorkshire, where he worked from seven in the morning till midnight training horses, sometimes rogue racehorses which hadn't come up to scratch for racing and therefore had to be made ready for service in the Army. He was still not out of his teens when he had a tumble while working for a banking family. He was jumping a hedge when the horse fell and did two or three somersaults over its rider.

'I was off work two years and the doctor said I would never work again. But I met a pal of mine and he said there was someone needed at Princess Mary's, and not to say anything about being sick. I went there as nags-man, to ride anything.'

Still in his early twenties, he stayed with Princess Mary three years. Then he was employed by a horse-dealer, which, in retrospect, he looked upon as a mistake brought about by ironical pressure of circumstances: 'I didn't want to go there. I hadn't worked for a dealer in all my life and I wouldn't work for one again. But he kept coming into the area, pester-ing me to go to him. Our head man found out that he kept coming after me, said I was after another job and gave me my notice. I went there and then. I stayed three years with the dealer. Then he went bankrupt.'

It was hard work during those three years with the recklessly busy dealer. They would arrive together in Ireland at six o'clock in the morn-ing and buy horses before their competitors were out of bed. They bought a dozen at a time, and brought them back to England by boat. While they were catching up on their lost sleep, the horses were being groomed, ready to be hunted the very next day. If they didn't sell within three weeks, they went as Troopers in the British Army.

After financial difficulties curtailed this busy enterprise, Bertie Brass moved to Sussex, working for a hunt master who had only three horses. He stayed there nine years, but then got asthma so badly that his doctor advised him to go back to the Midlands – somewhat controversial advice in those days, when no one had thought of smoke-free zones, certainly not in the Midlands of England.

The next employer in the long chain that fashioned Bertie Brass's high standards was a tycoon who, with the rest of his family, wanted to be taught to hunt. He was seventy-five at the time and hadn't been on a horse in his life.

'So,' Bertie Brass recalled, 'I taught them to ride and they went hunting. The old man was jumping five-barred gates by the time I'd finished with him. He would always jump a five-barred gate after hunting, just to show them.'

But it was Bertie Brass, not his employer, who finally broke a thigh.

He got compensation and, for a most tedious and undignified period, worked at a sitting-down job in a boot factory. Bored stiff, he spent much of his time looking out of the windows and thinking of horses. A businessman relative of his former employer rescued him with another groom's job once he had become physically fit again.

His job was 'to take his daughter to school and learn her to ride'. But the gentleman proved, as Bertie Brass put it, 'very fussy – I always had to take her to school in a big car. I couldn't take her in a small one. I had to go to the works and get a Humber Super Snipe or a Jaguar.'

When the young lady became of age and married, there came the move to Ragley. This was on the suggestion of the young lady herself. Apparently Bertie Brass at first took some persuading: 'My old employer had always bought two of everything. If you wanted a horse, he would buy two. If he bought a Land Rover, he bought two. That was not so at Ragley.' Indeed it was not, for at that time Lord and Lady Hertford were fighting every inch of the way to keep Ragley alive, when many people believed that the days of the great estate were over. To a man of Bertie Brass's august standards, the principal advantage of working at Ragley was that he was able to introduce his own daughter to riding. She rapidly took to hunting, met an agricultural machinery manufacturer in the process, and added to the twentieth century's social mobility by marrying him. 'No, she never minded me being a groom,' said Bertie Brass, 'because it meant she could always ride a horse.'

In spite of Lord Hertford's love of horses, to Bertie Brass the 8th Marquess was a 'modern man' rather than a sportsman. 'He's got it all worked out. He is very clever. He has made it in the end. But I liked the old times myself. I have been paid for everything I have done and I have enjoyed myself. I don't think I would enjoy myself today. I think things changed after the Second World War. Have I liked being a servant of aristocrats for much of my life? I have been more or less like one myself. I have always had a well-paid job, and everything I wanted. Yes, it was a bit of a let-down when I came to Ragley and found no one to open the gates; but no one has servants these days. I have had a good life. I don't think anyone had any better. I have been able to hunt five or six days a week. Look at what that would cost today.'

As he made me a cup of tea in a traditional earthenware teapot, it was very obvious that Bertie Brass was not greatly in love with 'today'. Stable work was very different from what it had been, he said. There was no more plaiting work done to decorate the doorways and they didn't groom horses like they used to. He used to have to clean the horse three times – the quarters, the head and then the body. Today they just took the rug off and went all the way down the horse, and that was that.

Of course, he said, he supposed he and his contemporaries were fussy. A horse had to have warm water when it came back from hunting. That was all done away with now. The horses had to have gruel at one time and now that had been done away with too. They weren't so particular about exercise, either. Nowadays a groom would take three or four horses at once for their exercise, but in his time he had seen six huntsmen to one horse.

'Men,' he reflected, 'were cheap in those days, but a horse cost £26.'

I found some of the same nostalgic spirit when I went to the Ragley stables and discovered the present – and sole – groom helping Anne, the youngest member of Lord Hertford's family, to saddle up for her morning ride. It was a far from easy process, as the horse got nervous, fell on the concrete of the stableyard, and had to be walked very gently up and down by Phil Roberts before it became calm.

'In the old days I would imagine there would be five grooms,' said Phil Roberts wryly. 'Now there is only myself. But it is still a lot easier working here than in the Army – not having to get up at five o'clock, for a start!'

Phil Roberts, a carrot-haired unmarried man with a Midlands background and a Jack Russell dog called Judy, was in the Army for twelve years. This was after a boyhood in Leicester and Wolverhampton and a three-year stint working for a construction company in Thailand. It was in the Army he gained his love of horses. He was in the Blues and Royals, the élite regiment of the Household Division – soldiers who traditionally perform guard duties for the Royal Family. He spent six of his twelve Army years with an armoured regiment in Germany and Northern Ireland, the other six years as a Troop Sergeant working with horses.

Such a man was a natural for Ragley – a bachelor with little appetite for the cinema or other cultural pursuits, who liked working on his own and enjoyed the isolated freedom of his own flat above the stables. He lived in London for eight years while in the Army, but didn't miss it at all when he left it: 'Too many people. There's no peace and quiet, really. You couldn't get away.' He said he watched very little television, but went running three miles twice a week and played squash when he could find someone to play with. He was obviously a physical and uncomplicated man, who was apt, even in his spare time, to take his dog and mooch about a local paddock where they kept horses at grass.

The job of the sole groom at Ragley – who has extra help only in the hunting season – starts at between six-thirty and eight o'clock in the morning. First he mucks out the stables. This takes him three-quarters of an hour. Then he takes possibly two of the horses out for exercise, riding one and leading one. That will take him about an hour and a half (first he would have fed those horses left behind). On coming back, he will feed the two he has just taken out, and then exercise the remainder, again possibly two at a time, by riding or leading them round the estate. He will probably cross a couple of roads in the process, but there is never any urgent need to go outside the boundaries of the estate.

Lunch, in an hour's break, will consist of a cup of tea and a sandwich. There is no room for a heavy mid-day meal in the life of a modern groom – indeed, it is so often not the done thing among the countrymen of Ragley generally, that I almost came to the conclusion that if one saw someone there consuming lunch, it had to be either Lord or Lady Hertford or a paying visitor.

In the afternoons Phil Roberts will groom the horses, clean the stables again, and do any extra jobs that need doing, like varnishing the woodwork of the stables. The stables at Ragley almost dazzled the eye on the days I visited them: successive grooms tend to take pride in making the stables look spick and span their way, which is seldom that of their predecessors.

'When I took over, the first thing I did was to get the stables sorted out,' reported Phil Roberts. He used almost the exact words that his predecessor of many years ago, Bertie Brass, had used to me to describe how when he'd first taken over, he'd had all the plywood being used for stable dividers taken out and replaced with something much stronger.

Lord Hertford, said Phil Roberts, had put it to him that he might put the stables to rights, 'if he had time'. 'But ———it!' he commented enthusiastically, 'it was something to do when there wasn't a lot happening with the horses. I washed it down and stripped the old paint off and painted the ceiling and the walls. I have still got the doors to do. I have to finish the painting and get the carpenter to work on them. When it is quiet I spend an hour here and there on it. Next week, I shall have it all finished. Compared with the Army, it is a lot easier! You can please yourself as to what your next job is. I am more or less my own boss. I have got Lord Hertford's horses to look after, but I haven't got my own to look after at the same time.'

This comparative freedom of action is something highly valued by the sort of self-reliant fellow who is likely to adapt well to being almost certainly the sole groom on the surviving estates of the British aristocracy. It makes up for things like the lack of a tea-break in the afternoon, a privilege so beloved of the industrial shop floor. Phil Roberts said he worked straight through till five, when he went to his flat, ready to have his 'lunch' at six or seven o'clock in the evening. After the meal, he might pop down the road for a drink in Arrow, or he might be joined by his friend Bernard, who used to man the gate at Ragley and now tended to pop in for a drink with him two or three times a week. Otherwise he might take his dog Judy out for two or three hours rabbiting.

'She caught one last night,' is one of his proud boasts. Yet this nevertheless is a sideline. The centre of his existence – a fact which makes him well-suited to life at Ragley – is that animal which has survived as unexpectedly in an unsympathetic age as the aristocracy itself: the horse.

15
The
Contemporary
Gamekeeper

THE SHOOT is not quite what it was. In times beyond the memory of
those still living at Ragley, there were several gamekeepers employed by
the residing Marquess and a score of beaters from the estate ready, at the
tip of a cap, to beat the pheasants and drive the partridges over His Lordship's gun. There was not a sight of anything so plebeian as a businessman,
except perhaps a very well-behaved one as a guest of the Marquess. For
that he would have needed to be a good shot and well bred enough not to
commit any of the possible social solecisms, such as expecting hock rather
than port at lunch.

Today it is still possible to drum up a dozen beaters. But the 8th Marquess himself does not shoot; the only shoot over the Ragley estate is run
by an amalgam of Birmingham businessmen, professionals and local
farmers; and the single gamekeeper takes his pay cheque from, and doffs
his cap (if at all) to what is known, though without trans-Atlantic connota-
tions, as the Syndicate – not to the Marquess.

When I first met Ken Ward, it was at nine in the morning in his plain
brick-built cottage, a home rather different from the ivy-covered one now
occupied by the widow of his predecessor. The difference was, perhaps,
yet another sign of the times. He had just come back home for his breakfast. This always takes the form of either a cup of tea or coffee, and a slice
of home-made fruit cake. He had already been up over five hours, having
got up at three-forty a.m., a not unusual hour for him. It would have been
difficult to imagine him as the natural heir of Lady Chatterley's lover,
Mellors, D. H. Lawrence's celebrated gamekeeper who was helplessly

inferior to his master, except in his master's bed. It was true that Ken Ward was carrying the traditional badge of his now rare craft, a rifle; but the general aura was rather more of Ian Fleming's James Bond than Lawrence's Mellors. For a start, it was not a shotgun he was carrying but a Czech-made Brno .22 rifle, fitted with a silencer.

My townsman's innocence was affronted. 'Is that what you'd call a sporting sort of thing to use?'

'No, it isn't,' replied the compact, wiry and clear-eyed Ken Ward incisively. 'But I am a keeper; and my job isn't entirely being sporting. The gun is a tool of my trade. When I have got to kill something, I have got to kill it – not perhaps in the best sporting traditions, but kill it dead. That's to say a fox, a ferral cat, a stoat or a rabbit. With a silencer on it you can shoot close around young birds without causing them any disturbance.'

In such ways technology impinges on even the most traditional crafts. But though the constitution and the internal politics of the shoot over Ragley have changed tangibly with the years, and although unsporting silencers are now *de rigueur* if pests are to be eliminated without disturbing the painstakingly reared pheasants and partridges, the traditional crafts and way of life of the gamekeeper have perhaps not changed quite as much as superficial appearances, silencers and all, would suggest.

Ken Ward was in at least one sense born into his craft. His father was a Kent lorry driver, who was also a keen shot. So were Ken Ward's six brothers. They lived in a terraced house owned by the cement works for which their father worked, and it was situated on the edge of a marsh – good shooting territory. Ken Ward left village school at fourteen and went to work on a nearby farm when his older brothers, who also worked there, were being called up for the Second World War. He did general work as a farmer's boy. It was a mistake for a youth who was obviously a romantic before he also became a realist.

'I don't really know why I wanted to be a farm worker in the first place. I think it was the same as any lad wanting to be a train driver or a police car driver and then finding it doesn't live up to their romantic ideas,' he remembered. 'A year of farm work – and though I had wanted to be a farmer, I vowed I would never be a farmer's lad again.'

In fact he did – borrowing from shooting jargon – 'a whole rake of jobs' before becoming a keeper, all of them calculated to appeal at first glance to a romantic. He worked as deck boy first on a Thames tug, then on a private yacht, and spent two years in the Royal Navy. He remembered that, at the age of seventeen or so, he wanted to be either a keeper or a big game hunter. But both ambitions dissolved in the cold douche of reality: there was little demand for lads to train as keepers when men were being demobbed back into keepers' jobs from the war; and as for big game hunting ... 'Well, the world was a smaller place then than it is today, and you just couldn't hope to do it, not someone in my position.'

He was a builder's labourer, driving heavy building plant, earning good piece-money rates and struggling against boredom, when, at the age of thirty-eight, he saw an advertisement for an under-keeper at Ragley. He answered it, and got the job. For him it was obviously as if a giant mental and emotional door had been opened.

Militant trade unionists might well be appalled and baffled by the economics of the transition. The year was 1967, when money was worth several times what it is today. Ken Ward's last pay packet while he was driving the building plant equipment was £80. His first week's pay packet as under-keeper for the Syndicate was £13 5s. 'Why did I come? The wife and I talked about it. I was not happy in the work I was in, and we felt we could manage on less money. The kids were growing up and we felt we would be happier here. My interest was not in my former job, and my lifelong interest had been in keepering. I don't think that was because it was the nearest I could get to being a big game hunter. Oh no, I think the big game hunter thing was most probably just another young man's fancy.'

The move was certainly not made in the hope of an easier life. Ken Ward's wife works in the canteen of a factory, and it is probably as well she has a job of her own because the wife of a keeper sees less of him, on some days, than she does of her neighbours. His seven-days-a-week routine always begins before first light, which in summer time means very early indeed. The day I first met him, Ken Ward admitted that three-forty, though not unusual, might be a bit earlier than average: say by about fifteen minutes to half an hour.

He had risen a little earlier that day because he was having trouble with a fox. It had been seen on several occasions in Lady's Wood in Ragley Park. This wood is one of those into which young birds are released direct from their rearing cages; and for the first few weeks they just sit on the ground, where they are easy prey for foxes and other enemies of the Syndicate and its shoot.

Seven days a week, said Ken Ward, he had been down to that wood early to protect the jukking birds. For a moment I thought he was over-stressing his point by recourse to colourful language, but the word was 'jukking'. It means, in effect, birds in transit between the rearing cage and full mobility. 'I have been out early to all the woods where the birds are jukking,' said Ken Ward, 'to keep him away. He gets the smell of you, he don't like it! If you get a look at him, he likes it even less! This has been going on since I have been putting the first birds in the wood.'

The .22 Brno rifle with the silencer, Ken Ward's early morning com-panion, is indeed a friend in need in this sort of situation. Though the offending fox was still eluding his gun at the time of our first conversa-tion, late in the summer, during the previous week another one had fallen victim to its silent efficiency.

Ken Ward was almost lyrical on the subject: 'For killing at close range, nothing beats a shotgun. But beyond 45 yards, a shotgun isn't effective. Here is a typical instance: last Thursday night a vixen was squawking somewhere near young birds. It was obvious it was calling to a grown cub. I couldn't see it in the darkness, but I was out extra early the next morning and went to the same wood. Just as it was getting light, I saw this vixen and a well-grown cub coming out of the wood, 140 to 150 yards away. That is three shotgun lengths, but with a .22 rifle, I managed to kill them both.'

One job that Ken Ward has done at Ragley for Lord Hertford, as distinct from the Syndicate which runs what is now called the Kennels Shoot, is controlling the deer.

There used to be dozens roaming about Ragley in the days when the private slaughterhouse by the stables converted them speedily into family fare; but they do tend to cause damage. Any damage costs too much to be tolerated at the pruned and efficient Ragley. Lord Hertford has tried to keep the number of deer down to about eighty, and it has been Ken Ward's responsibility to cull them by taking them out with a heavy rifle, rather than the Czech Brno .22. When I met him, he was planning to take out around thirty. But, as it was summer, he was postponing the start. As soon as a deer fell to the gun in summer, he said, the flies were at it and the carcass was no good for food. There is no room for such waste at modern Ragley: some of the carcasses of animals shot in autumn or winter are sold to a game dealer, some find their way to the dinner table at the Hall, and Ken Ward himself gets an occasional carcass, which he skins and puts in the freezer. One carcass lasts him a year; deer is better as an occasional delicacy than as a staple diet. Carcasses are hung by Ken Ward at the house of the previous keeper, Ted Addison, just up a gravel lane by the back entrance to Ragley Park.

Yes, I detected an element of the big-game-hunter *manqué* in Ken Ward: a predatory alertness, a suggestion that thought and action would occur together if he had his finger near a trigger. Rather surprisingly, he claimed that in fact, even as a youth, it hadn't been shooting as such that had primarily interested him when he went out on a shoot; and that at Ragley shooting was probably only 5 per cent of his job. His main interest was seeing how nature unfolded. He waxed even more lyrical on this subject than he had on the killing of the vixen and the fox cub and the taking out of the deer.

'For instance', he said, 'a fox walking the tightrope with two of your birds in its mouth! I saw it walking along this single strand of wire that is less than a quarter of an inch thick – surely a better feat of balance than that fellow who went over Niagara on a rope while carrying a pole. It was the top strand of a wire fence, a 6-foot deer fence, and the fox was doing a perfect tightrope act. It is a treat to see the way animals behave. I remember a stoat rolling an egg along the bottom of the wood with its front legs – dribbling better than any footballer would, taking it away to eat it. I've seen young stoats running all over oak trees hunting squabs – young pigeons – just as if they were squirrels.'

Ken Ward handed me a small plastic box containing a large, nasty-looking insect from which I instinctively recoiled, though it was plainly impaled with a stout pin to the base of the box.

He had found the insect, alive, in the birds' drinking water, picked it up, put it in a match box and slipped the match box into his pocket. When he had arrived home and reached into his pocket to examine it more closely, he had found that the creature was half way out of its box, and, given a little more time, would probably have been crawling all over him inside his clothes. He took it to an expert, who told him: 'That's a hornet.'

'I had always wondered,' said the doughty gamekeeper, 'what a hornet was like. If I hadn't taken it out at that moment, it would have got on to my neck and stung me rather badly. Hornets are definitely on the increase in the Midlands. I have seen half-a-dozen this summer. They are not as aggressive as wasps, but they have much more punch in the tail.'

Wasps can sometimes be more difficult to control than foxes. One wasps' nest was hanging on a branch of a tree in the woods, just above the spot where Ken Ward was intending to put the rearing pen of some birds. It was obvious that unless the nest was removed either he or the birds, or both, would at some stage get badly stung. Wearing protective clothing, Ken Ward held a plastic refuse bag under the wasps nest, while a friend gingerly hacked through the branch from which the nest was hanging. Eventually the whole lot dropped into the plastic bag, which was tied rapidly at the top before the wasps could take stock of the situation and counter-attack.

In a sense, all the clothing of a gamekeeper can be counted as protective as he goes about his arduous tasks. Ken Ward's habitual attire in summer is a brownish-coloured shirt and khaki drill trousers. Both are easily washed. As tending to young game birds can be a messy business, Mrs Ward washes her husband's trousers twice a week. This, not unnaturally, lessens their life expectancy. In the comparatively short bird-rearing period, from the middle of May to the end of September, Ken Ward may wear out five pairs of trousers. He has to buy expensive waterproof boots at about £60 a pair, as cheaper ones tend to fall apart under the strain. Even good ones last only two or three seasons.

This, with a country-coloured coat in the winter, is virtually the entire uniform of the gamekeeper. It is not dictated by thoughtless tradition: 'Every item of clothing has to be in country style, not in bright colours, and in the same class of colour. And I wear a hat not because I like it, but because you must always present a similar picture to the birds, otherwise you frighten them. I have to wear a hat when the weather is bad, so I must wear one too if the weather is good. If I went anywhere near my birds without a hat on, I would frighten the life out of them, being bald.'

The point was well demonstrated when Ken Ward took me down to the rearing field. There were two rows of breeders containing grey English partridges, which were fairly quiet. There were also two rows of French partridges, brown except for their red legs, and with a habit of flying round hysterically when I got within ten yards of their cages. Ken Ward could get close enough to pour their water only by wearing his hat and moving very slowly indeed: 'The Frenchmen are the wildest creatures I know, with strangers or with me. The Englishman is a much quieter bird.' It sounded almost like an expression of national pride.

The birds in the breeding field get their water from a pipeline attached to a hydrant at the cottage of the former keeper, Ted Addison. It runs into a water butt on the rearing field, where Ken Ward fills a watering can and pours it into the breeding cages. These cages have to be moved every other day because the birds foul the ground so much.

What with moving the young birds around, and preventing the foxes having the same freedom of movement, Ken Ward has ample opportunity to indulge his passion for watching the countryside. His first task of the day is to go down to the woods to feed the birds already there. Then he goes to the rearing field to feed the birds still in the cages. Later in the season, the partridges will be sent out to the nearby fields and the pheasants will be put into the woods, their respective natural habitats. That normally takes until nine in the morning, when Ken Ward goes back to his cottage and snatches his usual breakfast. The coops are then shifted on to different ground, which sometimes takes up a full day or even more. In the wet weather, precisely when it is most difficult and messy to move the birds, they have to be moved more often. By lunchtime, the water in the rearers has to be checked to make sure that each rearing cage has two or three gallons of water. Ken Ward's own lunch is usually a sandwich eaten in a half-hour break. Then more coop-moving, which lasts until six in the evening.

It is then time for him to return to his cottage to feed his three labradors, Ben, Biddey and Nell – working dogs and jacks-of-all-trades. By this time Mrs Ward has her husband's dinner cooking. He expects to sit down to it at about six-forty-five and by seven-thirty he is back at work, which will go on till nightfall.

'The rest of the day,' said Ken Ward, as he tried to quieten the hysterical French partridges, 'is my own.' It was a phrase, I began to realize, that I had heard more than once at Ragley.

Only considerable craftsman's pride could make such a life acceptable in an era when increased leisure time, irrespective of whether it will be enjoyed, has become the stock demand in industrial employment. Ken Ward even buys his own guns to kit himself out for his role. 'I have six shotguns and three rifles altogether. Some of the shotguns are an investment for my old age, because two of them are good quality English-made guns. Like antiques, they will never lose their value.'

The modern gamekeeper, as Ken Ward sees it, really needs a combination gun, both shotgun and rifle, so he can take out close and long-range targets effectively. But unfortunately these are beyond his means. The American combination guns cost only £200 or so, but Ken Ward dismisses them as 'bloody awful things', too heavy and cumbersome. The Continental gun is much lighter, except on the pocket: it costs about £500.

So Ken Ward and his kind make do with cheaper implements. The .22 Brno rifle cost £30 complete with silencer five years before he moved to Ragley; now it would cost over £200. A working Webley shotgun like Ken Ward's now costs nearly £100. An investment of perhaps over £1,000, on a modern gamekeeper's wages (the same as a skilled agricultural worker's), argues some dedication to the craft.

Blazing away at poachers with the implements of the trade is socially and politically out of fashion today, but part of Ken Ward's job, nonetheless, is to keep a wary look out for the caddish breed who try to bag a bird before the men who have paid to have them reared can do so.

'Poachers?' said Ken Ward. 'Generally speaking, this shoot is a small shoot. We don't rear large number of birds – 1,600 pheasants and 1,000 partridges a year. Yes, we do get poachers, but normally they are small-time chaps, the snatch-one-and-run merchants from the roadside, or the local who fancies a free meal. We make every effort to catch them, but the main thing is to deter them by being about as often as we can. Even in the winter, when the daylight has gone, I have come here and had my meal some nights, going round the woods and roadside and not going back home until two or three in the morning. Of course you can't be on duty all day and all night every night. You have to pick the days and night when you think it is more likely that someone will have a go at you.

The worst case that Ken Ward could remember was when seven birds were shot out of roost one night, within 150 yards of one of the rides (paths for horses) through the woods. Sometimes birds can disappear without anyone being the wiser, since it is obviously impossible to know each one. Often feathers are left clinging to the branches of a tree, or are lying on the ground at the spot the bird fell, and twigs and feathers are obviously riddled with shot. Sometimes the poachers shoot birds but then can't find them themselves, and the gamekeeper and his dog come along afterwards and stumble upon them.

It is impossible to say how much the Kennels Shoot has suffered at the hands of poachers. Ken Ward could not guess how many birds were lost each year, but suspected not many: 'I really have no idea, and I don't think any keeper does. On a small shoot like this, I wouldn't say many in a year. But larger shoots, where the gangs come in, can get a real hammering. They are up against professionals who do it for a living, and they can cause real trouble. The types who snatch one for the pot, as bad as that is, are nowhere near as bad as the gangs that come in.'

It is just as well that poachers are a relatively minor problem at Ragley because the keeper is stretched quite far enough without them – and all for between £70 and £80 a week at the time I asked.

'I think,' said Ken Ward, requesting me again to move further away from his excitable French partridges, 'that many townsmen would look at me and say, "He's nuts!" But I think it's in your blood. It's something that is either in you or not in you. I know that I would rather do this job at my relatively low wage than virtually any other job in the world for ten times that. Yes, really! The wife? She likes the countryside and is a very good and understanding woman.'

She needs to be. Working seven days a week, daylight to dusk, the gamekeeper doesn't have time for any sort of social life in the summer months. When one of Ken Ward's nieces got married recently, Mary Ward went to the wedding in Kent, but her husband was not able to go with her. At the time we met, he hadn't been able to take his wife anywhere for over three months, apart from a couple of hours' shopping once a week. Ken Ward thought carefully about this last point. 'No, not even a couple of hours,' he corrected. 'But it doesn't become a bore to me. My work, despite all its frustrations and disasters, is something I really like. It is always interesting to see things in nature you would not believe unless you saw them. I have known hens to fly at foxes when they are put into the rearing coops to hatch out the young partridges – they fly at the wire and drive the fox away.'

Modern farming methods, and new methods in forestry – for which Ragley is noted – cast a cloud across the gamekeeper's brow. Both are tending to destroy the natural habitat of the birds concerned. At least, that is how Ken Ward sees it: 'But I would not say there was a tug of war between Lord Hertford and us. The farming side and the forestry side have both got to show a profit in these modern times. I suppose that what the forestry office are planting now will become the woods of the future; but the natural habitat of the pheasant in the woods is the oak and nut coppice, whereas the tendency nowadays is towards planting conifers, because they are quicker growing and generally show a quicker return.'

Modern farming necessitates the use of combine harvesters, which usually means pulling down hedges to make bigger fields. This, coupled with the stubble-burning carried out today immediately after the crop is cut, plus the quick replanting of the fields, means that partridges tend to be driven away from the area. In the old days, most of the planting was done after Christmas and the stubble of the old crop remained there, to provide birds for even the traditional Christmas Eve shoot. Then – though the farmer himself may have failed to see the advantages of this – the seed used to be in the earth for quite a time as seed, in which state it was good food for the game birds. Today, thanks to chemical fertilizers, crops are soon growing and cease to provide free nourishment for the birds due to be shot for sport.

Ken Ward and his kind, it was apparent, try not to be bitter about the implications of more efficient methods of farming. 'The farmers know our views,' said Ken Ward, 'but they have got to make a profit, so they have to keep up with the times. They do all they can to help us, but they are in business and we are in sport.'

Yes indeed. But the politics of this situation is largely above the game-keeper's head, even when he puts on his yearly, free, tweed suit to keep up with the gentlemen on the shoots. The diplomacy and the agreements on policy are the prerogative of the Syndicate, often acting through the tenant fruit farmer Robert Hiller, or through another tenant farmer, Michael Bomford. The latter, I found, was a man in his late sixties, with the friendly gravitas and gold glasses of a family doctor, who officially runs the shoot on a day-to-day basis for the Syndicate, in any spare time he has left over from running his three farms at Ragley and two more elsewhere.

Michael Bomford lives in a very comfortable farmhouse at Dunning-ton village and his family have been farming at Ragley for generations;

his great-grandfather had 6,000 acres in the 1850s, though not all of them at Ragley.

The fact that it is Michael Bomford, a farmer, who now runs the Kennels Shoot is significant. In the old days the local farmers were not looked upon as gentlemen of the type who should be attending shoots, let alone running them. Right up to the outbreak of the Second World War there were three shoots at Ragley, all the province of the titled and the prosperous, the latter tending to include those involved in respectable sorts of business or the formal professions. When Michael Bomford took over Tothall Farm in 1938, and was invited as a guest to the shoots, the invitation could have been seen as the patronage which the wealthy sometimes confer on the appealing young; for Michael Bomford was scarcely twenty-one. The shoot he went on in those days tended to be dominated by very wealthy businessmen, including the owner of a coal business, the owner of a tannery and the owner of a spectacle frames company.

I could sense, as Michael Bomford talked to me in his comfortable middle-class living room, why he had been socially acceptable at that time. His manner was gentlemanly, and before the war and even immediately after it, this was a vital prerequisite if one was to be on nodding terms with the wealthy who came once a week, starting in late September, and shot their way through the season for nineteen or twenty shooting days.

Michael Bomford remembered that they were all driven by their manservant-cum-chauffeurs in Rolls Royces and Bentleys. There were then two keepers on the estate – Ted Addison and Norman Hanson. Even two was thought at the time to be something of a come-down as previously there had been three. There were also two separate shoots in operation – one at the north side of the Ragley estate, known as Cold Comfort Shoot; and the one at the south side, known, as it is now, as the Kennels Shoot. It was only a few years ago that the 8th Marquess stepped in and called a halt to the Cold Comfort Shoot. His reason for doing so is one that has figured greatly in many of the decisions he has made regarding Ragley: financial necessity. 'At the northern end they used to raise between 3,000 and 4,000 pheasants a year. I came to the conclusion that the value of the corn eaten exceeded the shooting rents. No shooting man will believe me, but it was a careful calculation. I am not one to turn away rents if they are offered, but I came to the conclusion I was losing money with it,' said Lord Hertford.

Such was the view of the 8th Marquess, not himself a shooting man, on the economics of shooting versus agriculture. Perhaps the fact that he is a hunting man (and therefore interested in the foxes that keeper Ward so diligently puts down) is a further complication; perhaps not. The undisputed fact, as Michael Bomford will tell anyone who is interested, is that the remaining Kennels Shoot has been subject to that process known usually as 'changing to remain the same'.

When Michael Bomford shot with the Kennels Shoot as a guest, it was made up of stockbrokers, a Judge, a High Sheriff and people no less eminent, but all getting on in years. At £2,000 a year per gun, plus shooting expenses on the actual days of the shoot, it was hardly a cheap sport. Future candidates did not loom large on the horizon. Gossip soon suggested that the shoot would go out of circulation altogether and this would have meant breaking with a tradition that went back many generations.

Generously for a non-shooting man, Lord Hertford called a meeting at which local farmers were asked to participate in the shoot, even if it was on the basis of having only a half, or even a quarter, of a gun. Lord Hertford himself, for a time, held part of a gun.

'Industrialists joined in as well,' recalled Michael Bomford. 'Lord Hertford and one other farmer dropped out later and were replaced by other people who took guns. We now have two farmers in the Syndicate, and eight guns, at nearly £2,000 a year each. Rent to the estate accounts for barely a quarter of that sum.' Members of the shoot, at the time I spoke to Michael Bomford, included a High Sheriff, a hooks and eyes' manufacturer, the director of an enamelware business and a quantity surveyor.

All these changes had to be handled with delicacy and tact, for it was generally agreed that a 'cad' in a shoot could disrupt the whole thing – the sort of fellow who wouldn't accept the shooting stand he had been allotted, or who started shouting at a gamekeeper who (the Syndicate were wise enough to know) was what is traditionally called 'a treasure'.

'In former days,' pointed out Michael Bomford, 'the shoot didn't change much at all. The real change only came about five years ago. We were trying to encourage people to approach the shoot in a more professional way with slightly different members. But we didn't want to attract people who didn't really appreciate the country and could be difficult. I think we have always had very friendly people and, generally speaking, a good atmosphere. But sometimes people can fall out among themselves, and you can get an awkward man in a shoot who makes life difficult for everyone. That has been avoided here. I actually run the thing, and although I am easy going, I like things to be just right. They all seem to get on well with me and take things from me. Remember they are not easy men to handle. They are somebodies who have done something successful. You can't treat them like nothings, you have to handle them tactfully . . . They would not stand being shouted at and told what to do. I have seen that happening in shoots and it doesn't go down well.'

No one, according to Michael Bomford, had ever been asked to leave the Syndicate having once been made a member, though a few people had come as guests and not been asked again. All members had willingly accepted the changes Michael Bomford had made. These have included spreading the birds out to all sides of the shoot, so that there are fewer bad days' shooting – a guest can hardly be invited by any self-respecting member on a bad day.

The shoot normally meets at ten in the morning, when the keeper and the beaters have already been there for half an hour. The keeper will have advised the beaters on how to do the beating (in the case of pheasants) or the driving (in the case of partridges). Generally speaking the head keeper takes the centre of the long line of beaters or drivers; but Ken Ward dislikes calling himself head keeper. 'Not in a one-man outfit,' he will say caustically. 'It's like being Field Marshal in a one-man Army.' All the same, it is he, in consultation with Michael Bomford, who will form the starting line of beaters or drivers and move them on, according to the wind and other factors, to try to make the birds fly over the line of guns. Usually there are between five and seven drives a day.

Any instructions or suggestions to the guns or beaters will be delivered by Ken Ward, but will be in Michael Bomford's tradition of diplomacy. Ken Ward is by now expert at making his voice heard at distances of up to half a mile without giving the impression of being a Sergeant Major. 'I would never shout at the guns,' Ken Ward will tell you. 'The only time you shout at the guns is if someone shoots low. When a covey rises and heads in the direction of the guns, I blow a whistle, so the guns know the covey is coming.'

When things go wrong, both keeper and gun need the patience of a saint. On no account must they start berating one another. And things can go wrong. A change of wind can send the birds in the wrong direction and farm machinery working in nearby fields can send the birds away from the guns. And a drive can be done most successfully except for the one fact that the birds have all moved elsewhere. The keeper has to use his knowledge of the ground, the nature of the wind and the flight lines which, generally speaking, the birds like to follow. Sometimes a shoot has to work hard against all these factors, which can make the going extremely difficult and touchy.

The new involvement of local farmers in the shoot, which a hundred years ago might have been resisted as lowering the tone of the proceedings, has had its utilitarian value.

'I changed things quite a lot, I think for the better,' said Michael Bomford. 'Really, until we farmers joined, it was very much up to the keeper as to what was done. A lot is still left to the keeper, but our local people have a great deal more say with regard to arrangements. Their local knowledge is a help to him.'

The gastronomic delights of shooting days have been changed as little as possible. It is true that Mrs Elspeth Addison, an excellent cook, stopped cooking lunch for the shoot after the death of her keeper husband, Ted. It is also true that the 1927 port, which a businessman knight invariably brought with him to accompany lunch, has long since run out. But the idiosyncratic cuisine of the day's shooting remains broadly what it was: very English and very masculine.

In the building where the shoot now have lunch on shooting days (originally built for fruit-pickers by one of the tenant farmers of Ragley) it is still a rule that port is drunk with lunch – there are no Continental corruptions, like table wine. Each member of the shoot supplies lunch in rotation, which is then usually served by a faithful character called Bill, who lives next door.

Members like their sherry and their pink gin and they have never rebelled in favour of claret or hock. As an aperitif, it *must* be sherry or gin. With the meal itself, they drink beer, and afterwards, in lieu of a liqueur, comes the sloe gin or port.

'That is traditional,' Michael Bomford told me impassively. 'Some of the members of the shoot like it.'

Later in the day, the members return to the building for tea and cake and a whisky – still no wine – before heading their Bentleys or humbler cars for home. This ritual applies to the eight days they shoot partridges and the eleven or twelve days they shoot pheasants. On Christmas Eve, the tradition is that the shoot has a turkey. But the same accompanying drinks are served.

Perhaps there is something to be said for the rather spartan drinking traditions of the Syndicate, even in these modern times. The gamekeeper has to control fourteen beaters to get the birds right over the guns, and the Syndicate members have to control their tempers when the place they are standing gives them (they may feel) an inferior view of the partridges or pheasants. Ideally there must be no recriminations, however slight the day's bag. The eight members of the Syndicate have bagged as many as fifty brace of partridges and as few as twenty brace, and the average of thirty or forty brace is better assured if all members are clear-eyed and not awash in wine. The presence of the local farmers, which might have been a cause of tension among other members, tends to increase the bag, since they know the terrain well; and this adds to the euphoria and amicability of the occasion. As many as a hundred and fifty head of pheasants have been bagged on a good day and the Syndicate try to average a hundred head.

'The little devils can be a bit difficult to handle sometimes,' said Michael Bomford. He was talking about the partridges (which are blown about by the wind and are more generally mobile than pheasants), not about the members of the shoot.

On the whole, then, the tradition of shooting at Ragley has survived, despite the unsympathetic British economy and a Lord who is not himself a keen shot; and it has survived rather well. The Syndicate can afford their good humour as much as their pink gin. So can the 8th Marquess, who gets his £4,000 a year rent plus a couple of brace of whatever the Syndicate shoot, however good or bad their bag.

And the faithful keeper, Ken Ward? 'Some of them,' confessed Michael Bomford, 'can't understand what motivates this chap. But he likes doing it, as we all do. I think between us we have both carried on a tradition and adapted to modern times.'

16
Forest
Strategy

*E*ACH OF THE FORESTS at Ragley has a personality all its own. Almost like a human being, according to some of the men who work in them.

I found Colin Bindley, Ragley's head forester, at Spring Wood, one of those he considers pleasant and welcoming. 'There is a lot of character to these woods. It is a pleasure to meet some of the woods, but not others.'

Colin Bindley and his three forestry workers sometimes personalize the woods, which chiefly run along a ridge in the central spine of the estate. Three Oaks Wood, full of old oak, is like an elderly aunt or uncle. Thorn Hill is such a mixture of trees – larch, birch, oak – that it is like a scatter-brained but pleasant girl. Berry's Coppice, with Japanese larch, is like a young girl wearing a spring dress and smelling sweet. Spring Wood itself, in which I found Colin Bindley mending a gate – helped by one of his workers, Cyril Tebb, an old hand on the estate – is a dowager duchess with a face lift. It had not been thinned for twenty years, but then work was started and the rays of sunlight began to penetrate.

This is one of the more attractive woods. There are others.

'Bush Wood is not nice. It is all poplar and they haven't been attended to in the seventeen years I've been on the estate,' explained Cyril Tebb, a short sturdy man with the ruddy face and square beard of a Victorian sea captain. 'That place is like a witch's corpse. In Pool Wood you are liable to trip into holes: it is one mass of briars and thorns and would be a wicked, or at least not a very happy person – a lazy witch, perhaps.'

There are workers at Ragley who insist that all the woods have one identity – that of a Cinderella. This, they say, is because most of the attention is paid to the farms. It is true that, when I first asked Lord Hertford how many woods there were at Ragley, he replied cheerfully, 'I don't know. I've never counted them.' Only after referring to the map by his office desk was he able to say, 'There are sixteen.' I thought at first it might be a studied piece of casualness, part of the persona he has exploited so shrewdly in 'selling' himself and the estate to ensure its survival. But eventually I decided that I could take it at face value.

It is certainly true that, whatever personality the woods may have in poetic terms, it is subject to constant change, and the change is for commercial rather than aesthetic reasons. Ragley has 1,000 acres of forest, 200 of them leased to the Forestry Commission, and the rest taken in hand directly by the Ragley estate. Each wood is divided into 'compartments', so that it may be carefully mapped and accurate records kept of plantings, and all of the woods are now expected to justify themselves in terms of the estate's survival. The financial turnover of the forests is, however, still less than visitors to the estate produce. But the forests are more *consistently* profitable than the tourist trade. The turnover on sheep, at about £8,000 a year, is on average about double the turnover on the woods; but there are always plans afoot to change the woods so as to increase revenue.

On his office wall, near the ceiling-high map of the estate, Lord Hertford displays Royal Agricultural Show silver medal certificates for Cockerham and Berry's Coppice, which were judged the best-managed woods in their show class. 'That was a great pleasure to me, as I manage them,' remarked Lord Hertford drily. The farms manager's writ, it is generally held, does not run to the woods; though he does tend to be consulted about any new developments to transform the personality of the forests into something more in keeping with the needs of the times.

'Will our discussion for Wednesday morning be all right, Milord?' asked Colin Bindley as Lord Hertford introduced me to him. The question had a very obvious urgency. It transpired that Lord Hertford and his head forester were enjoying a slight disagreement about the strategy for the latest personality change.

It concerned Christmas trees. The year before there had been a great shortage of Christmas trees (normally Norwegian spruce); and any forester who had planted in bulk five years previously, and been able to produce a good crop, would have made a financial killing that year. Hence the discussion planned for the coming Wednesday about exactly how 30 acres at Cook Hill would be planted with up to 150,000 Norwegian spruce. The plan was the first on such a scale in the living memory of Ragley, and since the tree plants could cost up to £1 each, a large investment would be involved.

'I want to put in about 150,000 trees at once,' said Colin Bindley. 'His Lordship has doubts about selling them. I haven't any doubts. I would plant them and get on with it. But he has got to pay for it, so . . . I think we have got to have a crop that large. Lord Hertford wants a third planted this year, a third next year and a third the year after. I don't want that. We would have to spray this place three times instead of once, and with weed killer at £20 a can, it would be very costly.'

It was plain that Lord Hertford was distancing himself from this enthusiasm. Not for a present-day aristocrat the grandeur of large-scale development when the future market was uncertain. The Marquess pointed out that the whole idea was to use a piece of land which was on a slope and therefore of little use for farming purposes (that is to say, he pointed it out to me, but tactfully refrained from doing so to his head forester, to whom the woods are, pardonably, the centre of the universe).

'It was used in the past for pheasant rearing,' Lord Hertford recalled, 'but we don't rear any more pheasants. We stopped three years ago. Someone set a snare, which is forbidden by agreement, which meant I was empowered to terminate the agreement. They caught my dog, which was pretty tactless of them. I heard him crying out and, luckily, got to him in time. It was round his foot, not his neck, fortunately. But we never allow the setting of snares, because it is so cruel. We came to the conclusion that, on the whole, the pheasants were eating a lot more corn than I was receiving in rent. We didn't think it worthwhile carrying on with it.'

Christmas trees might have seemed an ideal solution for the disused pheasant-breeding land, but Lord Hertford was proceeding with his usual business acumen. 'What worries me is whether we will find a market for the trees. There wouldn't be any trees to sell until the third or fourth year, so one is having to guess what the market will be like in four years time. If everyone is planting Christmas trees because of last year's shortage, then in three or four years there may be a glut. There is no point in planting the trees if no one wants to buy them. We would be aiming at a crop of about 50,000 trees a year at £1.50 to £2 each on the wholesale market, and that is a lot of money.'

Caution about the Christmas tree project was all the more understandable at a time when Ragley was involved in an extensive ten-year programme of thinning and clear-felling trees. Tens of thousands were to be removed altogether and new trees planted. But at the time I met the foresters there was a deep economic recession, which had hit the building trade – one of the largest purchasers of Ragley's timber – particularly hard. Prices of timber were low and Ragley was hanging on in the hope of an upturn. Oaks, Spanish chestnuts and beech were either still in the ground or being cut up, seasoned and stored in the hope that the building trade would soon pick up in earnest. Colin Bindley and his men were doing the ground-work to make sure they could take advantage of any revival.

Colin Bindley, a tall and gap-toothed man in his thirties, deep-tanned from working stripped to the waist on Ragley's exposed and windy acres, came to the estate in 1978. He used to work on the Forestry Commission's Keilder Forest, in Northumberland – the biggest man-made forest in Europe. Lord Hertford advertised for a head forester at the same time as Colin Bindley had family problems in the Midlands – his sister was dying of cancer and his mother, in her eighties, was far from well. Colin Bindley answered the advertisement and was taken on.

It was quite different, working on the estate of an aristocrat like Lord Hertford, said Colin Bindley. He painted a picture of Keilder that somewhat resembled that of a factory: the men were on piece work, cutting down and cutting up trees for paper pulp, helped by a big combine that cut the trees down like corn. 'If you scored more than fifty trees, you got a coconut. That was the feeling. Men were falling down with heart attacks. We had to fell a hundred trees a day and stack them. It is different here. You can devote your life to it here – and everybody expects you to, as well! You start at eight in the morning, and you never know when you are getting home. I come here and have my dinner and then I might go riding a tractor until ten at night, cleaning between trees.'

Such work is partly aesthetic. Colin Bindley and his team force their way through thick woodland, carrying a chainsaw. They hack away at the undergrowth and shrubs between trees, letting in the light and creating paths where Lord Hertford can ride his horse on one of his frequent excursions round the estate, an activity of which he never tires.

'You never get bored here,' said Colin Bindley. 'I should think I usually put in sixty-five to seventy-five hours a week. My wife works in the sweet shop at Ragley Hall, which makes a change for her.' He and his wife lived in a Tudor-style cottage called Evesham Lodge, near the gate of Hollybush Farm, with their thirteen-year-old daughter who had to travel several miles to school, and a ten-year-old son who went to school at Dunnington, near the boundary of the estate.

This country idyll was obviously highly agreeable to Colin Bindley. What was less pleasing sometimes was the fact that on a private estate he must work on a tighter budget than he would be allowed if working for an institution using public money. To some extent, this feeling may be based on professional touchiness of a sort one would encounter anywhere. 'The farm always comes first here – this is only a second-grade job, like,' Colin Bindley said at one point. 'Yet this is the only one that is paying at the moment, until they get the corn in again.'

There was also some feeling that a very, very good case always had to be made for acquiring new machinery. The Forestry Commission, said Colin Bindley, would give you a new piece of machinery if you simply said, 'This old one is knackered.' But at Ragley they would take the machinery away for three weeks to have it repaired.

No doubt, I reflected, such procedures would be more popular with Ragley's accountants than with its foresters; but it is through such rigid cost-control, and perhaps only because of it, that the Earl of Yarmouth will have an estate to inherit.

Colin Bindley, nevertheless, has suggested some reforms since he gained Lord Hertford's ear at Ragley, and he has carried out several changes suggested by Lord Hertford himself.

The fences are an example. According to Colin Bindley, the woods didn't suffer from vandalism at all, unlike the Adventure Park on the estate, which was a regular target. The only creatures who damaged the trees were not skinheads or members of other current cults, but the deer and rabbits – of which Ragley had plenty. In Pearson's Wood, the 24,000 Corsican pines were under regular attack. The deer used to be shut up in their own compounds, but when they were allowed to roam wild they became not only more prone to wandering but also more prone to increasing their numbers. For some time after the deer were released, the fences surrounding the woods remained 2 feet high – enough to protect them from rabbits, but not from deer. New plantations often tended to be nibbled, or broken down. Colin Bindley and his workers started to put 5½-feet tall wire mesh fences round all new plantations, the netting going down 6 inches into the ground to prevent rabbits burrowing underneath it. This protection, it was thought, would last for twenty years.

The planting programmes, I was told, had also been increased. This had been mainly for business reasons, but sometimes there had been an aesthetic spin-off for His Lordship.

'On the Old Reservoir site in Old Park Wood, we will plant Norway spruce and wild cherries in alternate rows,' promised Colin Bindley, 'so it will look nice from the Hall. Everywhere he looks from the Hall now, there are Corsican pines, so we will put Norway spruce and cherry over 12 to 14 acres. This he can view from the double doors of the stables. There are three oak trees in line, and these trees will be behind it. It will look very good.'

The trees that had been planted in some of the Ragley woods before Colin Bindley arrived were dismissed by him as 'rabbit food'; and, indeed, some of the 12,000 that had been planted had fallen victim to animal hunger. When he had first bought Christmas trees a foot tall instead of a few inches, others on the estate had thought that he'd gone mad. But such trees tended to last and they also produced a marketable crop more quickly.

Cyril Tebb, the ruddy-faced Yorkshireman who used to work on the estate of a retired Army Major and MP near York, had, I gathered, also given His Lordship the benefit of his advice on 'thinking big'. Plant better and bigger plants, and have a more reliable crop, and the money for it, sooner. That had been his message.

Such a gospel of perfection has been regarded with caution by the 8th Marquess who, everyone agreed, was a practical businessman first and foremost. It is likely that the woods of Ragley, which now produce 17,000 fencing posts at about £1 each a year, will increase this figure to some 33,000. It is also likely that there will be an expansion of the crop of 12-foot rails for jumping posts at riding events; of thick strainer posts for straining the wires of fencing; and of 35- to 40-foot-long larches for the building of hay barns.

But, in the personalized terms in which Lord Hertford's forestry workers sometimes think of the woods, forestry at Ragley is likely to remain more like a cautious young accountant than the spendthrift black sheep of the family. Such economic calculations are the basis for Ragley's survival today, though they might have seemed strange to the more feudally-minded Ragley workers of the past.

17
The Old Faithfuls

Jim Jelfs is one of Ragley's longest-serving workers and a man who finds it fairly easy to speak his relatively tranquil mind. His father also worked on a great estate – and he was a man who found it very difficult to repress his rather radical opinions. In those days, when the Squire had almost absolute power and the worker was expected to be grateful – and silent – for his crust and his tied cottage, it was a dangerous attitude.

Jim Jelfs, who carries out maintenance at modern Ragley in an era which could be a million light years away, recalled the situation which cast a shadow over his boyhood: 'I went to school, before I left at the age of fourteen, in more than one place. My father moved around a lot. He worked on farms and if he didn't like a job he moved on. He had worked on the land, been his own boss for years, and then met with ill-health. He couldn't settle down to being told what to do by someone else. In those days, if your face didn't fit, they would just say "You are fired", and that was that. Then they could take you to court, and just throw you out on the street. They can't do it nowadays. Father was taken ill and could not work, so they took him to court, and we had twenty-eight days to get out. We just put the furniture in some outbuildings. My sister was already in service, and I moved to an aunt's, and my mother and father went to his brother's.'

At this time Jim Jelfs was eighteen, his sister sixteen and his brother thirteen. The mysterious stomach complaint which kept young Jim away from work for long periods of time – 'one year I think I had only one National Insurance stamp on my card' – was possibly less understood in those days than it would be today. The eighteen-year-old worked on the farm where his father was working, then moved to another, then worked in a factory. Throughout all this, his stomach complaints persisted.

Jelfs, a small man with intelligently bright eyes and the habit of twisting his cloth cap in his hands when in conversation, recounted the story in tones of fatalism and incredulity rather than bitterness. 'I remember it was Christmas and when we were turned out we had nowhere to stay. We were looking for somewhere. My mother applied, on my behalf, for a job as a gardener here at Ragley. Someone from Ragley called on her and said the gardener's job was filled, but that they needed a bricklayer's mate and a plumber's mate. I came as a plumber's mate and my brother as a bricklayer's mate. We went into a tied cottage, two up and two down, rent-free. I am fifty-four now. Here they don't turn anyone out when they retire. They stay in the cottages.'

They do indeed. In the Ragley cottages, scattered throughout the surrounding villages, widows and widowers of old employees, as well as faithful old retainers themselves (some working part-time), form a little community. It is inevitably a shrinking community as age whittles away the survivors of a totally different social epoch, but its members cling to their memories, good as well as bad, and welcome the chance of chatting about old times with their contemporaries once in a while – usually when they are invited back to the Hall itself for some social occasion. This may be at the beginning or the closing of the open season, or at a birthday party for a member of Lord Hertford's family.

At the time I talked to him, Jim Jelfs was still working full-time at the age of fifty-four, and was proud of being the most senior Ragley employee in terms of length of service. He was taken on in 1945 and paid the going rate – about £4 for a forty-eight hour week. His brother left the job after two years, got married and moved away, leaving him alone in the cottage with his mother. When she died in 1964 he was left completely alone, an unmarried man with comparatively few chances of a social life.

The pattern of his life did change slightly when he said goodbye to the cottage which was overlaid with memories. But this was not so much by any conscious desire of his own but due, rather, to the modernization of the estate. In 1964 there was still no mains water or sewerage in his cottage and the estate wanted to sell the property rather than bear the heavy costs of modernization. (It was in the days when the estate was still managed by an agent, who possibly had less family feeling for the Ragley possessions than the then heir himself.) Jelfs asked if he could have another cottage which had fallen vacant, at Astwood Bank, Redditch. His wish was granted, to all-round relief. He was still living in this two-up, two-down semi-detached cottage when I met him; a reasonably contented worker earning £78 for a forty-hour week, and living rent-free in a cottage he was unlikely to be required to leave the moment he fell ill or retired.

I asked him why he appeared to be so contented. 'There is such a variety of jobs when you work at a place like Ragley Hall,' he said. 'Today I have repaired a door, done a little bit to a fireplace, made a toilet work and done one or two other little jobs. Then I started to lay the floor of the restaurant kitchen, which is a wooden floor with paper on top and then a cushioned floor on top of that. It's all different work. I have never thought of going to live in a town, nor wanted to set up on my own in anything. The job has worked out all right. I have been here so long on the Lord of the Manor's estate because he's been so fair to me. I could have made some changes in my life, I suppose – like not remaining single.'

In fact he married shortly after this conversation, but his was not an isolated comment. There is no doubt that the Lord in his Hall still finds it easier to have a satisfactory social life than the worker in his cottage. For the aristocrat and his family there are focal points (the cocktail party, the dinner, the Great Ball) where equal can meet equal; or, to be even more blunt about it, where women can meet men and vice-versa. For the faithful employees in their cottages it is still not quite so easy, especially at a time when rural bus services have been cut drastically. More than one dweller in a Ragley cottage has remained single, and it must have been especially difficult in the past for those with a spark of individuality to meet suitable marriage partners: a game of cards with a very limited pack.

For Jim Jelfs, the pack of cards is an all too literal one. One of his few social diversions, he said, was whist. He always went to whist drives at Astwood Bank, on Mondays. He ran whist drives every fortnight at Cookhill in aid of the village hall and he ran a tote to raise money for both the village hall and the old people of the village. He had been doing this for fourteen years. The cinema? The nearest one was at Redditch, and he never went. He went to Evesham cinema if he went at all and he vaguely remembered taking his sister and his nephew there to see a horror film. It did not greatly impress his countryman's soul. 'It was a load of rubbish. American. Most of them are, aren't they?' He looked quite surprised when, in fairness, I told him that the British, too, had made a sizeable reputation in that genre, indeed practically inventing it with Hammer Films. 'Oh yes? Wouldn't know about that.' A whole vein of British sub-culture was dead to him.

In previous generations, dedication to the great Hall could confer some benefits in terms of status, but it could well be at the cost of a degree of social and perhaps emotional isolation which rather fewer young people today would be prepared to accept.

For the daughter of such an important person at the Hall as the butler, life was not easy – especially if she happened to be, like Marjorie Crick, a sort of premature women's libber, with a penchant for riding motor bikes. Miss Crick was eighty-four when I met her at her immaculate, detached red-brick cottage in the village of Arrow, with its ivy trailing up the front wall and its neat tulips in the front garden. She was a very tidy and self-possessed lady who could press a cup of tea on you with all the informal charm of a duchess, coupled with the competence of a governess.

Even sandwiched precariously, as she had been, between the upper class manners of the aristocracy and the simplicity of the villagers, she could have met a suitable spouse to share her motorbike. But the odds were all against it. With no ill intent on anyone's part, the Hall did help to condition her to a life of independence, which had obviously stood her in good stead as a spinster but which might not have been easy for a husband to accept.

Miss Crick described life as the daughter of Ragley's butler with the cool precision of a lady who had appreciated her father's status as an important man within the local community – a 'character', and a man fond of a drink now and then – but who had determined to maintain her own sovereignty. And sovereignty is the right word. When I called on her unexpectedly at mid-day, she said, 'I think three-sharp would be more convenient', and closed the door briskly, if not impolitely. At three-sharp, she welcomed me with cordiality and tea, her thoughts neatly in order – she was plainly a spry example of a dying breed.

'My father used to be butler to a Captain. He moved to his job at Ragley when the present Marquess's grandfather was in residence. We lived in a flat in the stable yard. I would be about five. The flat had no bathroom, but we had a big open fire, and we bathed in front of that. There were three bedrooms and you had to go up three flights of stairs to reach them. There was a water toilet downstairs, so we had to go down three flights of stairs to go to the lavatory. We didn't see much of Ragley Hall itself, except for the chimneys. I expect, in those days, you rather stood in awe of the Hall.'

As a child, Miss Crick played with the children of other servants in the stable, through the shrubbery or around the slaughterhouse where the family at the Hall killed their own deer. Sometimes the Crick family would talk to the children of the Hall itself. One of them was called Daisy and was quite friendly with Miss Crick's sister, who was also called Daisy. This circumstance was thought to excuse a certain familiarity. The family as a whole were quite friendly.

'The only thing we didn't like,' remembered Miss Crick, 'was that we had to curtsey.'

Even this practice varied in depth of unpopularity according to who was at the receiving end of the curtsey. One of the ladies of the house, now long deceased, especially inflamed the pride of the butler's family.

'If she was there in the park,' said Miss Crick, 'we used to run a mile rather than curtsey to her. We used to hate it. At that time, we used to go to the village school at Arrow. If she came past, when we were standing in the lanes outside the school, we had to bob down. Even the school-master didn't like her. The others were all very nice to us; we used to be invited to the Hall when they had parties and things. The servants had a servants ball. The Marquess used to come round and open it and stay a little while.'

The particular incident of the Marquess's knee was so unusual as to brand itself into Miss Crick's memory for seventy-five years: 'I rode on the Marquess's knee one Sunday, coming from church. That was a great honour. I would be about ten. The Marquess and his family always used to go to church on Sunday morning, and my sister and I were in the choir. It was raining and they stopped to pick me up in the rain. There wasn't room in their Brougham, so I sat on the Marquess's knee. They were coming through the park when they stopped for me. That was the only occasion we got as intimate! It was just because it was raining.'

The separation from some of the other servants could be just as rigid. Miss Crick recalled her mother as being strict, and very insistent that the family model their behaviour on that of the Lords and Ladies. Her father, as butler and head of the servants' household, was perforce a loner. This strained emotional condition was sometimes relieved by a bicycle ride to Alcester, where the locally-famous Crick would swop anecdotes and drinks with his cronies till a late hour. Then he would ride the three miles back to the butler's pantry. He might also, on occasion, have a drink in the butler's pantry itself, with the footman and the underman.

Mrs Crick used to say to her daughter, 'When your father has had no drink there is no one nicer.'

The demands on Miss Crick's self-reliance became even greater when the then Marquess died of cancer in 1912. The estate was put into the hands of trustees, the Hall was put into mothballs, and the dignified Crick and his family were asked if they would move into the house and live there to keep an eye on it. It was a logical request, but for the family it meant an even more singular existence. They had servants' status, but the virtual run of the Hall's one hundred and fifteen rooms. They didn't particularly want the honour, but they fell in with the wishes of the trustees. It was the sort of thing one did if one was a servant in those days.

'It was a big roomy place and, with only us in there, it was very lonely,' said Miss Crick.

The family lived in the basement of the Hall, using the Stewards' Room – where the heads of departments had had their meals – as their living room. A lady would come in daily to help Mrs Crick with the cleaning. It was the only contact the family had with other people at the Hall.

Naturally, the place had a ghost. A lady's maid was reported to have been murdered on Spring Bank, the strip of ground alongside a stream in Arrow village. By some perverse logic, perhaps acceptable only to collectors of supernatural phenomena, she revenged this act by walking about Ragley Hall at all hours of the night; often – if reports are to be believed – wearing something like hobnailed boots.

'It was a bit eerie at times at the Hall. I used to be glad when I was inside my room and could lock the door,' confessed the butler's daughter. 'We heard creaking noises, and other things you couldn't account for. I remember my mother and I used to like to sit up after father had gone to bed. One night we suddenly put our books down and looked at each other. I said to mother, after we had heard noises in the passageway, "I thought Daddy had gone to bed. Someone is coming down here." We took an oil lamp and went to his bedroom. He said, "I've been in bed a long time, why?" We told him. Father said, "Serve you right, you shouldn't sit up all night reading." But we still didn't know what that noise was.'

Fortunately Ragley Hall was never broken into by more earthly intruders – possibly because, in those days, the very act might have smacked almost of social impertinence. 'Except,' said Miss Crick, 'by bats. They used to sweep over our heads. We didn't like that very much. This great big passageway led off to the museum and my bedroom and bats used to fly in it and sometimes into other rooms. They hung themselves upside down and we had to get them out. We got used to them eventually, but we made sure we put something on our heads before we tried to remove them.'

There was also an underground passage to the laundry yard, never used by adults though sometimes children played in it. The butler's family studiously avoided it. It echoed. Rumour had it that there was another underground passage that led to the church two miles away, but no attempt was made by the Crick family to verify this. Crick might be hail-fellow-well-met, especially after closing time, but not even as the doyen of his drinking set (to whom a good story was worth its weight in ale) was he ever recorded as going in search of the two-mile-long tunnel. Even today, it is easier not to believe in ghosts while one is on the Arrow main road in daylight than it is at dusk, when one is at the end of the mile-long driveway, approaching the isolated Hall.

Eventually Crick himself was taken ill and died at the age of sixty-nine. This left his wife alone, at least in the daytime, after Marjorie Crick had jumped on to her motor bike and ridden the fifteen miles to Evesham, where she was a shorthand typist. She enjoyed working and regarded it as leading her own life – something she had never quite been able to do when confined to Ragley. Then her mother became ill, and the independent minded daughter was visited by Lady Helen Seymour, mother of the 8th Marquess. Lady Helen tactfully enquired whether Marjorie would give up her job and her daily motor cycle rides and return to Ragley to look after her mother.

It was a kindly approach, albeit one that indicated how strongly feudal rural Britain still was in the 1930s.

'It was quite a blow to me,' admitted Miss Crick. 'But I agreed. Mother got better for a year or two and I more or less helped to keep the house tidy. It was full of furniture – all the pictures and books were there, but no people. It was quite a responsibility, but it was a lovely place to be, the grounds were beautiful. Unfortunately, though, I was confined to the house and I had her two dogs to look after; really, it was a very lonely life. When I look back on it, I think how extraordinary it was that I lived that lonely life there.'

Miss Crick invited me to have another cup of tea, looked a little sadly around her immaculately-kept living room, with its china cabinets and wood and silver biscuit barrels, and mused: 'No wonder I like living alone now. It really conditions people, that sort of life.'

The war had almost begun before the elderly Mrs Crick told her daughter: 'It's time we had a place of our own.' This time both the family situation and the national mood made the Cricks determined to have their own home. Eventually, just before the war broke out, they rented a house from the Ragley estate – detached, with three bedrooms, two reception rooms and a pleasant view of woods and the Arrow main street. When her mother died there at the age of eighty-four, Miss Crick stayed on in the house and went back to her shorthand-typing. When I had tea with her, she was still in the same house at an economic but not excessive rent, and maintained that she loved the surroundings but wasn't too pleased with some of the demands of modern-day living. For example, her big garden was really too much for her to cope with at eighty-four, so that she had to employ a gardener, and gardeners were expensive. Then, the bus service to Alcester, two miles away, had been cut, which meant that she had to have taxis every time she visited friends in the town or wanted to shop. One day, she thought, she might look for a cottage in Alcester itself, even if that meant leaving the borders of the Ragley estate.

The former butler's daughter was well aware of the business acumen of the 8th Marquess of Hertford: 'Do I know the present Marquess? In my opinion, you can't help but know him! He was very, very shy as a boy, extremely shy. In fact, he made you feel awkward to talk to him. But going to school and agricultural college, and mixing with boys of his own bringing-up, brought him out a lot. I think the public like Ragley Hall because it is homely. You see the Marquess walking about. In a lot of stately homes they get you into one room and talk to you, but they don't do that at Ragley. The public can walk around at their leisure. On a nice day they can have tea on the terrace and walk around the gardens, and they probably see him in the gardens if not in the house. He now likes people to talk to him and ask him questions. I don't think he is shy any more. He has the money-making business well in hand. He's got to make it pay, we know that.'

Life can perhaps be even lonelier for the old faithfuls if they have been married once, but now live on their own in the same Ragley estate cottages, contending with the death of old acquaintances and with the poor public transport that stops them making new friends.

I found eighty-two-year-old Alf Goddard in an old combat jacket, cracked shoes and working trousers, digging in his half-acre garden. He said he wanted to keep his mind occupied. He was forking up the border round his rose bushes, and discarding some parsnips which hadn't come to anything. His wife had died the year before, after a long and distressing illness. He had started working at Ragley Hall in 1924 and worked there as a tractor driver and gardener till he went on half-day working at sixty-five and then eventually retired. His garden would have done credit to a man half his age.

It was a sunny spring day, but Alf Goddard asked me to imagine the scene in winter: his cottage was near two others, but in an exposed position in the middle of the countryside. 'Lonely? In the winter it is the devil! If you had sat here of a night talking to yourself soon after you have had tea, you would know. You have got no one to talk to, you keep looking at television and time seems endless. Still, I have my health and strength, and I suppose I will have to put up with it. I live here rent free, after all, and will carry on as long as I can. I used to be able to read and thread a needle but now blood pressure has affected my eyes and I can only read big print. I don't have any hobbies – only the garden. No football pools. Never messed with that.'

To a townsman, Alf Goddard's present life might appear bleak indeed. He retired when he was seventy-three, having done eight years of half-day working (eight a.m. to one p.m.) for a wage of about £3 a week. Since then he has lived on his pension and his savings in an area where he sees few people and really needs to have some form of transport, which he lacks, to get him to the Hall for occasional social events.

'I know chaps who work on the estate, but they keeps coming and going. There aren't so many now, either, you know. When I started in 1924, there were between forty-three and forty-seven at the Hall. Now it would be a handful of casual workers. You've got to remember that Lord

Hertford wasn't even born when I first went to the Hall. For 28s 6d★ a week we had to mind our P's and Q's. But I don't know whether it's a good thing that times have changed. It's a job to know what this country is like today. They are more or less a lot of pigs, aren't they? I think someone said it wants another war to clear half of them out of it.'

Such views may or may not help to promote a full social life; but living in the same cottage for over fifty years (in his case since 1930) certainly does tend to foster a certain sort of conservatism.

'I go up to the Hall when I'm invited, and that's about all,' said Goddard. 'Otherwise I stay at home.'

Lord Hertford, I suspect, rather likes the thought of reunions. He is certainly rather good at inventing pretexts for them. One of them has been what almost all the old faithfuls described to me as 'The Muriel'.

By this, they mean the mural. During my visits to Ragley, it was being painted over a vast area of ceiling and wall in the South Staircase Hall by Graham Rust. It is entitled The Temptation. The intention was that it should be 5,000 square feet in area when completed. Christ and the Devil were to be painted on the ceiling, looking down at the scene below, which was to include pictures of the Marquess's four children with their godparents. Chippendale mirrors were to be incorporated into the design.

The progress of this work of art had been a source of no little wonder and comment to the old faithfuls, who had been invited up to the Hall at various times to inspect it and pronounce upon it. Lord Hertford was delighted that his 'Muriel' was such a constant topic of conversation among old servants of Ragley. He warned me in advance who 'Muriel' was, so that I was not unnecessarily perplexed by references to her many intriguing qualities when I was in conversation with old members of the staff.

Sure enough, the 'Muriel' soon entered the conversation I had with the retired plumber, Jim Hancox, in his cottage, about the last time he had gone up to the Hall. He was a remarkably young-looking seventy-two at the time, his hair neatly combed across his thin patch and his necktie neatly tied and dead central. Since he did not know in advance that I was calling on him, this was no special preparation for a visitor.

'We certainly went to have a look at that Muriel,' he said. 'We went on a public visiting day, but as ex-employees of the estate, we don't pay, and

★ about £1.45 or $3.75.

we can take our friends in.' He and his wife were impressed by 'that Muriel', and obviously grateful that the Hall could produce such subjects for discussion long after he had retired. Would working for a factory have proved as interesting in retirement? It was plain that old employees of the Ragley estate could still feel tugs of loyalty to the Hall and its people, a feeling that may not be so prevalent a few miles away in the factories of the West Midlands.

Jim Hancox, still living in the modernized cottage to which he first came fifty years ago, had retired four years before our conversation took place, when he was just sixty-nine.

'I came here,' he said, 'in 1931 as a lodger. The wife's grandmother was living here, and that is how I met my wife. She was in service on another estate. I was twenty-three and she was sixteen. She was brought here as a war orphan in 1915 and has lived here ever since.'

Mrs Hancox, a slender and alert lady with neat white hair, stood behind the living room sofa as I talked to her husband, supplying the relevant detail at the right time. 'Yes, I was three weeks old when I was brought here. It was before the cottage was modernized. There was a tin bath in front of the fire until fourteen years ago. Then we had a bathroom and a flush toilet put in. Before that, we had to go round to the toilet right at the back of the cottage, past the pig styes.'

'And then we had to empty the bucket up the garden,' her husband added.

'My grandfather,' said Mrs Hancox, 'was a bricklayer on the estate. He died before my grandmother and the tenancy went to her. They paid a rent of 2s* a week. I don't know how much they were paid – about £2 or £2 10s, I suppose. Of course, today you have to depend on the family for transport. There have been no buses here for three years and there used to be three a day. We see the children most weekends, and I still ride my bike. We have to keep going.'

Such a difficult lifestyle had nevertheless not made the Hancoxes great admirers of life in the industrial towns, with a Kentucky Fried Chicken or Chinese takeaway at every street corner.

'Financially we are better off now,' said Jim Hancox. 'But before the war everyone made their own amusements and everyone looked in on one another. There were no toffee-nosed people around at that time. You

---

* 10p or about 24 cents US.

enjoyed life a lot better. Today they keep up with the Joneses if they have to cut their own throats to do it – that is the attitude of people today. Then you get the unions. They are greedy, and what have they got for it? They are on the dole.'

A suspicion of trade unionism was widespread among the old retainers of Ragley – even those who were now living on state pensions supplemented by occasional payments from the Ragley estate.

'I started work in June 1926, just before the General Strike,' recalled Jim Hancox. 'I hadn't any interest in the General Strike. I think I earned 21s a week then, and paid 17s a week lodgings. I just got my 3s 3d, because my national insurance was 9d. I had 3s 3d to keep my bike in working order and to keep myself. You didn't get much to throw about in those days. But you enjoyed it. You weren't bothered about it. As long as you had a job, it took most of your life up, and that was that. You had to turn up at seven in the morning, and you left at five-thirty in the summer and five in the winter. It was a half-hour ride to work and a half-hour ride home again. You had a breakfast and took your mid-day sandwiches with you, and that lasted you until you got back home. Those days wasn't good, but everyone seemed more happy and sociable than what they are today. Today it is all hurry and bustle. It is only in the country that people recognize one another. In the town, you are knocked arse over head if you don't get out of the road; and no one knows anybody.'

In this close-knit country community, the occasional visits of 'the Boss' are much appreciated. If Lord Hertford happened to be anywhere near, said Jim Hancox, he might call in, to see how the family were. Other members of the family might stop in the street and have a chat. Lord Hertford had called when the cottage was painted up last summer, and his wife had called once. They had attended the wedding of Lord and Lady Hertford in 1956, and they had gone to the Hall for the Earl of Yarmouth's twenty-first birthday celebrations.

'Lord Hertford's mother,' said Jim Hancox, 'used to go round and talk to the people in the cottages. She would come in and sit down and say, "Can I have a little rest?" I suppose the present generation are far too busy for that.'

Despite the pull of the estate and its traditions, the Hancoxes decided that their four children should be 'independent'. The eldest, Dorothy, went in for office work at the Co-op. Margaret joined Needles Industries in Dudley, in the heart of the industrial West Midlands. John went to the offices of a German tool firm and Robert became a lorry driver. None have worked on the Ragley estate.

'You have got to adapt yourself to work on an estate,' said Jim Hancox. 'There are a lot of "ifs" and "buts" about the job. You have to be prepared to grin and bear it if they jump on you at all. When you are on the estate, they really want you at their beck and call. That is why they brought you there in the first place. We preferred our children to be independent.'

Jim Hancox had no grumbles about his own job: he was a general maintenance worker with plumbing experience at just the right time. It was irritating to be told (by the agents then running the farms) the way to do a job when 'you could see a better way to do the job than the way they had suggested'. But you did the job their way, right or wrong, even when it came to the water wheels or the pumps, about which he was supposed to know something.

Until the early 1950s every farm on the Ragley estate had its water mill or pump – there were no water mains to the twenty-two farms which then made up the estate. Jim Hancox often used to ride his bicycle the eight miles to Stratford-upon-Avon to repair a pump or mill, and, when mains water was first introduced, he put much of his effort into connecting up the farms as quickly as possible. Trenches were dug up to the property, and sometimes he had to spend a week on one job, then cycle the best part of twenty miles to different parts of the estate and start again. The process of connecting up farms to the mains was still going on when he retired at the age of sixty-nine.

'At that time,' he said, 'there were still some properties waiting for mains water.'

Jim Hancox was prepared to retire completely at sixty-five, but Lord Hertford called personally and asked him to reconsider; would he do half days at the Hall itself, cleaning the gutters, sweeping up leaves and mending potholes? In his complete retirement, said Jim Hancox, he still had, free, the cottage for which he previously paid a rent of £7.50 a year: 'It wouldn't pay the rates today.'

I heard the usual murmurs among Ragley pensioners about cottages needing a lick of paint outside; but the high costs of decorating cottages for which little or no rent is paid is fairly well understood.

'We do have a roof over our heads, which is the chief thing today,' said

Albert Richards, former head gardener of the estate, at his home. This was a lodge at the bottom of the drive to Kingley, a part of the estate where Lord Hertford's mother used to live, but which was later disposed of.

Albert Richards said he was really only accustomed to life in tied cottages. His father, a carter, lived in one. Then the family moved from that to a tied cottage on the Ragley estate, fifty-seven years ago, and the young Richards worked for Lady Helen Seymour. This was at what was called Park Hall, a part of the estate which was also later sold – though it was there that the 8th Marquess was born.

'We moved here to Kingley with Lady Helen,' said Albert Richards. 'She was a very grand lady, the idol of people round here. No matter what it was, an accident, anything, she was good, really good. When she died, we went back to Ragley Hall and took over the garden together. I altered the rose beds a bit. I often saw Lord Hertford, who called round. I first knew him when he was a baby at Park Hall, when I was with Lady Helen.'

This was a fairly typical example of the sort of personal interest taken in their aristocratic employers by the old faithfuls of Ragley. No doubt it is innocent, and may well seem feudal to many townsmen. On the other hand, the people who live their lives within the Ragley boundaries may read of street muggings, violence and breakings-and-enterings in the towns and rather wonder at the modern townsman's sense of liberated superiority.

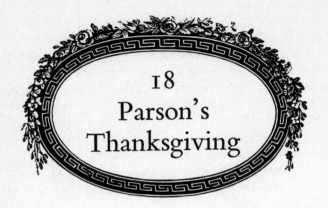

18
Parson's
Thanksgiving

ONCE THE PARSON was one of the great powers of country life, rank-ing between the squire and the doctor. It is not quite the same now. His power is eroded and he has to battle manfully for goodwill and Christian influence.

Ragley's parson greeted me at harvest thanksgiving with the cheerful briskness of a missionary advising a fairly friendly native. 'I will start delivering the harvest parcels to the over-seventies of Arrow at nine tomorrow morning. If you want to come with me, nine o'clock sharp. All right? Tonight's sermon will be called, 'Do you take milk with your tea?'

Here, obviously, was no identikit modern man of the cloth, all city-smooth unction and sociological jargon, prepared to discuss God as if He were a candidate in a local council election. Here was a real character. One should not, perhaps, have expected less from Ragley than a parson who had served in Borneo and Hong Kong, who now lived in a beautiful Georgian rectory next to his church and who could boast a steady eye with a shotgun on a rough shoot.

'Come to the service tonight because you think it'll be a bit visual, have you?' enquired the Reverend Arthur Stally, rector of St Nicholas, Alcester, of Holy Trinity, in the village of Arrow, and of Oversley and St James, in the village of Weethley. His living covers much of Ragley, and the 8th Marquess of Hertford is patron of the living.

At the time, when the congregation were still filing into St Nicholas Church for the evening harvest thanksgiving service, I wondered what

Ragley's parson, who is also Rural Dean of Alcester, actually meant. Visual?

I had no time to enquire at that moment. Dressed in his light green surplice, he was off to see that the 400 harvest parcels of fruit and vegetables were neatly lined up on one side of his church; that the standard of the British Legion, Alcester Branch, was in the porch; that the nest of six eggs and the farmhouse loaves were in place by the intricately carved fount; and that the little pyramids of tomatoes had not tumbled over. He was being sternly regarded by the vigilant white marble eyes of the Right Honourable Sir Hamilton Seymour, GCB, GCH, born 1797, died 2 February 1880 – immortalized in the entrance of Alcester's parish church by Sir Hamilton's son, Arthur Henry Seymour, another ancestor of the 8th Marquess.

There was a time in England when the squire, the parson and the doctor ruled country society as a powerful trinity. The doctor may have had his divine right to rule dented by the National Health Service; but within reach of at least some of our great Halls the squire and the parson are still linked together in a chain of influence. Ragley is obviously such a case. This became clear as the Churchwarden of St Nicholas, Kenneth Humphrey, a compact man in a blue pin-striped suit and country green shirt and tie, courteously explained to me the social connections that existed today between church and Hall, parson and squire.

Alcester, it appeared, had a Lord of the Manor at the head of its traditional constitution, a structure rather different from those of the boring new district and county councils that attend to such mundane things as drains, education and pavements.

'Lord Hertford,' said Kenneth Humphrey, 'is Lord of the Manor and supports as many functions as he can. He joins the processions if he is around. It's an enormous advantage that Lord Hertford's name is just there. A real live Lord as Lord of the Manor adds something and it must assist when it comes to fund-raising.'

Various local trusts and good causes are funded by a sort of local council called the Court Leet, which goes so far back (to around 1200 AD) that Alcester locals will boast of its antique origins without in the least knowing what they are. Every year Court Leet elections are held to appoint a High and Low Bailiff. Unless he does something disastrous, the Low Bailiff usually becomes the High Bailiff the following year. During their period of office both men take part in local ceremonial and fund-raising so that, for instance, between six hundred and seven hundred food parcels can be handed out at Christmas to all people over seventy years old, whether they are in need or not. The Steward of the Manor, appointed by the Lord of the Manor, acts as go-between betwixt the Lord of the Manor and the Court Leet.

The fruits of this feudal co-operation are many and curious. A proclamation is read through the streets by the Town Crier. There is a Town Criers' competition, in which Alcester's own Town Crier once came first in the best scroll section, fourth in actual crying and unplaced in the best-dressed award.

'It's become pretty traditional,' explained Kenneth Humphrey, who happened to be that year's Low Bailiff, 'that the High Bailiff has a ball at Ragley around June, for which Ragley Hall is hired from Lord Hertford at a concessional rate. It is very much a prestige event and there is usually a good demand for tickets. I think there is a definite connection between Hall and town. For instance, something that has happened in recent years is that the High and Low Bailiffs are usually entertained to dinner by Lord Hertford before the ball at nine o'clock. We went there, and as far as we were concerned, it was a most notable occasion, and one we will remember for the rest of our lives. Lord Hertford takes an interest in Alcester, and he has done a lot to restore Ragley to its former splendour since he came here.'

By now I was almost having to pinch myself to remind myself that Birmingham, with all its twentieth-century wealth and concomitant problems, was less than thirty miles away. It might have been in a different universe. The city, and its values, was to seem far away for the rest of the evening, except when one of the servers refused to let me, an unidentified stranger, hold the collection plate as I put my contribution into it. The experience made me, a townsman, immediately feel more at home.

It was true that harvest thanksgiving service began traditionally enough, with nothing especially visual that I could see:

> Come, ye thankful people, come
> Praise the song of harvest-home!
> All be safely gathered in,
> Ere the winter storms begin . . .

But with that sermon, 'Do you take milk in your tea?' the proceedings tooks off in an idiosyncratic, theatrical and undeniably effective way, fully worthy of the barn-storming tradition of the country clerics of old. The Rector and Rural Dean took as his starting point the current harvest festival and finished with an appeal to give generously for the purpose of digging wells in India. Quite a feat. He punctuated his argument by boiling up a kettle, making a pot of tea and drinking it – all directly beside the pulpit.

The argument went something like this. In England, we all came together at this one time of year for the harvest thanksgiving. But in Northern India they were always reaping their harvest, which was why in Alcester we could get our cup of tea. (Parson drinks cup, says to congregation: 'You didn't think it was genuine, did you?' Small boy from congregation: 'Oh yes we did!') Both the harvest in England and the tea crop in India required one thing. What was it? Small boy at back: 'You need water.' Correct. Now we in England lived in a place where there was plenty of water, but in India they had to dig wells and digging wells cost money . . . And so on.

'We collected £34.70 for digging wells in India,' the Rural Dean told a local newspaper reporter the next morning. This was after teasing him, in what was obviously a congenial and expected ritual, about having a leader of the Plymouth Brethren for a grandfather. The reporter also happened to be a Court Leet Constable and, I gathered, a Methodist.

I asked the Rural Dean what the letters BMA, listed after his name in a reference book I had consulted, actually stood for. 'Ah! It means Borneo Missionary Association. I remember I went to an event at one of the universities in Wales, and the bill for it was sent to the British Medical Association. They are, after all, a rather better-known BMA than we are.'

The distribution of the harvest parcels had a certain military precision, with an assembly of local ladies acting as well-trained troops.

In the church, the ladies were allocating areas of activity to helpers. A large piece of chipboard was laid across the tops of pews and lists of people over seventy years of age were pinned to it, each covering a specific area of the parish.

The parson and I began to load up the boot of his family saloon with harvest parcels. Almost all were in fruit baskets of some sort. Some had handles. Some had transparent plastic coverings. Many contained carrots, leeks and onions; whereas in previous years, before the economic recession set in, they apparently used to be filled with canned foods. But even in hard economic times, the appeal by the children of St Faith's Church of England School, and other local schoolchildren, had produced two hundred and fifty of the total four hundred harvest baskets.

At one time it was decided to distribute money rather than parcels, as it was felt that this was more in keeping with the times. However, it turned out to be rather too clinical and so the parson restored the ritual of the handing out of harvest parcels.

While the loading up was in progress and the willing ladies were setting off on their own delivery rounds, the Rector recalled for my benefit how he had come to Alcester in 1966, after an interview with Lord Hertford and his mother. He thought that Lady Helen had had a great influence on his appointment: 'She was a most charming and strong personality. She had her feet very much on the ground and knew what was going on around her. I had considered another living at the time, one at Stone in Staffordshire. I took photographs of both places, went home and developed the films, and considered them carefully. I chose Alcester because it is what I call a Heinz 57 Varieties parish – you have got absolutely everything here. If pastoral work is your business, then variety is what makes it go.'

Of course, said the Rector, he would like to see more of his patron. But Lord Hertford did come to remembrance day and other 'classic' services; and he himself was very keen to perform the classics as well as the more popular, updated type of service which might include tea-drinking.

'But,' said the Rector, as we set off on the harvest parcel distribution in Arrow, 'we do have many varied activities here. I take the Friends of St Nicholas abroad for a weekend, Arnhem or somewhere like that, and for the tenth anniversary we are going to Fontainebleau. We raise money for church restoration that way, and you have to remember that when you talk of getting it decorated you are talking about £50,000. We hold a Midlands Conker Competition round the church itself for a Silver Cup.'

The first recipient of a parcel from the Rector that day was Dorothy Harwood, the seventy-three-year-old widow of a Ragley worker who had been on the estate since he was nineteen. 'At first he was a forester in the woods, and then the war came and he drove a lorry because all the other men had gone to the war and after that he was a bricklayer until he died,' she remarked to me, because the Rector himself already knew her personal history. Indeed he was knowledgeable about the history, foibles and misfortunes of most of his elderly flock of Ragley tenants. He nodded understandingly as she told her story again.

The Rector handed out two parcels to each of the over-seventies. He took care not to sound patronizing when the old folk showed pleasure and surprise.

'You know,' he said, as we trooped up yet another cottage garden, 'you can never assume these old people you talk to have done nothing in their lives. You must never talk down to them. I remember once going to the Isle of Skye. The old fellow who handed me my ticket, whom you might have thought had never been anywhere, had been to Vladivostock – he had been with the White Russian relief forces in 1917. I had rather pompously assumed he had never lived anywhere other than Skye.'

Outside the cottage of a ninety-three-year-old widower, Joseph Knight, the Rector looked for any smoke coming from the chimney. He was surprised to see none. 'Every day he has a fire going, winter and summer. A day without his fire going is a rare one.' The parson obviously took great pride in his flock; even if they but rarely flocked in his direction nowadays.

The old man inside the cottage thought the day a rare one, too, when he got his two parcels of apples, carrots and leeks. 'Thank you very much, and good morning to you!' he said, raising a finger to touch a non-existent forelock; he was almost completely bald.

'Yes,' said the Rector, back in his car, 'it is still the squire, the parson and the doctor here, in a way. But look at these cottages we're passing now, they don't have much to do with church life. They've been done up and sold off to all sorts of people – the owner of one is the son of an engineering company executive. You have an enormous range of wealth here now. On the one hand you will find people earning vast sums of money, and then on the other you will find villagers like Mr Knight, who has been retired for most of his life here. That old school over there was once the Ragley estate office – now it's a kitchen and bathroom design centre. He's a very good chap there now. But the place is a far cry from the collection of tied cottages that formed the traditional village years ago.'

Parcels were distributed to the over-seventies, the zealous cleric pointed out, quite irrespective of their individual wealth or lack of it. This was partly because the gift itself was not the whole point of the exercise. It was the act of remembrance. He would be going to a relatively well-off family in Alcester later in the day. The man had recently sold off his garage business, lived in a splendid house, and certainly didn't need a harvest parcel.

'But we still give him a parcel,' said the rector. 'It's the tradition.'

Some of the villagers I talked to said pointedly that they would like to see the parson rather more often. To others he was obviously an august figure, to be regarded with awe at a comfortable distance rather than with familiarity. Arthur Randall, who retired nearly twenty years ago (after working on the gardens at Ragley for twenty-three years) and has lived in the same half-timbered cottage for fifty-one years, said contentedly: 'The Rector never calls unless it is something special. He doesn't bother you at all.' A parson of today, even in a village like Arrow, has to be sensitive to people's feelings, hoping to give the impression of being neither an absentee nor a pest.

Alcester's parson, I did not doubt, was well able to jolly along even the shyest parishioner. He seemed almost to welcome the invasion of Arrow by householders from far away: not only from Birmingham, England, but in one case, from Atlanta, USA.

'These cottages,' said the well-informed Rector as we passed some recently renovated buildings, 'are owned by a family from Atlanta, who come over here for their holidays. They are looked after by Mrs Randall. I don't mind this sort of development at all, on the whole. They frequently take an active part in village life, and they all come to church and present us with new vision and ideas, a new angle. You *could* say they don't contribute towards the social fabric, I suppose – but we are not likely to start burning things down like the Welsh Nationalists.'

But it was the old 'locals' who really occupied the parson's thoughts on that harvest parcels delivery day; and they were usually people who had been in Arrow a very long time and had its interests very much at heart. One retired employee of Ragley insisted on finding some conkers in his garden for the conker competition at the church. They liked to think, too, that someone had their interests at heart as they faced the long winter evenings, many of them living on their own.

'I could never understand why my Fred made such a fuss about getting his £1 from the High Bailiff's fund at Christmas time,' said Mrs Elspeth Gwynn, widow of a Ragley farm worker, as she took her own little share of the Ragley harvest festival. 'But as I get older myself, I realize that even if it's only an orange or an apple you get, what matters is that someone has remembered you.'

It is perhaps at harvest thanksgiving time that country people of all social levels most remember their reliance on one another, a reliance that the townsman perhaps neither wants nor needs. If the villagers, old and young, need their parson, their parson also needs them. If they need their squire, the squire needs them no less. Indeed, some might argue that he needs them rather more.

'The defence of Ragley today,' said Ragley's parson, having handed out his last parcel, 'is based on the fact that there is farming still going on around it, which is a reason for its existence. Remove that and what have you got? A large house on its own. The farms and the people of the farms give Ragley Hall a reason to exist today.'

This bond of mutual need, perhaps appealing to something deep in the British character, however anachronistic it may appear to some, arguably gives a great country estate like Ragley its continuing strength – in an era which could probably not be more unsympathetic. It has not, perhaps, prevented the figurative autumn of the Hall, but it has so far held off its bleak winter.

19
Shades of Autumn

GREAT ESTATES like Ragley die a little, at least in the eyes of the casual observer, when both summer and the visitors have alike disappeared.

As I drove towards Ragley in the early morning of a late September Sunday, I heard the ominous tones of the weather forecaster on the car radio. 'It will begin sunny but later, I'm afraid, there will be showers of rain, some of them heavy, and temperatures will remain low.'

It was suddenly autumn and, equally suddenly, closing day of the Ragley season. When I reached the gates of Ragley, no gatekeeper was in sight and so I opened the black and gilt gates for myself. Unlike a sunny afternoon in the peak of summer, there was only one couple waiting patiently for the gates to open, an American and his wife, who I advised to come back later. There was still a couple of hours to go before the gates officially opened to the public for the last time that year. The American and his wife climbed patiently back into their car and started the engine. 'Might as well get the heater going, I guess,' said the man. 'But we'll wait.'

It was very much that sort of day. Once inside the gates there was little sign of activity, except for members of the Ragley Sailing Club who were making for the boating lake in Ragley Park, on which they have a long lease. Crews huddled in their oilskins as they raised their sails. It was a good day for sailing. A chill wind cut through the shallow valley to the west of the house, which holds the boating lake. It gave some idea of what Ragley could be like in a winter nor'easter. In the Adventure Park, most of the amusements had been taken away and the two Lunarworlds (the rubber inflatables in which children jump and climb in the summer months) were now two sad-looking parcels on the grass, ready to go into winter storage.

Soon the gatekeeper, Jack Smith, came into view in his red Ford Cortina. He was wearing a thick tweed suit. His absence from the gate when I arrived was soon explained.

'There's a back way near here where people can sneak in,' he said, without getting out of his car into the cutting breeze. 'You have to watch that they don't sneak in without paying.'

Jack Smith had kept his eye on it for a time. But it seemed the day was too chilly even for interlopers hoping to get in free. I went back with him to his lodge for a hot cup of tea. Over it he said that the now dying season had taught him a lot about the attitude of the general public when it came to visiting a stately home. 'The best, from my personal point of view, is the British working man. He has worked out exactly what it is going to cost him before he reaches the gate, and what he is going to get for his money. He pays, and that is that. No bother. The man in the latest registration letter car will ask you what it is going to cost, and you say so much for the Park and so much for the House, and he often waits and thinks about it. Sometimes I say to people, "Would you mind pulling over and making up your minds so I can see to the rest of the queue, and when you have made up your minds, I will let you have what you require." '

On this autumnal day, Jack Smith was to have no problems. There were no queues. There was a financial as well as meteorological chill in the air.

Shortly before the house was due to open for the last time that season, Fobbester, the dignified butler, was still in his shirt-sleeves decorating his flat. His wife, Iris Fobbester, the cook, was in the kitchen-cum-butler's-pantry, on her own except for Lord Hertford's golden spaniel William. Lord and Lady Hertford were away attending a country house ball. There was an end-of-term feel to activities in the kitchen. There would be only three to lunch in the private dining room next door, and Lord and Lady Hertford would not be there. So Iris Fobbester was grilling some pork chops instead of roasting the more usual Sunday joint. She had cut her hand, anyway, and was finding it difficult to handle things. She was thinking about setting off on a welcome holiday in a few days' time – golf at Wentworth.

'Then we go back into the usual winter routine,' she told me. 'You can go into the garden and relax from now on, and you can take the dogs for a walk without having to bother. We always have afternoon teas for Lady

Hertford in the closed season, which we don't have in the summer when the place is open. They are served at five in the library. If the whole family is here we will set up the Cadogan table – a round table which folds up when not in use.'

The cook does not totally lose contact with the public in the closed season, however. There will still be dinners for individuals and various firms – the professional entertaining which the surviving British aristocrat has now mastered as a fine art. Once recently, said Iris Fobbester, she had got a standing ovation from the British Airways people who came to dinner. She was asked to go through and Fobbester insisted she went. They all got up and toasted her. 'Sometimes they send for me, but they don't often toast me. It was very nice.'

Only a trickle of people came into Ragley when the gates were finally opened that day. One of them sat almost on her own in the tea rooms. She was on a sentimental journey which was as autumnal in mood as the day itself. Audrey Hellawell, now retired, first visited Ragley in the 1950s when she was with the Warwickshire County Museum, helping the curator, Miss Jocelyn Morris, to do a complete inventory of items in the Hall before Lord and Lady Hertford started to implement their revival plans.

'I am on holiday alone,' she said, 'and I have relatives in this area. So I thought I would come up from Stratford-upon-Avon and look at Ragley and then go and see the relatives in time for tea. When I saw this place in the 1950s, it hadn't been lived in for some time. It was grey and very cold. There was lovely furniture, but it was under dust sheets. It was an interesting experience to see the things in the house. Not depressing, I wouldn't say – rather a challenge to bring the place alive again. I suppose we spent about a week here. I haven't been back here since it was opened to the public – I have been living in Cheshire. But I've read about it and how it has been developed. I think it is very nice indeed – beautifully done. I heard someone here say it was a life's work; and it certainly is.'

Behind the counter of the tea rooms, the longest-serving lady, Kathleen Hanson, was dispensing her last cups of Ragley tea for the year. She told me she had been serving in the tea rooms for twenty years. Her husband had come to Ragley when he was seventeen, first of all working under the gamekeeper and then becoming head keeper of the Cold Comfort Shoot, which had now been discontinued. She used to make lunch for

Lord Hertford's shoot, and she still prepared the lunch for a shoot occasionally. When the tea room closed, she would confine herself to spending three mornings a week on cleaning work. She used to do five, but found it too much, what with having to be in the tea rooms in the afternoons as well.

Was life going to be easier for her in the winter? 'Well, I enjoy my work, and if you enjoy it, it isn't a burden, is it? I'm certainly not thinking, "Oh, thank goodness it's over." I enjoy it because I enjoy meeting people. And you need all kinds. It was rather funny yesterday. Two gentlemen stood in the tea rooms' counter queue, talking. One walked past without paying and I said to the second man, "Are you going to pay for the gentleman who has just gone in?" He said, "I may as well, someone has got to pay." Then he went and sat down in a different place to the other man! He wasn't with him! By the time I got there and apologized, he said, "Well, we're in the same party. Don't worry, I'll twist his arm for a gin and tonic on the way home." '

Sad as the approaching winter might be in some respects, it would at least relieve Kathleen Hanson of her frequent bus-driver dilemma. Drivers of coach parties are supposed to have a cup of tea and a cake on the house. 'But if you look at a man and say, "Are you a bus driver?" and he isn't, it is a bit embarrassing; and they don't always show their badges. But, on the whole, I really enjoy the work.'

In the sweet shop Cynthia Bindley, the lady in charge, was looking at a handsome iced cake which had been presented by the departing restaurant manager with 'many thanks for help and support during the year'.

In her own office, Maureen Lawrence was already brooding about possible new ideas for the next open season and saying how difficult it was to find any which were economic and didn't destroy the character of the house. A narrow gauge railway through the surrounding woods would be nice, but would probably cost half a million pounds and would it pay? It was all right having an exhibition of Crown Jewels; they had lined the walls of the Great Hall, which could also be used for other events. But an exhibition of larger objects in the Great Hall would prevent it being used for other events. 'It becomes quite a problem, thinking up what we can do next,' she admitted.

In the souvenirs shop, Molly Stephens was having sherry with two visitors who were finding the occasion very sad indeed. It would be their last visit to Ragley until next year – they had been coming as often as three or four times a week during the summer. Frederick Bacon, a retired chartered accountant and his wife, Irene, certainly deserved their goodbye sherry with the staff. As we walked to their car on the park afterwards, Irene Bacon feeding the peacocks with diced wholemeal bread as we went, they explained that they had been coming to Ragley regularly for five years.

Why such consistent devotion? 'I think what set us coming in the first place,' said Frederick Bacon, 'was that there is such a variety of domestic animals. We feed the birds on the lake, and we're very fond of the mountain dog Roland and the beagle. The tea amenities are good. It is one of the best amenities in England, tea on the terrace on a sunny Sunday afternoon. Then we see the crops sewn and cut and several broods of peacocks reared from babyhood. It is an estate; but it is intimate enough to know everything about it.'

The Bacons originally lived in London, but at the time I met them they were retired and living in a flat in the stockbroker belt of Birmingham. Perhaps they found their life in a flat a little restricting?

'I do think it makes it easier for us to decide to come out,' said Irene Bacon, 'put it that way.'

'Here at Ragley we have the advantage of country gardens, but with someone else having all the trouble of them,' laughed her husband. 'We find it quite a home from home, as a matter of fact.' One could see why he found the notion rewarding.

'We are always careful not to intrude,' said Irene Bacon. 'We always remember it is Lord Hertford's home, not ours. But in a way we do feel like part of the family. It is quite a wrench today. It costs us £10 a week in petrol to come here. It sounds silly to you, perhaps.'

Not necessarily, I assured them. Stately homes like Ragley do exercise an almost hypnotic influence after a while, seducing people of almost any class into identifying strongly with them and their occupants. I sensed it myself. This is perhaps one of the secrets of the longevity of the British aristocracy. Whoever you are you begin, after a period of exposure to Ragley, to pat the giant mountain dog almost as if he were your own, and to regard anyone who deposits litter as aiming an insult at you personally.

It is fortunate that this type of emotional worship, although particularly English in nature, is also to a degree international. Ragley's fortunes depend on it.

Two of the last visitors to disappear into the autumnal evening were

Americans: Dr Joel Warren, a visiting research scientist from Florida, and his friend Bill O'Brien, a lawyer, who for years had rented a summer holiday home at the nearby village of Broadway.

'I would give anything to see Ragley as it was originally, as a stately country home,' said Bill O'Brien.

'I would give anything to have enough money to turn it back to what it *was*,' said Joel Warren. 'I suppose most visitors would say they enjoyed it because it represents a style of life long gone, and which will never come back. I enjoyed it because it represents it in great detail. It is a slice of the whole social cake of England. By looking at the house and its furnishings, you can tell what it felt like to live at that period. I haven't seen excessive modernization in this place. This atmosphere of life going on has a wonderful allegorical value.'

Ragley and its farms, forests and people are certainly an allegory of the survival of the British aristocracy, albeit in a newer and more commercial form. All the people who work in and around Ragley feel it. Visitors pay money to experience this feeling for themselves. Time and time again they say that what they most like about the Hall is that a real live Lord and Lady live in it.

The part-time staff who fade away in the winter months were already packing up for the last time that autumn evening. Violet Brooks, at her desk in the study, had torn her last admission ticket for the year. She confessed that she would, in a way, like the change from always having to be on her best behaviour with the public, who could be rather demanding sometimes.

'But on a day like this you do feel a bit sad that it's all over,' she said. 'I am looking forward to the spring. When we have got over Christmas I always think, "Oh, if I'm asked back to Ragley again, I will be pleased." We always wait for the letter saying we are wanted back and we're relieved when it comes.'

The British aristocracy itself, I reflected as I drove from Ragley towards my own home, has certainly not survived by waiting for invitations. It has written out its own invitation to survive; and it has often done so, as at Ragley, with a flourish, a certain shrewdness and a diplomatically quiet success. If the British aristocracy have had to become showmen, farmers, or curators (or all three) in order to survive, then their defence could be that all three are honourable occupations that produce benefits for the whole community.

And in future? Ragley left me with this intriguing thought. If British heavy industry continues to decline as it has in recent years, and there is a swing back to a more agriculturally-based economy, who is to say with absolute certainty that the power and influence of the landed aristocracy and the lesser gentry will not increase? This might seem to some to go against the grain of that equality which has been making at least nominal progress in other parts of the world, and of the meritocracy and love of the entrepreneur which underpins much right-wing political philosophy in Britain. But many things have gone against those two philosophies and survived with diligence and bravura.

As I drove away from Ragley, the vigilant gatekeeper was characteristically *still* giving me the once-over to make sure I wasn't one of those people who alone constitute a real and undisputed threat to the Ragleys of England: those parasites who expect to hang around the place without either working or paying. Some might say that in their vulnerability to the less scrupulous members of society, the modern aristocracy are as endearingly human as the rest of us.

20
Future
Prospects

THE RIGOURS of winter, literal or figurative, cannot destroy the optimism and almost casual sense of indestructability exhibited by the 8th Marquess of Hertford, his family and his staff. Ragley was under deep snow in the winter of 1981–82, but the harsh weather did not produce a mood of defeatism. On the contrary, it seemed to stimulate that resilience so vital to the survival of a great estate like Ragley.

'We had quite a funny Sunday, just before the snow, when it was freezing hard,' Lord Hertford told me cheerfully. 'I was showing some people round, and we had just got to the Prince Regent's State Bedroom when I heard what sounded like a waterfall coming from the bathroom beyond it. A pipe had burst away from the washing machine above the bathroom and water was coming through the ceiling.'

The 8th Marquess busied himself trying to stop the waterfall. 'While I was doing that the cook came through and said there was another flood in the kitchen. This was caused by a frozen pipe which had burst in my daughter's bedroom above the kitchen.'

Had these and other assorted calamities made him have doubts about the long-term future of life at the Hall? The 8th Marquess quickly dismissed the question.

'It was,' he said flatly, 'what you would call an entirely normal winter Sunday morning in a country house.'

Such resilient sang froid is surely inconquerable. Or at least it may be argued that it deserves to be. The sentimentalist might well want to leave the matter there. But, at the social and political levels, the argument will no doubt continue. All one can hope is that any criticism levelled against great country estates like Ragley is informed criticism tempered with some understanding of what aristocrats like Lord Hertford are trying to achieve. I can only hope that my own understanding was deepened by my acquaintance with Ragley. It was difficult to see how the removal of the 8th Marquess could considerably improve the lot of any of the people living on or around the Ragley estate, however 'morally' desirable this might be in the eyes of some politicians.

In any case, how much semi-feudal sway does the 8th Marquess really command? The nearer they are to the Lord, the more warmly his circle seem to speak of him. Fobbester the butler and 'Mrs Fobb' the cook, certainly feel great affection for Lord and Lady Hertford and their family. This warmth thins out a little when it comes to Lord Hertford's tenant farmers who have, every three years, to renegotiate their rents with him.

This phenomenon is not, I think, to be explained simply in terms of sycophancy. There are more plausible and complex explanations. Those who choose to dwell, as it were, in the house of the (temporal) Lord are obviously, in the first place, prone to think well of him. Their application for employment would be eccentric if they didn't. In the second place, they are more exposed to his charm. This, in the case of Lord Hertford and many of his fellow aristocrats, can be considerable, even if one senses it could falter if faced with too much outright opposition. I myself felt the charm, even if I also sensed its brittleness on some vital issues – notably the vulnerability of the Ragley balance sheet and the need for this to be offset by constant work on the part of everyone concerned, Lord and worker alike.

I had only one significant conflict with Lord Hertford in the course of writing the book. It started on the day I began my visits and finished on the day I ended them. I could meet and talk to whoever I wished, he said at the outset (I would have proceeded on no other basis); but I was on no account to hinder them in the course of their work. Work, to Ragley, *is* survival; and Lord Hertford was determined it should not be impeded. Nor did he fail to monitor my conduct in this respect. When I kept his son and heir, the young Earl of Yarmouth, talking for two hours at a stretch about his work in the lambing season, I was afterwards told very politely by Lord Hertford that there was 'something on his mind' he wished to discuss. Only my firm declaration that the two hours at once had been exceptional, and not the way of life we could expect throughout the preparation of the book, did he relax. On another occasion, when I was talking to one of the estate's longest-serving farm workers, who was in the middle of cutting the hay, His Lordship himself arrived on the scene ten minutes after I did, pointing out that the hay had priority over me.

This preoccupation with an uninterrupted work-flow may have inconvenienced me from time to time. It certainly did not support the caricaturists' view that the British aristocracy have all become self-indulgent and lazy élitists, frightened of dirtying their hands on the more mundane tasks of life. Some, at least, are obviously to be regarded as 'good' employers, not only in the sense that they pay adequately but also in that they know what they are doing. That, in other words, they are no longer only gentlemen but also professionals.

Tenacity in pursuit of survival has been the hallmark of those aristocrats who have managed, in some ways, to preserve the lifestyle of their ancestors. The strange thing is that enthusiasm for the maintenance of the status quo, albeit at varying levels of emotional commitment, is evident all the way down the social line on the estate, as it would almost certainly not be on a factory production line. Grumbles were usually minor. There may be feudal overtones to the relationships of many of the workers with His Lordship, but no workers would do anything but laugh unbelievingly when I asked them whether they had ever seriously considered moving out to one of the industrial towns nearby. Of course, they said, they might make more money, and they might more easily be able to thumb their noses at the foreman or manager than they could in a fairly closed community like Ragley. 'But this is a way of life, not just a way of making a living,' said one veteran. The remark had the ring of truth.

Is it a way of life that can continue? Is there hope for the next generation, let alone the ones that will follow? Those closest to the 8th Marquess, and noblemen like him, are unlikely to revolt against his remaining power. In practice it has become too limited, too much subject to social counterpressures for that to happen.

It is true that many of Lord Hertford's present-day workers still live in tied cottages. But several widows of ex-employees also still live on the estate where they have always lived. Either through inclination or regulation, or a combination of both, the Lord does not cast them out into the cold, cold snow. Several old retainers still occupy cottages on the estate and the tenant farmers, who can perhaps be regarded as the 'middle classes' of the estate, are protected for three generations by law. The 8th Marquess might, I would think, *like* them to leave so that he could farm the land himself and make more money from it than he can from rents. He is restrained by simple humanity, by the law, and by a lack of ready cash to buy them out. In short, by his awareness of the realities of the whole situation. The Earl of Yarmouth expressed to me his interest in acquiring as much land, inside and outside the present estate, as possible. He may or may not, when his time comes, find himself able to do this. If he does not, the obvious question would be: would a young man, thwarted in his ideas of expansion, be content to devote his life to maintaining the status quo?

Several of the Ragley old hands I talked to were guarded about this. One remark I heard more than once was, 'Will Harry think it worthwhile to put the effort into Ragley his father has done? That's something that none of us know.'

The future of the estate depends in some measure on His Lordship personally. No doubt the farms, a respectable 3,000 acres, plus one of the most modern dairies in Europe, could continue somehow without aristocratic ownership, though they continue very well with it. And the forests would presumably be attractive as investments to untitled commercial producers of Christmas trees and timber for gates and fences.

But there is little doubt that, to many workers, the contact with an aristocratic employer is a bonus – though it would not compensate for unrealistic wages or incompetent management. Some of Ragley's professionals were quite capable of making the odd, dry comment about His Lordship's foibles. Even these people plainly relished the fact that they were able to do so about a Marquess rather than about a mere Mister. One does tend, after all, to have a more assured audience, over dinner table or pub pint, for an anecdote about the nobility than about mere misters. It may no longer be a decisive card for the nobility to play, but it is a card of sorts nonetheless. I must admit I was interested to discover the stirrings of this starry-eyed impressionability in myself: such factors must help, marginally, to keep His Lordship's estate going.

But what about Ragley Hall itself? The inner citadel of so-called privilege? It was designed by Robert Hooke, has been in the same family since it was built in 1680, and has continued in family occupation through the 1750 James Gibbs alterations to the windows and Great Hall and the 1780 building of the Palladian portico by Wyatt. But surely the prospects for the survival of the Hall itself are rather more doubtful than those of the estate?

True, it is hardly likely that any other family – even a family of rich Arabs – would be able to take it over and make their home there. And, isolated as it is in its own grounds, one mile from the main gates, the Hall is not the most convenient building for conversion into an office block, though it would certainly be a picturesque one. Ragley Hall might face demoltion if the family's strong *will* that it should survive does not itself do so. But it would be either a very brave or a very insensitive man who would, without a heavy heart, give the final order to demolish Ragley Hall.

Lord Hertford was once advised to do so, and to build a smaller house on the site. He found that the advice was very much in conflict with his ideas, his sense of destiny and his strength of will. Even a descendant who secretly welcomed such advice would, I think, have a shaking hand when actually trying to implement it.

Would the inhibition be objectively justified? Only the future will provide an answer to that. What is clear at present is that the aristocratic owners of great country estates are subject to the same pressures as the rest of us, in at least one respect. They must now justify themselves not by their backgrounds but by their results. As the 8th Marquess of Hertford has proved so effectively at Ragley Hall, for the time being at least, he and his fellow aristocrats should be well capable of doing so. But the pressure of willpower required is ceaseless, and the final result may depend heavily on individual temperament rather than family background. It is a strange and unexpected endorsement of the democratic view that in the end human character matters more than social class.